TARMAC WARRIOR

Dedicated to My Girls. With a Father's Love.

Thanks to:
David Monoghan who talked me into sharing my story
with you; Esther Rantzen for her kindness and for making
me focused; Oggy for reading the new typescript every
morning before going to work.
Hon. Prof. Ian Hancock (USA) for his contribution,
support and friendship; Pat Rose (USA) for her technical
advice, belief and encouragement.

Also:
Stipendary Magistrate Grey and HM Prison Chelmsford,
for giving me the 'Time' to complete my transcript; Julian
Davies who provides unlicensed and bare-knuckle fight
fans with a brilliant web site at
www.geocities.com/unlicensed2000

TARMAC WARRIOR

BILLY CRIBB

MAINSTREAM
PUBLISHING
EDINBURGH AND LONDON

First published in Great Britain in 2001 by
MAINSTREAM PUBLISHING COMPANY
(EDINBURGH) LTD
7 Albany Street
Edinburgh EH1 3UG

ISBN 9781840186758

A catalogue record for this book is available
from the British Library

Reprinted, 2007, 2010
This edition, 2002

Contents

NOTICES

At this point I want to make it clear that I am not related to the great fighter Tom Cribb. Although I am a Romani I am not a Gypsy fighter and have never fought on the Gypsy circuit.

Glossary

ASSUTI	Sleep	**FLOAT**	Horse transportation lorry
ATCH	Camp or Stop	**GAD**	Shirt
ATCHINGTANS	Stopping place	**GATTER**	Beer
AVRI	Out from	**GAVVERS/GAVMUSH**	Police
BAR	Pound	**GORGIO** (pronounced 'gorger')	
BENDY	Tent formed by tree/branches		Someone who is not a traveller
	and tarpaulin/sacks	**GRAI/GRY**	Horse
BOK	Luck	**HEDGECREEPER**	Inferior Gypsy
BOKKI	Unlucky		(derogatory)
BOX	Horse trailer	**HOKKAPENS**	Lies
BROUGUES	Trousers	**HOLDING** Having large amounts of cash	
BUTTI	Work	**HOTCHI/HOTCHIWITCHI**	Hedgehog
CADIE	Hat	**JOEY**	Small coin
CHAI	Girl	**JOGRAY**	Gypsy stew
CHAL	Man	**JUK**	Dog
CHAVVI	Boy	**KEL**	Have
CHAVVIES	Children	**KER**	Do/Make etc
CHINS	Cuts	**KOR**	Fight
CHIRIKLO	Bird	**KOSH**	Piece of wood
CHOKKERS	Shoes	**KUSHTI**	Good
CHOOMERS	Kisses	**LEL/LELLING**	Take or get/Getting
CHOR/CHORING	Steal/Stealing	**MAS**	Meat
CHUCHI	Rabbit	**MOCHARDI**	Unclean of mind,
CLARET	Blood		habit or way
COSH	Firewood	**MONGED**	Begged
DELLED	Gave	**MONKEY**	Five hundred pounds
DIDECOI	Form of Gypsy	**MORA**	Bread
DIKKED	Saw	**MOT**	Tea
DIKLO	Knotted kerchief	**MOULDER**	Lorry
DINILO	Mad	**MUI**	Mouth
DORDI	Dear me	**MULLER**	Kill/Ruin
DROM	Road	**MUMPLEY**	Inferior Gypsy
DUKKERING	Fortune telling	**MUSH**	Man

MUTTERING	Pissing	SHIRTED	Taken by police
NIX	Nothing/Nil	SKIVING	Dealing in
OLL	Eat	SKREEVE	Motor vehicle
PANNI	Water	STARRY/STIRIBEN	Prison
PAVEE	Irish Gypsy	TOOKEN AWAY	Sent to prison
PEG	Sell	TOTTING	Dealing in junk or scrap
PETER	Cell	TOUG	Trouble
POSH-MULLERED	Half-killed	TRAILER	Motor-drawn caravan
PUKKER	Speak	TRASHED	Frightened
PUV	Field	VARDO	Horse-drawn caravan
RACKLI	Woman	VASS	Hand
RARTI	Night	VITTALS	Prepared food
RAT/RATTI	Blood	VONGA/WONGA	Money
ROKKER	Speak	YOG	Fire
SCRAN	Food		

Introduction

I was encouraged to share my life with you by a man called David Monoghan, the head of a TV production company. We first met through Lenny McClean when we filmed the banned documentary Bare Fist (*The Sport That Wouldn't Die*) and became friends. It was David's excitement at my stories that first urged me to start making notes.

During that same period, I met Esther Rantzen who kindly set aside time for me in her BBC office and gave me some great advice. These were her words: 'You are a visionary [a polite way of calling me a dreamer]. You need to re-think your position and become more focused; explore your life experiences and see how they can help you help others.'

It was Esther's words in my mind and David's excitement in my heart that eventually made me commit to writing a biography.

I begin the book in my early teens, during the summer of 1962. This was a time when I remember Gypsies having more freedom than they do today, although small groups still suffered attacks at the hands of irate villagers and drunken young men in cars. I start here because this was the turning point I remember so well. An attack on my sleeping family brought hatred and pain to the surface from somewhere deep inside me.

Taking you through 17 years of my life – from a peaceful family existence around England's leafy lanes to my drug-crazed time in the control of the USA fight syndicates where my dreams turn to nightmares – your feelings toward me will change several times. You will love me, hate me, laugh with me, despise me and sometimes maybe feel sad for me. But by the end of the book I hope you will at least understand how I became the person I did.

Enjoy my life . . . I did!

Billy Cribb
July 2001

ONE

First Blood

Her scream tore me from my sleep. The darkness hurt my eyes as I strained to identify the shadows by their horrific cries, as my family floundered in their panic. Light pierced the darkness as a simultaneous explosion of glass brought down the blind of the trailer window. The offending missile continued its journey, destroying my mother's proud display of crystal. My mother's arms appeared to extend twofold as she reached out, gathering her brood close to her. My dad cursed loudly as he fought the effect of his startled awakening on his co-ordination.

'Where's me poxy brogues?' he screamed in anger, as he searched frantically in all the places he would normally lay out his clothes for the morning. Giving up, he pulled on his boots and crashed through the trailer door into the light beyond, grabbing the large baseball bat that he kept behind the door for just such an occasion as this. I peered through the broken window. It was the skinheads from the neighbouring village, their drunken jeers filling my siblings with the fear of a thousand years of systematic abuse. The revving of their engines and blowing of horns, the loudness of their music – we could feel their frenzied excitement as they bayed at our trailers.

'FUCK OFF SCUM!' they shouted, 'DIRTY BASTARDS! TRAMPS! . . . TORCH THEIR FUCKING CARAVANS!' These were all words we knew too well. The thought of burning to death terrified us all, it had happened all too often to families in the past and the reality had become an inherent fear within our community.

I recall with horrifying clarity the stories told by my grandmother of the night she and granddad awoke in their trailer parked at the roadside to find it engulfed in flames. Locals had set their homes alight as they slept. She wept each time she told the story, yet always felt compelled to tell it, as if helping us avoid a similar situation. It was almost as if she felt that she herself was to blame for being there, rather than the arsonist who set her alight.

My father's voice was joined outside by those of his brother, Darkie; his brother-in-law, Bendy; my cousin, Joey and granddad, Alf. Darkie was a fearsome figure amongst Gypsy men with his unusual strong, green eyes that would pierce the soul, the mass of black curls crowning his bronzed face, and the short beard hiding his pearl-white teeth that shone when he laughed. Tonight, however, those teeth were biting down hard on his lip as he shouldered his shotgun. I stood looking through the jagged reminder of our attack in the window. I saw a flash as both barrels of the yogger were unleashed and a thundering echo was sent back from the surrounding trees.

The jeering stopped instantly and turned into cries of fear. There was a scramble of panicking feet, followed by the sounds of car doors closing. An engine wound into life and revved hard. The gearbox crunched as it tried to find the gear that would carry its occupants to safety. The loud music began to fade as the screeve spun in its tracks and was aimed towards the A12 heading for Colchester. The second vehicle lay crippled by the shower of leaded shot delivered by my uncle's hand upon the trigger. Steam poured from the bonnet, creating a ghostly haze as it filtered through the car's headlights.

My gaze was fixed on the shadows of my elders as they 'rewarded' our abusers who had now been abandoned by their gutless army of 'friends' to face retribution. I could see the brothers beat on the skinheads without remorse or rest. There was a barrage of fists, heads and feet flying from all angles towards our attackers. They tried to fight back, bless 'em, but quite honestly they were fucked. What they didn't give thought to before their cowardly deed was that Gypsy men are born to fight. It's in our blood – the survival instinct that has allowed this hidden minority to live amongst you for a thousand years, still retaining its identity and culture.

The skinheads were badly beaten – or well beaten, whichever way you want to look at it, I guess. This was their reward for venting their racial hatred on our sleeping family. Their bleeding bodies fell across and alongside their equally battered screeve.

My lips tightened across gritted teeth. My anger at this intrusion distorted my face and my hands were clenched tightly into fists. I looked at my family. As I did, the sadness of their faces filled my eyes with tears. I had never felt such mixed emotions before, although I found in later years that these would not be a stranger to me. My tears fell upon my clenched fists as the fingernails dug into my palms, drawing blood. I reached out to comfort my mother.

'Don't let them hurt you, my son,' she whispered, 'Your tears are the jewels of your soul, spend them wisely.' Her words came softly through the darkness and were to stay with me forever. Mum was always full of little phrases of wisdom, she got them from her mother who was the child of a Jewish girl made pregnant by a Romani boy. That side of the family came out of Cumbria and the other side were from the borders of Scotland and England, in Northumberland. The story goes that my great-grandmother was banished from her family having become pregnant and began to travel with the Gypsy boy's family. That baby they had was my gran. So all these little words of wisdom were what mum called her 'Jewish jewellery' and came from her side of the family. So I am in fact Jewish–Romani. The Nazis would have had some fun with me in World War Two, wouldn't they!

I moved to the trailer door, still open from my father's exit. My father and Joey put their arms around my tired grandfather to console him. He was far too old for all this; he had earned some peace for what was left of his life. Granddad hated the abuse of another human being. It was beyond his comprehension, yet he had suffered it all his years in some way or another. He was a very quiet man, gentle in his ways and soft in his speech.

'Clothes tell folk who you are,' he would say. He was always immaculate in his dress; he didn't have a vast wardrobe, you understand, but what he did own was always clean and of the best quality. A diklo (a silk kerchief also known as a 'Kinsman scarf') would be tied neatly and in the traditional manner around his neck. He had one for every day of the week. Shirts were always clean and lay crisp across his vast chest. Red braces supported a heavy pair of cord trousers that shrouded his shiny dealer boots. The trousers, incidentally, also came complete with a huge leather belt, which, along with the braces, shows you what a cautious man he was. Finally, the finishing touch, an old trilby cadie that had to be steamed weekly, sitting just-so, tipped cockily over the left eye.

'I hide the left 'cos that's me truth eye,' he would say. 'The right eye needs to be out to tell a lie when it comes at me.'

All was quiet outside. Mum put the kettle on (mum's medicine for every occasion was a brew). Dad and the brothers bundled the beaten skinheads into the back of their wounded car while granddad brought his lorry round to the opening. The huge boom on the back of the lorry reached over the car and the hanging chains were carefully stretched to embrace the carcass. There were familiar crunching and whirring sounds as the car was lifted quickly on to the back of the lorry. Granddad and Darkie climbed into their respective seats and almost ceremoniously drove off into the night air. It wasn't until weeks later that I learned the end of the skinhead story. Granddad and Darkie drove them to the fens of Norfolk. I don't know if you know this place but at night-time it is as deserted and as bleak as hell: flat, wide-open spaces, field after field with little-used roads that were no more than lanes back then.

The skinheads were stripped of their clothing – every stitch – and were sent to roam the dark plains of deepest Norfolk. Two were crying like babies. I was told humiliation is often a far better punishment to inflict than a beating, and had we not been Gypsies they may have had the choice – however, we do like to give good value and so they were given the hiding *and* the humiliation. Hopefully it would be a long time before these men engaged in other acts of mindless aggression. The car? Well, the car was first operated upon by Dr Darkie the car surgeon. He carefully removed the radio, the tyres and the battery before dumping it in the 'fen drain' (a sort of man-made river that acts as drainage to the fen area and runs all the way through it).

It was the early hours before the men returned. None of us except the baby had gone back to sleep, of course. We sat and talked about the night's events while Dad patched up the broken window the best way he could as a temporary measure. When our family was complete once more we hooked up our trailers and hit the road. It was still dark and so the younger of the chavvies slept in the back of the van. That was how the summer of 1962 started for this 13 year old.

By the time morning broke we had travelled about 80 miles and were atched on a farm in Kent. We came here every season to pick hops. I loved hop picking; we got to play with the chavvies down from London, those who lived in houses. It wasn't often we got to play with outsiders. I felt great when I was around these cockney people; they were always happy and down-to-earth, no airs and graces. They never judged us or looked down on us, not like some other townsfolk. Yes, I liked Londoners. They picked up a lot of their slang from the Gypsies too, words like 'kushti', 'bar', 'stir' (from our word 'stiriben' for prison), 'muller', 'joey', 'chored', 'mui' and lots more.

The London chavvies all thought we Gypsies had it made: no school; on holiday all the time. That's because we were in trailers; they didn't realise that these were in fact our *homes*. Funny, isn't it? No one ever saw the hard life we had earning a living. Okay, so we had no school – well, not all of the time. Mum got us in where she could but most places wouldn't take us because of local objections generally. The parents of the gorgio kids objected to their chavvies attending school with 'dirty Gypos'.

We had to work, and work like our parents – it was expected of us. We became almost adult at around the age of 12 really. It was just the way it was, and although I would have loved to go to school more, I also loved to be with my family.

Our time hop picking was magical for us; it was in fact a time when we could play and work. It was a land of fantasy amongst the huge arches of vines, and the imagination took us wherever we wanted to be.

It was during one of those hot magical days when I first had to defend the honour of my family. I was running through the vines when I caught sight of a gorgio boy push my sister to the floor. I knew instinctively what I had to do: I had to defend my sister's honour, and also my family's. I was her protector. My legs were already taking me to her side before my brain told me where I was heading. I was to have my first real taste of blood. I launched myself at the boy across the vines. We rolled and fought for what seemed to be hours, blood and snot spread across our scrunched-up faces, fists and feet flying like steam hammers, sometimes finding their mark but often missing completely, wrenching muscles in the shoulders and hip.

My opponent dropped to the floor exhausted and I sat on his chest. I had as little strength left in me as he had in him, but the defence of my sister's honour drove me on.

There was no force behind my punches at this stage. It was all that I could do to lift my arms. I just let the fists fall heavily and repeatedly into his face, until eventually I rolled over and fell at his side. It seemed that forever was going to pass us by. We lay there looking upwards, the sun spiralling through the vines warming our aching faces as the blood crusted nicely. One of us spoke, I can't remember who, and the whole experience became almost surreal. There we were lying on the floor, staring into space, chatting happily when only moments ago we had been bludgeoning each other with every intention to maim. We became inseparable from that day.

There's very little I can say to conjure up a picture of the boy who was to mean so much to me, he was just so *ordinary*. Smoke (as he was called) was very quiet but would at the same time always assert his presence. He was not submissive, he just didn't make a fuss about issues like I did. He would dress very much as I did all day except I had long trousers and he had shorts. I remember ribbing him about that often, especially when I was losing an argument – it always got him beat. The family he lived with were not well off. His parents were both dead. A car crash. The way he tells it, they were walking down to the chip shop when a car mounted the kerb and just wiped them away, missing the pram that he was safely riding in. Smoke spoke of them often and always as if they were still alive. He never referred to them in the past tense. I thought that was a bit odd, but looking back I guess that was how he handled being an orphan.

This was my first real friendship outside the Gypsy culture, a friend from a world I would never belong to or understand ; a house dweller. Gorgios or flatties, we'd call them. This friendship hepled me realise that I was as good as those people which gave me great reassurance because from the way I had been treated at schools, I was beginning to doubt the fact. The family had always assured me I was better than gorgios in many ways. I could run faster, climb higher, work harder and I could drive a car. They, however, hadn't a clue. Okay, so they could read and write, but where was that going to get you in the real world? 'Oh yes, I have it all,' I remembered thinking to myself in a very smug fashion.

That summer was the beginning of a new world for me as adventures were to unfold and I became a man. After all I was nearly 14 and as Dad would remind me, 'Yer fuzzy bits are coming in.' This meant I would have to cover up in the trailer when my sister was around, Gypsies are very strict and secretive about pubescence.

The Londoners who'd come for the hop picking would live in their little huts provided by the farmer, sleeping on a palliasse, a sort of duvet-cover filled with straw. We, of course, were to carry on living in the luxury of our trailers. The family groups would park close together at night and there would be a communal fire on the Gypsy encampment, with good old songs being sung and music playing. Our women would be cooking, usually a jogray, or 'joey gray' as it is also known, which was a stew with plenty of meat, usually chuchi or kannie if the old man had nicked one. Bendy would have a pheasant or two on hand that he had poached. Often the same food would taste different to the time before; it all depended on the kosh used. I told Smoke that Bendy had eaten a juk once. He puked up everywhere. (You gorgios would believe anything about us . . .) The men swapped stories of their travels, the trading they had done and other such manly boasts. The greatest stories would be about a good kor they had seen or great stallion they had owned and sold. This was the measure of a good man.

No one could tell a story like my granddad Alf. (I never did know why they called him that, his name was Elder, like all of the eldest sons of his line of ancestry.) Granddad's yarns would hold you spellbound from his first intake of breath and would be full of humour, we would hang on every word.

My new-found 'brother' from the outside would sit with his jaw almost resting on his chest as granddad told his tales. Sometimes they had a familiar ring but then they would take a different turn to the last time you heard them and they always had a new ending. The tales grew with the enormity of the imagination but my little house dweller knew no different; he hadn't heard them before. Smoke loved being with us, it was like a fantasy world to him, where chavvies walked and talked with the adults on an equal level. Well, nearly.

I was never usually allowed to bring an outsider to the fire but mum had really taken to my pale-skinned friend. Sometimes he really pissed me off, with his manners and his showing off with words, but I soon stole back my place in my mother's light when I would show off how far I could spit!

Our women always appeared to be working. I am sure mum woke up with a duster or cleaning cloth in her hand. Gypsy women are so home proud. Mum would get us dressed and make us breakfast in the mornings, work all day on the farm or some other job, then come home and clean. She would then cook more food, wash and iron, put us to bed and still have time to give us the love and games we would never forget. I can never remember mum sitting down, but I can always remember her laughter. Her life was full, with her family around her, food on the table and her Royal Doulton china in the cabinet. Yes, all was right with her world.

I remember the plot cooked up when mum was desperate to get a set of Royal Doulton crockery she had seen while out with auntie Ruby shopping. It was so typical of a Gypsy woman, so cunning. She had saved some wonga from her dukkering but was around 200 pounds short of the amount needed to buy her full set of fine china. Dad put his foot down that day and said no. It was decreed by the man of the family that he needed another stallion and one of the Rooney family in the town of Tilbury had just the horse he thought he needed. How could dad possibly afford to pay out for mum to have a few plates when the thing the family needed most was standing at Tilbury waiting for a man with the right wonga and slap of hands to seal the deal? The plot now began to hatch. For days mum badgered and nagged dad about all manner of things but none of them to do with china – just things to try to get him in a temper, to put him on edge, until the day came to hit the right button, that final push. Mum told auntie Ruby that dad hadn't the wonga to buy her the china she wanted. He wasn't doing right by her at all. Ruby told Darkie, dad's brother, and of course Darkie told dad (just as mum had guessed). Well, no good Gypsy man wants it known that he hasn't the wonga to buy for his family, let alone have his wife talking about him behind his back.

Mum sat in the trailer and waited for the explosion. Sure enough, it came through the door, taking everything in its path. There was my dad storming around the trailer, a dark cloud looming above his head, lightning in his eyes and thunder in his soul. The table was set for our supper and he wiped it clean with one swoop of his large arms and as he did so he caught mum square across the bridge of her nose by pure accident. The air turned all shades of blue, mum's eye immediately began to swell and discolour, and the tears flowed like a dam had burst.

Then – silence. A stillness descended that by its contrast moved me. I was overcome with a sadness that the normality had gone from our home. Where was the laughter that normally filled the air? Where was the chatter, the love? I hated it, this feeling. The silence seemed to go on for an eternity; for once I was pleased that it was bedtime. We chavvies lay as still as the air on a frosted night, we could hear each other breathing. My brother and I lay opposite each other. I swear I could hear his heart beat and the blood wash through his veins. Suddenly my eyes met his and for absolutely no reason I felt the horrific, overwhelming compulsion to giggle. I fought it but it fought harder and came out as a stifled cough of strangulation. 'Oh God, help me please', I prayed. My heart beat faster, the laughter was building up; then my brother Jed started.

Us chavvies rammed pillows and bedding into our mouths to stop the onslaught of laughter. We were quickly losing the battle. And then it came. Soon the whole trailer was a fit of hideous giggles, snorts and grunts as laughter spewed from our mouths as if we were of one mind. We were DEAD! Dad's bedclothes went up into the air and we scrambled in the darkness to find the door to freedom, falling over each other as we went. We spent that night in the van.

Do you know, there's nothing like a bit of trouble to bring unity. This little rabble who would normally enjoy the usual bickering of siblings were now united in their plight. We were never closer than at these times. I loved it, we would chew the story over and it would grow. We would become very brave, saying things like, 'I'm not trashed of him,' and 'Yeah, just let him come in here then, see if I care,' or 'He can't catch me anyway, old git.' We laughed and talked till dawn.

The birds eventually warned us it was morning and as I peeked out of the little square windows at the back of the van I noticed the trailers gradually beginning to come to life. Dad emerged quietly that morning. He opened the van slowly with his key and told the young-uns to get to their beds. I moved forward. 'Not you, son, get in front, we're off,' he said. He threw me a bundle of clothes. 'Let's catch 'em while they still have sleep in their eyes.' The very next thing I knew, we were on the road and heading towards the town.

We would be tree lopping that day – always a great adventure as well as a good earner but bloody dangerous with my dad. He had no fear and expected me to be the same. He sometimes forgot I hadn't his strength or his head for heights. I felt like shouting, 'Dad, I'm a *kid* for fuck's sake' – but never did, of course. We stopped on the way. Dad was all-forgiving; he couldn't have been nicer. He bought me a breakfast as big as myself. I ate every scrap and two mugs of mot. This was going to be a kushti day, I could feel it. We got to the job and the lady was really nice. She made us more mot and gave us some cake. It was nice cake although mum made better. The trees were a doddle. Dad did all the climbing and I did the trimming and loading up.

We were done by midday and got into the van. I thought dad had taken leave of his senses. We were heading towards the town centre and we had a dodgy tax disc in the window of the Bedford van we were driving. It was out of granddad's old lorry, also the plates were off an older Ford Thames van that granddad scrapped months back. Was he mad?

We parked at the back of the big old Co-op store. Dad hated paying for a parking ticket. Usually he would park anywhere and just throw away any penalty ticket he got. None of our vehicles were ever registered to us anyway, so how could anyone enforce a fine? We left the van and walked through the precinct. Right in the middle of a store window was the reason for dad's detour. Mum's Royal Doulton set, the one that all the fuss was about. There it shone in all its glory. He had gone into town to get what she was after. As always, mum had won the day – in her own little way and without dad even realising.

We came home that day with boxes and boxes of the stuff. Dad had the biggest grin on his face, he knew he'd done good. And mum? Well, mum's black eye shone with a glint of cunning! She had won, her carefully laid plan had worked and she had her prize. Well worth a black eye, she thought. Dad never could handle guilt, poor sod. He never saw this one coming – still, he was happy as a pig in shit: we still ended up with the Rooney's black Hackney stallion in the trailer outside. Dad had had the wonga all the time, we knew that, he just wanted to hang on to it. It was a treat to watch dad haggle for a horse. The buyer and bidder would stand for ages, hands held out as each man slapped the other as he made a bid. Dad always pleaded poverty to mum but in truth, he always had enough wonga for everything. He just didn't like to waste it on silly things like household essentials!

Things always seemed this way, we always seemed to get everything that we wanted from life. I don't know if it was because we worked so hard or because we all pulled together, but whatever it was it worked.

You see, when wonga was earned by any of us, we would put it on the table at night and it was collected in a huge crystal jug. Dad would be the banker, the man in charge so to speak (mum said he could be). And whatever was needed was usually found one way or another.

Very soon the family was back to normal, bad feelings don't last long in our family, you can't afford to not talk when you all rely on each other for a living and live at such close quarters together. It wasn't like you could go to your own room to get away from anything.

I awoke with the feeling that another great day was about to enter my life. You know those days when the bed feels just right, the pillow is soft and folded around your head, the duvet is plump and seems to hold your body like a grandmother's hug?

My breakfast was my alarm clock that morning. I could hear the bacon calling as if to say, 'Up you get, young Pickles'. My sister Lolly was arguing with my brother Jed about something that was nothing to do with either of them. The twins were lost in their own little world of insects and worms; baby Sharla was at mum's side as always; good old mum was cleaning every piece of her china *again*. And dad? Well, dad and me, we had our new stallion to play with, didn't we? Grooming him until he shone and trotting him up to show off. I knew that today held no boyish adventures for me. We were preparing to leave and move to another site. The work was nearly done here and news had reached us of a farm where they were paying more money for fruit picking than most of the other farms around. We had to finish off the week here, though. If we didn't then we wouldn't get back on next year. It was a sort of unwritten contract, a rule that we lived by and that was understood by all concerned.

Little did we know at that time that there wouldn't be another season on this farm; that the farms were to be automated. Machines were taking the place of men. Men, who had kept things operating efficiently all these years. Automation was to bring other problems too, not just financial. Sometimes the older travellers were allowed to stay on the farm where they had been working to see the winter out. But as the farm work dwindled through automation they had to go back on the road, or worse still into a house. This was just the beginning of the chain of events that have, over the past 30 years, taken away the traditional ways the Romani used to earn their living. Machines were moved in – and we were moved on!

TWO

On the Move

The whole family was out that morning on the move, even my baby sister, Sharla. We had a good breakfast; mum always made sure of that, and we were ready for the best day's work man had ever seen – at least that's how we felt at 6 a.m. I picked like a madman, basket after basket of hops; I lost count of how many.

I was big enough to work alone; the twins worked together and poor old Jed was stuck with Lolly. Everyone did their bit and worked hard all day but we laughed the whole time as dad and granddad carried on their bickering and joking around, always egging each other on.

Granddad and dad pulled down the vines so that everyone could reach them, then we would pick all of the hops from those vines, racing to fill the wicker baskets that we worked with. As the baskets were filled we would empty them into huge tubs where the farmer stood. He would count the amount of baskets that were emptied and would pay the picker accordingly. The incentive for us kids to pick like mad was to beat each other with the total amount, but for me personally it was to pick as many as my father. The other adults? Well, they wanted the wonga.

Darkie and Bendy had already moved on. They hadn't really settled in in the first place. They always had some little deal going on somewhere. They were more interested in getting to Horsemonden for some trade. I hadn't been privy to their money-making schemes yet but I was due for initiation, I felt it.

The brothers were always flush with money, in fact I am sure

Darkie had developed a limp by carrying a roll of cash on the same leg all the time. Their vans and cars were always immaculate with what I assumed to be revolving number plates, as they never seemed to have the same number on for longer than a month at a time.

Romani families work as a well-oiled machine. We look out for each other all of the time, always maintaining the immediate family, and without intrusion enjoying the intimacy of the extended family.

The end of the week had arrived all too quickly. The vines hung bare and the tractors had began to move in preparing the soil for the next crop. We were packed up and set to move on. My gorgio friend and I stood staring at each other, neither knowing what to say or able to understand the feelings we held for each other.

Mine was a feeling that I had only ever had for my family. It was a feeling quite unnatural to hold for an outsider, it made me feel very uncomfortable. I wanted to throw my arms around him as I would a brother that was going away, but that sort of demonstration just wouldn't be the thing to do.

We said very little but what we did say must have been important to us both at that time, I guess. I can't recall the content of that short goodbye, but I know I held out my hand. We shook, turned our backs almost simultaneously and walked away from each other.

I wonder what his name was? Such an important time in my life deserved more considerate remembering. I just called him 'Smoke', since he came from London and that. What else would I have called him? I didn't even think to ask his name. He must have had one, I thought. But then what's in a name? He didn't have to have one to be my friend.

That's another thing we Gypsies do: we give everyone nicknames. As you've probably guessed by now we don't stick to conventional tags; we kind of make them up as we go along. Traditionally, our names have mostly been taken from the Bible. Gypsies have always been religious. They were Catholic as they entered Europe just to comply with the acceptability of regional preference, but at the time you read this book we have a huge proportion of Pentecostal ('Born Again' Christian) members in the community who hold enormous meetings all over the world.

Uncle Bendy got his name from the tent they used to sleep in as children. The tent (or 'bendy') was made at the roadside from tree branches bent over and covered in canvas. When Bendy was a kid, his folks travelled in a vardo, which is a horse-drawn trailer with either a bow or flat top, sometimes made of wood and painted in an ornate manner, sometimes just with canvas sides. He was one of 12 kids, and of course the vardo was nowhere near big enough for them all to sleep in. Sometimes they slept under the trailer and sometimes in a bendy. Even when he had the choice of staying in the trailer during the colder months, my uncle would always choose to stay in the bendy, hence his name. Dad was called Pickles because he used to drive round the housing estates with his old horse selling all manner of pickled goods like onions, cabbages and herrings. I was called 'Little Pickles' for obvious reasons. Darkie was so-called because his vans and trucks always poured out black smoke because he ran cherry (red diesel). As opposed to the fuel you would buy from the garage, it carries no tax and costs about a quarter of the garage prices. It is meant for farm machinery and other off-road vehicles such as earth-moving equipment, dump trucks and cement mixers. Darkie was also very dark-skinned, more so than any of us. My sister Lolly was so-called because mum ate loads and loads of ice lollies while she was carrying her. And my sister Bambi was named after the film. See? It all makes sense.

Smoke had somehow changed my life. We had touched each other's souls during those formative years. I had found out that the strange people who lived in houses could be our friends if they wanted to. I learned that the gorgios were like us in many ways and not from Mars after all. Most important, to me anyway, I learned that I was at the very least their equal. As Smoke and I parted we had no idea that our paths would cross again under very different circumstances.

Whenever I attended schools I'd been put in a 'special' class and that had marked me. Even when I was put in an ordinary class it was traumatic, bearing in mind that most travelling kids did not even have basic literacy skills. Everyone around you recognised that the lines and squiggles on the blackboard said a word and you tried to pretend that 'you knew that' when it was quite apparent that you hadn't a fucking clue. That is humiliating to say the very least.

I already felt different and not to know words when even the littlest kids knew them made me angry. The kids would call me a dunce and say that I was stupid or thick. My only answer would be to hit them. I knew I was good at that and they couldn't beat me. I thought that I was winning by beating them up. I couldn't answer in any other way.

I always became so excited when we moved our camp; our life really was a series of adventures: a new town, new people, new places to explore, the scenery always changing. It really is no wonder that the settled folk often decided to create their own travelling community, the 'New Age Travellers' (who I believe now refer to themselves as 'New Gypsies') and leave behind their controlled lives. Even when we went back to a more traditional stopping-place our excitement was just the same. The surroundings may have been changed, old play areas might have taken on a new identity as visitors imposed their own ideas and adaptations.

As we pulled out of the farm gates, Darkie came toward us in his old Ford D300, a bright red truck that you couldn't miss (he'd painted it while the maintenance crew were in the area doing the mail boxes – I'll give you one guess where the paint came from!) This truck had a multitude of uses. It was a three-way tipper and I believe this one had been 'acquired' while my uncles were working in Derbyshire. Darkie went out one night and came back with it in the early hours: it cost him a quick repaint, a change of number plates and a bit of welding. (I don't know where he found a commercial sales pitch open at 3 a.m.) Then, of course, we didn't see him for a few weeks. He went off to Cumbria, where our family came from, to find work for a while, to sort of gain a bit of history for his new vehicle. On the back of his truck there was a huge elevating boom with a grab bucket, which was especially useful for lifting small plant and machinery from the roadside or on sites. Darkie would lift the machinery high and place it in the centre of his high-sided lorry. Whatever he 'won' (he always called choring a 'win') could not be seen unless you actually climbed up to look in the back of the truck and you'd have to get past Darkie to do that – not an easy task.

'Change of plan,' my uncle shouted through the cloud of smoke surrounding his lorry. The men climbed down from their vehicles and huddled around the rear end of Darkie's truck. The big aluminium back was opened sideways and I could just see a yellow object inside. It appeared to be a huge generator – not, I might add, an item Darkie had owned the day before and to take an educated guess, he probably didn't own now . . . In fact it was not unlike the piece of machinery that the farmer had had behind his old barn. I glanced backward at the old barn wondering if it still hid the machinery I was thinking of. I wanted to be included in the huddles that go on between the men, that wonderful world of secrets intrigued me.

The meeting was soon over with the slapping of backs and all men were back to their vehicles to drive off again, this time the opposite way to the planned route. Darkie thundered off in a haze of blue smoke and our motors pulled in behind him. We choked on the fumes as they came pouring through the air vent of the van. Mum's complaints prompted dad to pull out and overtake the offending vehicle.

'I don't know why he puts that stuff in his tank,' mum said. 'The smoke it gives off is as good as a neon sign. Those gavvers are going to pull him over one day. They can confiscate the motor for putting cherry in and he'll have nothing.'

'Just as well he didn't pay for the truck then, init!' said dad with a big grin. Mum just looked at him in disgust; she preferred things to be straight.

'Why aren't we going on to the farm?' said mum.

'Darkie's got a bit of business up the road. It's best we go with him; there's another farm that way for apple picking and we can go on to the fair,' replied dad.

'You know what? I'm sick of being involved in your brother's business, especially when it affects ours. Is he up to something again? 'Cos if you're involved there'll be trouble.'

'Shut the fuck up, you do your business and I'll do mine,' said dad. 'He's my brother,' he added.

'Yes and these are your chavvies. Think of them first, not him or his selfish needs. He just does what he likes and you follow.'

Silence fell for a while. Darkie was often the cause of tiffs between mum and dad. He always saw us right, though. I remember when dad's back was out for months – he couldn't move and so couldn't earn. Mum went out dukkering but it was Darkie that always came round with wonga to put on the table, and auntie Ruby made sure that when she'd filled her cupboards, enough flowed over to keep us going. The family always saw each other right.

I looked out the back window of our van and saw Darkie turn off to the right.

'I think we've missed our turn, dad!' I shouted.

'Why's that, boy?' he replied.

'Uncle's gone off to the right, I thought we were going there together.'

'Darkie's got some business down that way, he'll meet us later,' said dad. Obviously mum's words had sunk in as dad continued on our journey and left Darkie to do his business.

An hour passed and soon my nostrils swelled with the smell of apples, my nose stung with the intensity of the sweetness. We were going apple picking. I hated picking apples, it was real hard work – although I loved the smell. I would sooner cart iron than work with apples. The boxes were heavy and I always got stung. My stomach griped as it was systematically filled with unripened fruit. I always had the shits and my arse felt like it had been wiped with sandpaper as the apples left my body almost as quickly as they went in.

The good thing about it, though, was the wonderful pies that my gran made. We would pick berries and she would make pies the like of which you couldn't find elsewhere. Blackberry and apple, blackcurrant and apple, gooseberry and apple, apple sauce . . . So I was kept between apple heaven and arsehole hell for the whole season.

We were set up in minutes. The trailer was levelled, and water was fetched in the bright stainless-steel churns. We always used stainless steel bowls for cooking and storage. We never used plastic as they would score and harbour germs. One thing we Romani were good at was hygiene and personal cleanliness. There was no room for dirty habits in our culture. You'd never see a dog or cat in a trailer either. These things were governed by mochardi, a law of physical and mental hygiene that the Romani lived by.

The chavvies were soon off exploring. Mum was boiling the kettle as you'd expect, with Sharla constantly chatting at her side, and the twins were off into the twilight zone of their own imagination. I'd swear they were bloody aliens. Jed was probably up to no good and Lolly would be there with him just egging him on, and when he got caught she'd be the first to tell mum about it.

Dad and I got down to business. We made our presence known to the farmer and we got to know what was expected of us and when. We figured out where we would be working and got the baskets sorted, and we let him know that there would be another three trailers arriving behind us shortly. We'd just settled down for some scran in the sun when there was a roar of diesel as Darkie's big red truck hurtled through the gateway, towing his Dutch-built trailer behind him. It was a 28-foot bulk of: 'Look at me'. The outside was as ornate as the interior, full of polished chrome and coated aluminium panels. The inside was spotless. There were cupboards with panels of cut glass; work surfaces were figured walnut polished to the highest shine you could imagine and the seating was off-white leather with navy piping, still with the manufacturer's polythene covering in place. The carpets were soft and deep and the same colour as the seating.

Darkie and Ruby had no chavvies. Mum said she 'hadn't been remembered by God' but I think God knew exactly what he was doing. I could never imagine having them as parents. Darkie was strong and cold with the heart of a lion, the appetite of an elephant and the roar of an injured tiger with a temper to match.

Ruby was a huge lady. We often joked about how she struggled to get herself through the door of her trailer, and about how the Dutch must have welded girders in their bed to hold two such enormous bodies. But one thing that sticks in my mind about her was that she was so house-proud. I believe she and uncle Darkie had discovered how to hovver in their trailer. Nothing appeared to have been walked on nor sat in. Nothing was out of place. When she travelled all her china and glass was carefully wrapped in paper and stored. When they arrived at a new destination and settled for a while she unwrapped her treasures and placed them in their pre-ordained spot for maximum display. Ruby boasted all of the time and anything she bought was rammed up your nose for months. But I loved them both. I just couldn't live with them.

Uncle Darkie leaped from his truck; his every move was always exaggerated. He was so dramatic and his presence was known about at all times. He strode up to my dad and put a wad of notes in his hand. Dad turned quickly and secretively away – not from me, but from mum. Obviously he had had some sort of business with my uncle and that big yellow generator (which, incidentally, had now disappeared from the back of the red truck).

We sat that night under a full sky. I remember how warm it was; the apple-scented night air mixed with the aroma of grannie's baking. Granddad and the boys had been drinking, just enough to make them silly. The stories flowed and the laughter rang in the night.

We had visitors also. Hughie Burton and his missus sat with us that night. Hughie was a big man from the North and his reputation as a bare-fist fighter was as big as the man himself. To some he was known as 'Uriah' but he always insisted he was Hughie. I think it would be fair to say that Hughie was the greatest fighting man that lived amongst the Gypsy men of that time – along with my uncle Bendy, of course. But those two never did fight each other. Uncle Bendy became great friends with Hughie in the strangest way. For years before they became friends they searched for each other – at Appleby, Barnet and Epsom – so as to see who the better man was. No matter where we went Bendy would let it be known that he would be there to fight Hughie. They never seemed to be there at the same time though, except for the one year at Appleby.

Bendy was having a bit of trouble with some Irish travellers. There were around 20 men standing but Bendy would never back off, he fronted them out all the way. Bendy stood alone with the Irish jeering at him. He waited for their move forward but it was slow coming, when a mountain of a man come out from a neighbouring trailer. We didn't know the man but auntie Sylvia for one was glad of his appearance. I think Bendy was relieved also. Although he wouldn't step back, he knew by the sheer numbers that he would have been beaten. But he also knew that there would be some Irish blood blessing the hills of Appleby before he ever went down – and that was enough for him.

The two men stood there. Neither spoke except to confirm that they would stand or fall together. The Irish moved away slowly, even though they were tooled up. They continued jeering and promised a future visit but I remember granddad saying, 'If a man lays a threat he won't do the deed,' and I always found this to be true. If a man's going to hurt you he'll do it without warning and usually there and then. Why should he put himself at a disadvantage by giving you a warning?

When the Irish disappeared, Bendy and the man who we now know as Hughie walked slowly away. Bendy invited him back to the trailer. They pulled out the scotch and drank it empty. Neither were drunk though, they were both sound and determined men. Uncle Bendy and the Burtons became great friends and stayed so from that day. Uncle Bendy's only regret was that he and Hughie never knew who was the better man, as they were soon such good friends they never did choose to fight.

Morning came at last and the day started as it always did. Dad and I had a fry-up breakfast after scrubbing up and while we ate the kids washed up. We would leave, after which the kids ate breakfast, joining us later. Mum would follow after she had cleaned from top to bottom and got Sharla ready. Lolly was approaching an age where she could expect to have the trailer to herself. As her body began changing she would be allowed a special privacy.

Our culture was quite Victorian in sexual matters and the girls would always be chaperoned when going anywhere. They would also be taken from any form of schooling while going through puberty so as not to be mixing with the lads.

Lolly was a very quiet girl apart from when she taunted Jed, but that was just their way: they fought all the time but would gang together should any of the rest of us start on either of them. They were inseparable and knew almost everything the other was thinking or feeling.

I was extra protective of my sister. Although she was only ten she was extremely pretty and had many a second glance from young men even of around 18 years old. Lolly had the biggest hair you could imagine. Jet black it was, shining like a well-groomed stallion. Her thick curls tumbling down to her waist and her smooth, dark skin were perfect frames for her porcelain-like teeth and saucer-like green eyes, which were her biggest asset. I must say she was very mature looking for her age and could possibly pass for 15. There was many a time I stood toe-to-toe with a man twice my height and width but fuck 'em, they weren't going to have thoughts about my Lolly. They knew their place.

I recall the day at Cambridge Fair in the summer of 1961 when one of the Scarrot family was after Lolly. She was in the market with the twins and the Scarrot boy tried to talk to her. Fucking cheek. And he knew I was about. That was taking the piss. I flew at him. He didn't know what hit him. I punched him straight in the mui and he went down like a sack of shit. Next thing I had his two brothers over and we stood toe-to-toe for ages but none of us wanted to fight. I didn't; I'd had my man and had no quarrel with the other two but they obviously felt obliged to shout for their brother – who now had nothing to say 'cos his tooth was broken and he was aching. I stood my ground long enough to show I wasn't trashed and then grabbed Lolly and the twins, turned and walked away slowly, waiting for a crack around the back of my head. But it never came. They knew I was right to defend the girl.

If I had caught a gorgio boy looking at her I would have mullered him without a second thought. A Gypsy boy was bad enough, but even he would go through a series of tests – almost a ritual, but the end would be the same: they would never get near her, not while I had fists and the breath to carry them.

Lolly's teeth were beautiful, but I would always remind her of when she had a smile like a piano keyboard and half of them were missing. She didn't mind losing her teeth; she was making a fortune putting them under her pillow! It was funny one night when Jed decided to wait for her to sleep and then stole her tooth from under the pillow and put it under his own so that he would get the wonga. Mum and dad rooted around for hours looking for that tooth, they looked in the bed, under it, around it . . . no one thought of looking under Jed's pillow. They still left her the wonga, though. Jed was shocked when he woke up and found this bloody little half-rotted piece of tooth still under his pillow and found out that Lolly had the money. He was so angry that he had no breakfast that day and went around the site trying to sell the tooth to one of the younger Gypsy boys. In the end he sold it to one of the Grey boys, the son of a Scottish traveller, who gave him one shilling for it in return for a verbal guarantee that he would get at least two shillings and sixpence if he put it under his pillow. That tooth was around for ages and ended up having several owners.

During the hop-picking season we usually parked very close to Horsemonden fair. The whole family loved a fair as all travelling groups do. The sleepy village of Horsemonden came alive during those days of trading. There were, of course, other fairs too. We had Priddy, Lea Gap, Cambridge, Barnet and best of all Appleby. There were lots of them but gradually it's being made tougher and tighter to enjoy fairs since they are being stopped by local authorities. I don't know why. The local economy must boom during the days travellers visit – especially the pubs. These were the fairs that Gypsy folk visited every year. The traders returned regularly, in fact you would see the same traders at every fair so they would always treat you right 'cos they knew they would see you again and wanted repeat custom.

Mum looked forward to the fairs enormously. She could renew her pans and soft furnishings in traditional wares and the more she paid for them the better she felt. She had to have the best. There was also a chance to catch up on gossip from around the country, see more distant family members and generally have a chat with other women, allowing her world to grow. Of course the kids would love it, the horses, the trotting, stuff to buy all over the place, dukkering and trading going on – such excitement. I personally loved to watch the boys race their sulkies (horse-drawn, two-wheeled training carts).

Dad and I were especially looking forward to the first fair we could get to, to show off our new stallion. He was truly magnificent and worth every penny of the monkey we paid. This was where he would start earning his keep. He would be serving as many mares as we could show him to.

Every man with a ready mare would want this boy of ours to mount it. We would charge 25 guineas a time to mount and he was well ready. We got him to the fair and stood him square, his manhood clearly intact, his nuts hanging like a sack of coal, his dick beating against his deep chest as it rose and fell with excitement. He knew why he was there. A good stallion would see you through and earn his wonga. We would take him all over the country for stud fees and expenses but it was always better if the mare was brought to us. I remember the many times I had to get hold of his 'old man' and guide it in. I hated that bit, but it was all part of the job. Apart from anything else it was bloody dangerous. We always had to be especially careful not to let him damage a mare's back with his hooves or come off sideways. That could split her, and damage him of course. This big black stallion we had was extra-special. He looked good and stood well at stud.

Horsemonden fair was to be my first real step toward a career as a fighter. No more would I scrap in a childlike rage for reasons unbecoming a Gypsy fighter. I was coming up to 14 years old now and could not live off my father's reputation. When people knew a fighting man was around news would spread and challenges would go out at the fair.

Dad would take all comers but there was a challenge from a new lad on the scene. He was around 16 or 17 and dad felt that he couldn't take the challenge from this boy, he was far too young and inexperienced. Dad would do him in seconds which would not do his cred any good at all. It would not be a good fight, so of course he didn't want it, but not wanting to insult him he spoke to the boy to set up an alternative arrangement that would keep both men happy.

'I tell you what, lad,' said dad. 'You fight my boy first and if you get him beat I'll fight you the next morning.'

Well, this got the old man out of it all quite nicely but I was well and truly landed in the shit. I now had to fight a man who I had no dislike for. I'd never met him before, he hadn't done anything to me, had he? I was never really a violent sort of kid. Whenever I had fought in the past it had been for a reason; someone taking the piss or abusing the family or encouraging it by bullying like Smoke did to my sister. Now I had to go in cold. I was not angry with him, I was not embarrassed and I was not in pain. How was this going to work? My motivation to hit this poor boy was clear – family honour. But why would I want to hurt him? Although I had been around the fighting all my life, I still didn't understand.

All was set. Dad had made the arrangements for the following morning: 6 a.m. on the field behind the trailers. I knew the procedure. I had watched dad many times. There would be the pep-talk at night, and a good sleep from an early bed. On waking I would eat a huge fry up, take a dump and make my way to the spot dedicated to the event. That's the way dad did it so I would do the same. 'I will make it a tradition,' I thought.

Dad gave me the pep-talk, I went to bed early as planned but to my horror I couldn't sleep. I was crapping myself – not for fear of fighting the man but through fear of losing and letting the family down. Dad was my measure and a difficult measure to stand beside. I tossed and turned until 5 a.m. when dad shook me. I pretended to come out of a deep sleep but actually I was still wide awake. Mum cooked breakfast and kept giving me this strange stare, like a dog that had just been kicked. I knew she didn't want me to go through with this but she knew I just had to. I ate my breakfast. It choked me to swallow it. I went for a dump but couldn't even fart.

'Fuck this,' I thought. 'Things just ain't working right.'

Off we set, granddad and the brothers at my side. They were all rooting for me. I began to feel great. No one was going to be tough enough for me. The family made me feel like I was the best thing since sliced bread. (*There's a thought: what was the greatest thing before sliced bread was invented?*)

I could see the crowd already formed ahead of me on the green and noticed the men had formed a ring big enough for me to knock this man around till his insides fell out. Hang on, though, was this *me* thinking such evil thoughts? I had found a new person inside myself. I never had such an urge to hurt someone in all my life. What was happening? I had changed my personality in the 100 yards since leaving the trailer. The brothers were advising me how to handle the fight, dancing around in front of me and showing me the 'right moves'. But I knew what to do.

Get in fast and get it over. He was mine and I knew it. I wasn't going to waste my time hurting my hands so that I could entertain the crowd. This was for me and my family. I had to win and I had to do it good. I got to the makeshift ring, my sleeve buttons undone and in the traditional manner I tore off my shirt from the centre. Button after button flew into the dew-laden grass. I had arrived. I felt great, like someone famous. The man inside me loved this new recognition, for me it was like being at a proper venue with the crowd cheering.

Then it came, from absolutely nowhere. My breakfast arrived on the floor in front of me. I had thrown up. Dad was covered, granddad was covered, Darkie was heaving at the sight and smell – it was a shambles. I had disgraced the family. Granddad held out his hand and just looked. For the very first time we shook hands. He wasn't ashamed of me. I was a man.

Dad said, 'I remember that feeling, fucking pucker, init?' I realised I had done no wrong. They had expected this from me, it was a part of the ritual I hadn't known about. Now I was ready. But oh *no*! 'What's happening now?' I thought. As I stood bare-chested in my track suit bottoms, I felt an unnatural movement in my pants. I was getting a sodding *erection*. For fuck's sake! What was my body doing to me? How big was this thing going to get? Was I going to be able to hold it down? Was I fuck. There it stood for all to see, floundering around in my tracksuit bottoms while I skipped about warming up, trying to ignore it. The brothers were hooting with laughter, which made me angry. I wanted to hit out at anyone. They were ridiculing me in front of around a hundred men. 'This isn't what families do to each other,' I thought.

'Shut up!' I screamed. 'Shut the fuck up!'

That was the first time I had sworn at my father. He went straight-faced, just for a second, then burst out laughing again.

'Boy, that happens often,' he said. 'That thing down there has a mind of its own for a start. You'll soon find that out at all the wrong times. When you fight, your body and mind will churn around and curdle your insides. You will have feelings bigger and better than anything you've ever experienced. Including sex.'

I found it frightening. My body had its own thoughts. I was actually aroused by the thought of beating this poor bastard to death – not in a sexual way, but in a way far more satisfying, more fulfilling than I could ever have imagined. My mind belonged to someone else. I was possessed by another personality very different from my own. This was fan-fucking-tastic. Muscles started to swell, veins began to rise in my arms and chest. I felt myself taken over with a strength I had never known. I wanted this more than I had wanted anything in my life.

The boy came at me like a rabbit from a burrow. First blood was his. I didn't expect him to be across to me so quickly. As he made his first strike, he also made his first mistake. He allowed me a minute to gather myself and clear my head. I squared up nicely, remembering everything I had seen dad do, everything he had taught me. Now was my time. He was going down my way, fast and hard.

He came at me again. Instinctively I crouched low, making a small target. I am only five foot five in any case; he was about five foot nine. I had a distinct advantage immediately; I could work close and inside. I just waited for my chance. He tried to go dirty. We had already set the rules: this was supposed to be a straightener. There should be no dirty fighting, no tools and no interference from the crowd.

He tried to nut me but me being so low he just toppled forward. Mug. I had him. I stepped to one side as he toppled past and I bashed him as hard as I could across the back of the head. He crashed to the floor. I allowed him to rise and moved in close again. My heart was in my mouth. I knew I had the man where I wanted him. It all felt so right.

I worked hard on the lower body, draining his energies. Then I came down on one bent knee and thrust upward with my right fist, using every ounce of power my body could muster. My feet left the floor. I had immediate access to the chin (what fighters call 'the button'). Hard and upward my fist went, burying itself into his hard, square chin. He was knocked out on his feet. As he floundered forward and to my left, he looked at me as if to ask 'Where am I?' That's when I made my move and came across with a right-hander into his face.

His nose exploded right there before my eyes. I had gone deaf to the crowd; I could no longer hear my family's roars. I couldn't hear anything but the explosion of flesh. I felt his skin burst open and the warm blood spurt on to my chest and face. It was over. He crumpled and lay motionless on the floor. I had beaten him fair and square – without tools, without fighting dirty. My pride was intact and the family honour had been upheld. Suddenly, out of my silence, I was bowled over by Darkie and my dad.

Their faces were alight and the screams around me immediately recreated the excitement of the fight. I instinctively knew then that this was now to be my way of life. I had become a man and would not look back. The brothers held me high and carried me on their shoulders back to the trailer. On the way they threw me into the cow trough. I didn't care. The claret from my opponent coloured the water and I bathed in it. The glory was mine and would never leave me.

We eventually got back to the trailer. The chavvies were all over me. I was a hero. Mum, on the other hand, just looked. There was no smile, no hug. She looked me over for damage and boiled the kettle for tea. Why did she not revel in my victory? Instead she looked so sad. She had a distant stare that took away all of my excitement, took away the thrill of the battle. I stood there wishing that I had never fought. Look what it had done to mum. She could see a life that I didn't yet know. She knew where I was going and the many aggressors I was to meet. At every fair now I would meet a challenge. At every fair she would go through the same pain that she had been through with my father for so many years, but now she had two of us to worry about. But she needn't worry, I thought. I had become invincible, *why didn't she know that?*

Wherever we go I would have to fight, it was our law, it was the way. And I wanted every bit of it. I was frightened of no man!

Bring 'em on! Let them bleed and fall at my feet.

THREE

Independence Day

As it happened, mum never really had to worry at all. That winter we joined the many travelling families around the country who had become settled. It was becoming increasingly hard to maintain a travelling life as stopping-places were dwindling and traditional work became less and less. My family had bought a large piece of land near Long Buckby in Northamptonshire, which was a really handy spot because we were about two miles from the M1 entrance (well, if we used the service ramp for the police we were). It was brilliant to be able to get to so many towns and find work. We were to make this our home for good. There were a couple of old shacks on it. Dad decided that he would buy several plots all together.

The initial idea was for us to pass the winter there without always being moved on by police. We only travelled during the months of April to October anyway so this would do us nicely, but mum had other ideas. She was more interested in getting us educated and putting down roots and I think she was worried about the older members of the family on the road. Things were getting tough for gran now.

By the time I was 16 years old I had my own trailer. I had to put up my share of the cash for the plot I lived on, we always pooled our money anyway The whole family mucked in to get the site ready. The councils never supplied enough transit or permanent sites for travellers to stay on. At one time the government was giving 100 per cent funding to councils to provide sites. Counties were always complaining about travelling communities stopping on farm land and old industrial estates, moaning about the cost of moving them on and the inconvenience to locals. When the counties had the opportunity to solve the situation with the government giving them funding, most of them decided that they perhaps didn't have a problem after all. If they provided sites, they would be seen to be encouraging travelling groups to come to the area and they didn't want that. Instead they declined the grant and kept on complaining.

Well we had this piece of land now. We weren't bothering anyone. In fact, before we arrived, there were infested outbuildings, debris tipped by local house dwellers all around, like old beds, garden rubbish and the like. The site was a proper tip. The locals obviously couldn't be bothered to take their rubbish to the council amenity sites so they just dumped it there.

Dad and granddad got an old JCB machine and levelled the site. Jed, Joey and I built beautifully ornate brick walls for the frontage in good old yellow stock bricks, laid it out real pretty, we did. Joey was a good bricklayer; we just laboured really. The bases went down for the trailers (they came to a pretty penny, as much as any fine bungalow would cost). Then we built little toilet blocks that would run to a cesspit that we made from the back of an old milk tanker. Water and electricity were run in and connected, and we were all set for the winter. We didn't need a council to look after us. We provided for ourselves. We had no dustmen or made-up roads (even though we paid rates), we kept the unmade road level ourselves with a machine. Rubbish was taken to the civic tip. We weren't interfering with anyone.

Then it started. The council were on us like flies on shit. Planning department, environmental agency – they were all there poking around making noises but not one of the bastards had a good thing to say, or one sound piece of advice. We didn't know what they wanted from us and they didn't tell us. If only someone had taken the trouble to sit down and explain, we would have done what they asked. We may have needed help with the forms and so on, but we would have done it. That's the trouble with the local authorities generally: they talk their own language and expect you to understand. Anyone who has tried to better their property by making alterations to it I am sure has had similar problems with either the planning department or building control. We weren't going, though, so the council had to shape up and work with us on that one. For the time being we just ignored them and kept putting in planning applications and appeals at the advice of someone who charged us a fortune to handle it all for us. I think in retrospect we might have been better just going along and actually talking to the people, then doing it ourselves. It would have made it more personal. It seems to me that while you're a number people treat you however they want to. If you become a person they can relate to, I reckon you have more chance.

Now we were all completely independent and sort of settled, the family members gradually began to earn their living in more individual ways. My brother Jed and I had come up with a great new earner. We went up to the Worcester carpet mills with our big old removal van and loaded it up with end-of-the-line runs. We could buy carpet for as little as 30 pence a square metre if we bought the full roll. We'd bring it back to Northampton and park up the van on our new site. The old van served as our warehouse. Each day we would load six or seven rolls on the smaller van and drive around the county 'on the knocker'. Driving around the towns we'd pull up at an office block and work the whole building, knocking on doors and introducing ourselves. We dressed up in smart blue boiler suits and walked in with carpet swatches made up of the stuff we had with us or what we had back at our 'warehouse'. Our story was that we were fitting out one of the office suites in that block and we had a load of carpet left over. If we took our carpet back to the warehouse, we said, we would get a bollocking for over-ordering and so we had to sell it off quick.

'We're only asking ten shillings a yard; this is, of course, only a fraction of its value,' we explained. 'This is office quality, worth around twenty pounds per yard.'

The office girls would fall for it every time. We had order after order. We even ended up fitting some of it. Can you imagine their faces if they had known they had Gypsies in their houses fitting carpets? We had knock-on sales from neighbours who turned up while we were there. We sold thousands of yards of carpet and our lorry just about got to know its own way up and down that motorway. We worked the same story in shops, building sites and garages. We were even stopping people in the streets eventually. We did really well out of it; I was able to buy a good old Range Rover trimmed up with real wood and leather seats. I loved my four-wheel drives as do most Gypsy men. And the punters? Well, they had a bargain also. The carpets were of first-class quality and it would have cost them twice as much in the shops.

The carpets kept us going for ages. We lived like kings, buying designer clothes, clubbing and drinking. Mum and dad had everything they wanted, including a new touring trailer for when the travelling season started again. Not that they asked us for it, we were pleased to give it to them. I suppose we were showing off, really. Dad was earning well for himself anyway. Our gifts were a sort of loving boast. Eventually, though, the carpets slowed down. All the lads were on to it and some started taking the piss, spoiling it for the rest of us. They would sell poor-quality stuff, something with a thread snag in the middle of the roll or a colour run. At least we made sure we sold near-perfect stuff. The gorgios soon caught on and began to steer clear. The last bits we sold to the Asian families in Leicester, Birmingham, Bradford, Manchester and East London. It was like a network. Do a job for one family and they tell everyone they know. We were getting bulk orders from them. They drove a really hard bargain, though. I suppose that's where we got it from, our bargaining skills, I mean. The Romani are said to have come from India and moved through Persia into Europe a thousand years ago, eventually landing on English shores around six hundred years ago.

Soon we started talking again about different little ideas we had to make money. Joey stumbled across an idea while he was out hawking. He went into a café on the A2 and got chatting with a lorry driver who did the Europe trip twice a week. The lorry driver came up with watches to sell. This was another good deal while it lasted. We would buy a thousand watches at under a pound a piece. I would put five or six watches at a time in a plastic bag and go around building sites, factories and pubs with them, telling the men I had been shoplifting. I always made a point of telling them that I wanted to keep one of the watches, and this one would then become the most desirable of the bunch. It would fetch real good wonga. The watches would sell for around a fiver and would make me a nice killing each day. I would probably sell between 40 and 50 watches on average a day. Psychology didn't only work with fighting, I found. We learned to work on people's greed and dishonesty. If they thought the watches were nicked then they wanted them. If I had said they were just being sold cheaply, punters would have resented me for earning a profit and wouldn't have bought them. We sold in a way that created an illusion, looking around all the time in case we got nicked. We used the same little trick with tools, gold and radios. It was a doddle.

As all things did, though, the selling came to an end – but we were always prepared. You just knew when your run had expired and we would have another plan ready for action. Tarmac laying was our next big earner. We really thought that we had arrived with this one. I was really organised now. The biggest wonga would be with the office blocks and big factories. I would drive in with the Range Rover wearing a real smart suit. I always telephoned for an appointment first with the managing director or proprietor. I claimed to be an 'estates maintenance supervisor'. Most of the old factory units were on large estates and each estate would have a maintenance program. I would have a properly measured and scaled plan of the factory site and car park that we'd get made at a little architect's office down the high street of Oadby, a small village near Leicester race track. I took along my own sketch for the architect to work from, with measurements taken at night (although as we got better at it we just went along in the day with our little yellow jackets or dufflecoats on). I would even get coffee and biscuits from some of the office girls. I was looked after. Once we had got our appointments the rest was plain sailing. Getting in was the hardest bit.

Our story would go like this. As a representative of the maintenance programming committee it had been decided, after having a recent survey, that the car parks required emergency maintenance. The site was shared by several other factory units and the costs would be broken down. Everyone would be charged a proportional amount relative to their square footage. Furthermore, it had been agreed by the civil engineering company that completed the initial works on the site, that as the work was required inside the maintenance period, they would stand 50 per cent of the cost.

The director would love all this. It looked like they were to get a new car park for next to nothing as their neighbours were coughing up and also the job was underwritten by a maintenance failure contract. I would produce a contract of about 30 pages (far too many for any busy businessman to read). This contract would, in fact, be full of shit. I would skip through the details, taking our man to the last page. I said I understood how busy he was and offered to condense the content of the document. I would show him the cost of five pounds per square metre. This was peanuts and they knew it, but the old greed came in to play again. It always works. I asked them to sign the contract so that we could get the programme in the pipeline and that work could start in around three months. They would be invoiced three months after that. The guy would always sign reading that last page very slowly and carefully, after all he was no mug.

What they didn't read was the carbon page underneath. The carbon copy showed the cost of work at *fifty* pounds per square metre. This copy would accompany our invoice, which arrived one month after the signing. There would be a note with it, saying that if the invoice was paid within seven days of receipt they could deduct 20 per cent off the total bill with a VAT adjustment (even though we weren't registered for VAT – that gave us another percentage profit, didn't it?). The company would wish to take advantage of the discount and clear the debt within the seven days. The larger companies had accounts departments that paid their bills. The managing director never even saw them so we had little chance of a tumble. But even if they did complain we had their signature on the order and they had a copy on file showing identical details. (The original contract went 'missing'.) By the time three months had gone by we had hit all the larger companies in the area and moved a hundred miles away to work on the next town – always at random and never in a pattern so the gavvers would never know where we were going next.

We made thousands and thousands. We never even had a smell of tarmac, let alone actually *lay* any. Joey bought himself a Rolls and Jed had a BMW – silly bastards. The gavvers weren't stupid, it would be obvious something was going on if we kept it up like that. I'd had enough. The boys started on smaller companies and I could see it was all going to fall apart. They were bound to get caught. Smaller companies were more hands-on and would scream out when the job wasn't done. They were more likely to see every penny that was going out as most operated on tight budgets.

Granddad always said: 'Boy, when you're in front always take time to look behind you and watch what the gavvers are doing.' The way I saw it I was in front, I had my fortune tucked away, I had what I wanted and I hadn't been caught. Now was the time to stop. So I did. I walked away and wiped my hands. The boys of course kept on going. Greed, you see. It was hard for them to give up a good thing and they couldn't imagine themselves getting caught. Eventually it happened, the gavvers moved in on them in West Bromwich. After a couple of adjournments and probation reports, it ended up with Joey getting four years, and little Jed getting six for being the front man. Still – with the time they did on judge's remand and with a bit of time off for behaving themselves, they were sure to be out and about in 18 months and 24 months respectively. Not too sad for the amount of dosh they had tucked away. The police never found that. I was gutted for my little brother, though, this was the first real personal disaster that he or I had experienced. This touched me inside, deep inside. I had always been there for Jed. He relied on me, I felt like I had let him down. I also knew, though, that it was his own bloody fault, but my guilt got the better of me.

Mum cried, I could do nothing. Dad just went quiet on me. He did that, it was so annoying. He would just go inside himself and deal with things in his own way. Don't get me wrong, he was always there for us and dealt with all the problems as they arose but we could never share our feelings with him.

I felt a little something inside me switch off when they took Jed down. When I looked I didn't see the young man that he had become, I just saw this little ten-year-old boy, his face all smiley with a line of snot pointing to his mouth. I guess it's like that when you are grown up, your children or your younger siblings always remain little in your memory. When they do wrong you see their little child's face, not the stupid young twat they really are. Why should I feel bad, though? I *told* them to jack it in. I had the wonga I had made from the tarmac scam but I wanted to keep it intact. I had worked hard for my wonga and the only way to keep it was to keep working at something, keep it topped up.

Dad had been doing real well with granddad, tree lopping and landscaping. They had their little thing going but that really wasn't for me. I wanted to move around further afield while they seemed to be settling in for good.

Old Darkie and Bendy had been working the road contracts for several years. They were real tarmac contractors now with no dodgy deals. I pulled in to Darkie's place and asked for some work. Of course I knew he couldn't deny me, although I did get an hour's lecture on not fucking it up or taking the piss and was told that there would be no favours. If I got out of line I would get a slap and so on. The usual family stuff. But I knew the job was mine.

I always got on well with Bendy. We had this thing about horses, you see. Sometimes Bendy would go all over the country buying horses, although his favoured place to buy from was Wales. He loved his Welsh section A and C ponies; good ponies that would make sound family pets or driving cobs. He wasn't bothered which. He knew how to buy and to sell. He never went wrong. I remember one time Boy-Boy, my young cousin, got on a pony that took off with him on it. He was a good rider but the run affected his confidence a bit. That pony was a favourite of Uncle Bendy's but when it ran off with Boy-Boy, he mullered it. Shot it dead, his own finger on the trigger. He wouldn't have let anyone else do it. Bendy wouldn't have anyone's life threatened. He was very protective like that. Even though he loved his horses, if they were a danger in any way they would have to go. He knew when they would never come right.

FOUR

Drom to Nowhere

My first job for my uncles was on the A1. We stayed in our trailers at the roadside and moved with the road. We'd start work at 5 a.m. and often work in shifts on a 24-hour rota. It was knackering but the wonga was good and Darkie always treated me right in that respect. We were to work here for months, always on the same road but never getting anywhere. 'The drom (road) to nowhere', Darkie called it.

I was a good worker, which surprised me! I always thought I would be a lazy bastard but I seemed to have matured since Jed and Joey had left the scene. I was always the one looking for a fast buck and an easy ride but this time I really settled to my job. Several months after starting work we had got as far as Hemel Hempstead. We used to go to the same old café all the time. It was clean and the portions were man-sized. We also went for the entertainment.

The bloke who owned this café, Mano, was Spanish and his wife Anietta was Italian. Whenever they argued (which was every lunchtime) they went off into their respective languages. We thought this was hilarious, not only because it sounded funny but because to our thinking, surely neither knew what the other was saying, so how did they know if they were winning or losing?

One day, I was having a bit of dinner in Mano's place. Us boys were over by the corner having a laugh and joke and a group of hauliers were sitting by the door. The group kept looking over, giving the odd sneer followed by a short burst of laughter that we just knew was a piss-take.

I began to bite. My dinner began choking me and my chest filled with a tight, stifling feeling, as if it had been stuffed with clouds, floating and bubbling inside me. Darkie told me to calm myself as he took a sock off his right foot and dropped a pool ball into it from the pool table next to where we were eating. Bendy never used a tool at all. His fists were, after all, lethal weapons. He wasn't a big man, not like Darkie, but his punch was so severe that when it hit his target, the man would be sparked for sure.

I took a sauce bottle and slid it up my sleeve, ready to drop it into my palm and plant it on anyone's head that popped my way, but the guvnor of the café saw me so I slid it back on the table. I didn't want him to think I was choring it. We had seen this kind of thing many times before: you grew to sense trouble brewing and made yourself ready. We were a loud bunch and often people would take offence at our presence but it was just the way we behaved. We kept it all between ourselves and any jokes were inoffensive. (In any case the gorgios wouldn't understand a word we said even if they did hear it.)

We rose as one and moved to the door. The hauliers grew quiet and never looked up. I was the last out and felt a thud on the back of my neck. I reached backward and felt a squishy mess, the dirty bastards had thrown mashed potato at me. I screamed a warrior's cry, the cry of a banshee and hurled myself back through the door. I didn't want to know where the tattie came from, I wanted them all.

I landed on their table and took the crockery clean off it. Darkie and Bendy crashed through the door behind me and we let them have it fucking good. There was claret everywhere. Bendy got a tooth embedded in his fist. The table at which the hauliers sat was shattered and was lying around the motionless body of a fat, bearded pig of a man.

People sitting at their tables moved back to one end of the café – after all, it wasn't their fight and in any case we had no intention of hurting them. Another three bodies lay scattered around the café, as each of the remaining men tried to take on his own defensive position. One ended up with his head squarely in the middle of the glass cake display on the counter. Another got a gash in his head that looked like a bloody rasher of bacon stuck on it and the last ended up sporting a lump the size of a football behind his ear where it had met with Darkie's sock. It didn't take us long to silence our abusers. Fucking served them right.

A familiar sound moved us to run as fast as we could. The siren of a gavver's screeve pierced our ears. 'Too late!' shouted Bendy. 'They know who we are in the café, let's just ride it out and see what comes our way.' The gavvers piled into the café. There seemed to be hundreds of them, running around like chickens with their heads chopped off. There were big, hairy Alsatians going mental at the end of a chain. I couldn't get away from the bastards. One copper bashed the backs of my legs with his stick, then cracked his cuffs across my head as I went down. I felt one of the dogs get hold of my leg. The handler screamed at it – it let go and grabbed my arm and held tight.

The gavvers shouted, 'Stay still!' Needless to say I did without question. Fuck, those dogs! There were gavvers grabbing and pushing. There wasn't enough of us to go round them all. Their adrenalin was up and they got so over-excited that they even pushed each other around. They didn't know who to get hold of or what to do until a ranking officer took control and pointed us all out after talking to the wounded men.

The brothers and me were stood up with our backs against the window. We were all cuffed and marched out to the three vans waiting in the car park. 'Fuck me!' said Bendy as we were pushed into the daylight. 'It looks like a gavvers' ball out here, there's hundreds of 'em!'

We looked and started laughing. There were three vans, two dog vans and four cars – with two more steaming up the road. What the fuck did they think was going on? As soon as you mention the word 'Gypsy', the world falls in.

Off we were hauled to the police station and banged up in a tiny cell apiece. A gavver came to see me.

He said: 'You're going to get it now. You're going to leave here with more than you came in with.' I spat in his face, I could do nothing else as I was cuffed to the thing they laughingly called a bed – a wide wooden plank with a three-inch thick, green plastic cover that they called a mattress. He slowly walked to the cell door as he wiped the gob off his face. Then he turned sharply and shoved his truncheon into my stomach with the force of a steam train. I felt my dinner rise to my throat but I wasn't about to let him beat me – *or* waste my dinner. I stood up, looked him in the eye, swallowed sick and grinned.

Again he thrust into me with the stick, this time bringing his elbow down on my middle back. I am ashamed to say that I went down with a thud to the floor. I felt his boot find my kidneys. Again and again the dirty bastard abused my body. I say 'my body' because he wasn't going to get to my mind. I blanked the absurdity of it all. Those lorry drivers were the cause of my pain. I accepted the abuse from the police. It had become a part of being who I was. I was, after all, just an 'old didekoi' in their eyes.

I promised myself that I was going to sit at that café until those hauliers returned. I couldn't beat the police force but I could beat the shit out of those no-good bastards. I counted the blows the gavvers blessed me with and vowed each one would grow twofold when the day of retribution came. I was a man possessed by revenge. The beating finally got the better of me and the police deprived me of the lunch I had eaten earlier. It went everywhere, up the walls, over the bench and floor and over the gavver's uniform. (I saved that bit for him and aimed it well.) Luckily for me, the duty sergeant had a mop and bucket so I could enjoy the rest of this eventful afternoon clearing up my vomit. Unfortunately they appeared not to notice that I was also caked in the stuff and I had to sit like that until around 4 a.m. the next day when they unlocked the doors. A young, spotty police officer said: 'Get the fuck out.' I didn't need telling again – I was out of there like shit off a shovel.

It turned out that they had known all along that the hauliers had started the ruck. The man who owned the café spoke up for us and several witnesses in the café had supported his story.

'Why did they keep us in then?' I asked Darkie.

'For sport, son, for sport,' he said solemnly.

The next day and for several days to follow I sat in the car park of that café. The brothers thought that I was mad but I had made myself a promise and I wasn't about to break it. After all if I couldn't trust myself then who could I trust?

My day came. A tanker with 'Thomas Alan' printed on the side came thundering up to the café, pulling up in a cloud of dust, its big wheels skidding on the gravel surface. Then there was another and another. My stomach turned, it knew what was coming. I stood squarely across the threshold of the café entrance. It was like a western, only the whistling music and the tumbleweed were missing.

Three men walked towards me across the car park, obviously unaware of my intentions. I saw the uncles pull in quietly in Darkie's van. They had seen the lorries pass them and knew that they had to hurry down to me if they wanted a little of the fun. As the first man came within reach of me I planted a fist square in the middle of his fat, ugly, piggy-eyed face. Blood spat outwards like an exploding orange, saturating his beard. His two mates jumped like wallabies and turned to run.

'Come here, you dirty mother's cunt!' I shouted, expecting them to stop, but of course they didn't. I chased them and kicked one straight up the nuts from behind. He went down like a sack of shit. I bet he had a lump in his throat after that. I followed through with several more well-placed kicks, wanting to muller the bastard. I turned and stood on the neck of the big man that I had already decked. I'd always been told to hit the big one first, then that would trash the rest of 'em. He had in any case been the real cause of my exploding head. I had felt such pressure waiting for this day; it had given me a headache that I knew wouldn't lift until I had done my job. The thought of revenge filled my every waking moment and my dreams enacted the damage I was to inflict on these men.

The third man had got to his lorry and began to wind the big machine up. Darkie, thinking quickly, drove his new transit van in front of it to stop him leaving.

Bad move! The big old Scania lorry ate him alive. That man was *leaving* and the fear that made him leave couldn't be matched. The side was ripped off Darkie's transit like it was a sweet packet being opened. Darkie sat there stunned and Bendy was crying with laughter.

'What the fuck are you laughing at?' I said. Bendy was holding his stomach with laughter.

'You know this is the funniest thing I have ever seen, it's like it was all in slow motion. I haven't had time to move yet and it's all over. I had just got out of the van and in that time you had demolished two men, put the fear of God into a third and had had the side ripped out of Darkie's van. That's what I call destruction!' Bendy replied in short breaths.

'Oh you think that's funny, eh?' screamed Darkie, 'Well, this is going to be hilarious.' And with that he leaped from his van and knocked Bendy spark-out.

What a fucking nightmare, I thought.

Bendy began to come round quickly. Darkie only managed to put him down because he wasn't expecting it; I think it was the surprise that got to him. He was still laughing as we pulled him up. There were no hard feelings, they always carried on like this.

Well – I had had my revenge and I felt satisfied. I could get on with my life again. As we three stood in the car park deciding whether to go in for a cup of mot, a big-looking mush walked slowly towards me from the shadow of an articulated lorry filled with scrap iron.

'Here we go . . .' I said and prepared myself to go again. I took a stand and waited for him to come close. He noticed my preparation and spoke up.

'Woah up, mate!' he said with a broad, booming cockney accent. 'I don't fight for free. You're a little bit handy with those fists. How would you like to go again – for money?'

Darkie was on him like shit on a blanket. 'How much and when?' he asked without even looking sideways at me (after all it was only my fight that was being called on).

'Back of this car park, Thursday morning, 6 a.m. We'll fight for a monkey,' replied the man.

I spoke up quickly before Darkie took over – he had a habit of doing that. I wanted in on every deal.

'Who'll I be fighting?'

'Me,' he replied and walked away with a swagger. 'Bring your money.'

'There we go boy,' said Darkie. 'I've got you a fight there, that's a nice little earner.' I looked at him sideways.

'What do you mean you got me a fight? The man came to me, how did *you* set that up then?' I said.

'Fuck me,' said Darkie, 'Can't please some people. Are we going to get some work out of you now, you crazy bastard?'

We all just looked at the gash in the side of Darkie's van and noticed the lilting suspension, looked back at each other and began to walk back to the job.

Later that day Darkie towed his van up to the town of St Albans and then reported it stolen. This led to a nice little claim on the insurance. Bit of a 'cunning stunt', if you know what I mean. Mum always said that if Darkie fell in a pile of shit he would come up smelling of flowers. He always had the knack of turning a bad situation into profit. 'Positive thinking', he called it. Positive bullshit, more like.

Well, I had a fight to prepare for now and I was really looking forward to it. The uncles talked about nothing else. It got on my tits in the end, I didn't want to listen to them too much, it would make me too confident. They thought I was the mutt's nuts anyway.

Thursday came at last. We were already at the café around 4.30 a.m., having our breakfast and waiting for the hour to come. I went for a dump. The usual routine. *Nothing*.

In the car park, the drivers began to congregate. Everyone in the world seemed to know what was going down; at least every lorry driver. The rear of the café had a pea-gravel area. I remember turning to the uncles and saying 'Oh, fucking *lovely*. If I go down on this I'll have me skin ripped off of me.' I had a look at the make-shift ring. It was all quite professionally laid out really considering it was just an old back yard to the café.

The ring was made up of four big red Propane bottles with lorry rope tied to each one. The makeshift seats at the corner were old blue milk crates turned upwards with a towel laid on them. Bendy was my second and the café owner came out to be referee. This is all very civilised, I thought.

We were now just waiting for my opponent. Then along he came, lumbering slowly around the corner. I remember thinking, he's going down quick and hard – he's far too slow, and big enough for me to run all over.

Then, without warning, *whup*!

'Oh fuck. Here it comes,' I moaned. Without fail, I puked at a fight. I just have to puke, it makes me feel so stupid but I can't get control of it. Bendy had the bucket all ready for me. It became part of my 'sports equipment'.

I looked up at the other fighter as I finished puking. He just smiled. 'I think he's more nervous than me,' I said to my uncle trying to boost myself.

We were both now in the ring and ready for the fight to begin. The referee shouted 'Fight!' I jumped out of my corner. The big man came across. I hardly noticed him coming. There were two hits, I didn't feel either one of them. He hit me and I hit the ground.

I woke up inside the café, the big man sitting next to me with a wet cloth covering his hand. 'You've got a hard head, son,' he smiled. I jumped up quick ready to fight on.

'It's all over, boy,' said Darkie. 'We're inside now.'

It took me a while to gather myself but I eventually calmed down when I felt the café owner's daughter, Gina, rubbing the back of my neck. Her smooth hand rolled backwards and forwards. Her neck-rub reached every part of my body – and I mean *every* part. I had to admit it, I'd had a thing going for her for months now. I was just too scared to say anything.

'Just rest, son,' said the big man. He held out his hand. It was like a shovel. 'Denny is the name,' he continued. 'I have been working this circuit for years and I can see something you have that's worth my time. You just need to slow down a bit, you do things in a hurry. You need to learn some simple psychology.'

I looked at Darkie. 'What the fuck's psycho . . . psych . . . whatever he said?' I asked. Darkie just shrugged his shoulders.

'Slow down?' I said, 'I thought *you* were going to be slow but you came across to me like the wind!'

'You should never underestimate your opponent,' he replied. 'Always consider them to be as skilful as you are – then try to out-wit them.'

We sat and talked for hours and we went on to become quite good friends in a sort of distant manner. Denny was a great influence on my fighting technique. I began to use my brain as well as my hands. He taught me some moves of the street fighter, moves I had never seen on the Gypsy circuit – they were dirty but were to stand me in good stead during the fighting years of my life that were to follow. He also taught me some boxing techniques and gave a new power to my punching by using the hip more. As a travelling boy I never managed to learn to box; we couldn't get into clubs most of the time, because we travelled of course. Not like nowadays – they love to get the Gypsy boys in the clubs because they're good, and in any case Gypsies are more settled and better able to join boys' clubs. In more recent years, as Gypsy boys began dominating the scene in youth amateur fighting, it was decided that Gypsy and travelling boys would not be allowed to box in the schoolboys championships. This is how they did it so as not to leave themselves open to accusations of discrimination. The exact determination of 'schoolboy' was changed from the accepted definition that you were of schoolboy age. Only those who went to school regularly were eligible to fight. Now everyone knows that travelling families don't go to the same school regularly because of the nature of their parents' work opportunities and their cultural desire to travel. They go when places are available, though they go to school as the law requires.

This was a clever piece of discrimination by legislation. Another ruse that skipped round racism is that sign you often see on public houses: NO TRAVELLERS. Now this could mean anyone really, couldn't it? The sales rep, the lorry driver – in fact, anyone on a trip. But we know who they mean, don't we? And we can't take them to task over it.

(Note: As this book goes to publication there has been successful prosecution taken against the use of the above type of sign. Romani people have been in the UK for six centuries. It's time to realise that we're here to stay. And our culture stays with us.)

FIVE

My Heart Runs Cold

I was back to work the next day and I couldn't see a thing. I had a black eye the size of a cricket ball. Darkie took one look and told me to bugger off back to my trailer. He knew, of course, that I wasn't going to be any good to them that day. I wandered up to the café. Perhaps I could grab a game of pool with someone. Most of the drivers had got to know me during those months on contract and I had met some half-decent blokes – for gorgios anyway! I found the café really quiet; empty in fact. So I bought myself a cuppa and began to knock the balls about on the pool table.

I got chatting to Gina. She was beautiful. I had become besotted. I recalled her gentle touch after the fight, the touch that reached parts of me even Heineken couldn't get to! We talked and talked, listened to music and played pool. I had never met anyone like her before.

Uh-oh! What was I doing? It looked like I was falling for a little gorgio girl. We got on so well that day and her mum didn't seem to mind us talking. In fact she gave us a few little smiles. I hadn't yet had a real girlfriend. 'Poor bastard,' I hear you say – no girlfriend, and me 18 years old.

Well, I began to get real brave. My heart was pounding in my chest as I forced out my burning question: 'Want to meet me for a drink tonight?'

'Sure,' she said.

'Course I'm sure!' I replied naively.

'No, I mean *sure I will*,' she confirmed.

I was a mess. I wasn't handling this at all well.

'Yes! She said "yes!"' I thought to myself.

We carried on playing pool for a couple of hours. I felt kind of awkward all of a sudden and I completely ballsed up the game. Gina beat me hands down. I used my loaf though and I let her believe that I was being the gentleman, allowing her to win. I kept dropping the cue and forgetting my go. This was how it went on until the lunchtime rush came and she had to go back behind the counter. I just stood for a while looking at her. I felt my mui fixed in a very stupid grin but I didn't care. She had said *yes*!

I skipped off back to my trailer to get myself prepared. I scrubbed my face till it was as clean as a new pin. I felt that I was shining from head to toe. I put on a suit for the first time in God knows how long. I was all done and ready, sitting on my bed waiting to meet up with the little gorgio girl. It wasn't even dark yet; it was only mid-afternoon. I was so keen I hadn't thought about anything else but getting ready. I took off my suit again and decided to have a good clean around the place in case I brought Gina back.

I looked around. Shit, I thought. It's a shambles, what will she think of me?

I cleared everything away – clothes, newspapers, bedding, crockery and cutlery – the lot. I simply wrapped it in a sheet and piled it in to the shower section of the trailer. Hid it away in one swipe almost. I heated up a bowl of water and scrubbed the tops and walls, tied back the curtains and swept the floors with the good old stiff brush that mum gave me. I didn't recognise the place. I looked around once more and was satisfied. I then just sat back and listened to the radio.

Bendy came knocking at my trailer door around seven. 'Fuck me, boy,' he said, 'It smells like a brothel in here!'

'Well how would you know what one of them places smells like, uncle Bendy? I'm sure auntie Sylvia would love to know,' I replied.

Well, that sent him out with his tail between his legs. Just the mention of auntie Sylvia frightened Bendy. She was just a small, dark-skinned woman; very gentle and loyal, but God help anyone who crossed her. They were, of course, very much in love. They had been for many years before they got together. They were both part of the same extended family. Gypsy women are extremely loyal but do have a sharp edge to their tongues and a temper to back it up. I remember auntie holding off several policemen, bailiffs and officials when they tried to take uncle Bendy's lorry from him one year. A man had made a claim in court against Bendy, but he never went to the hearing simply because he said he didn't owe anything, and that was that. The man got judgement against Bendy and sent the bailiffs to seize the lorry.

Auntie jumped into the lorry. Inside was an old gallon-can full of water. She promptly locked the doors and poured the can all over herself telling the police that she would set light to herself if they came any nearer. They didn't know it was just water. If they had thought straight they would have realised that there would be no place for a petrol can in a diesel lorry anyway. We laugh about that story all the time, it's still one of the family favourites. Auntie Sylvia daren't have let those men take Bendy's wagon, he would have gone mad. She had to stall them until he got home. And there were no mobile phones in those days either, so it was a long wait.

Darkie came in shortly after Bendy left. Bendy must have gone back and said something. He came in all smiles and grins.

'What you up to then, boy? Got a little rackli lined up, have you? You watch out for them little gorger girls. They know too much for the likes of you.'

'Leave off,' I said sheepishly. 'I'm a bag of nerves as it is.'

'Where you going off to then?' he said.

I felt the shock of pain go up the back of my neck and hit me behind the eyes. I stood frozen with my mouth gaping.

'What's up?' said Darkie.

'I didn't arrange where to meet! I just asked her out tonight. She said yes, and I left. I don't even know what *time*!'

My uncle began to laugh. 'You daft git,' he sniggered.

I had powdered every bit of my anatomy. I had even put balls of cotton wall soaked in cologne down my pants (well, you never know!) 'I am dressed like a pox doctor's clerk with nowhere to go!' I said.

Darkie, Bendy and myself sat for the rest of the night playing cards as usual. I kept losing, of course. My mind wasn't on the game. I kept jumping up and looking out the window in case she came by to see where I was. I even went up to the café for a walk a few times; maybe she'd be waiting there, I thought. But no. She didn't show. I had really messed up.

Instead of me feeling the caress of a woman's gentle touch, instead of the sweet smell of her body, instead of her soft voice – I had that fucking pair passing wind, slurping gatter and bashing me around the back of the head every time I dealt them a crap hand. My first attempt at dating and I ballsed it up. Prat!

I lay awake all night. My anticipations of earlier were catching up on me, if you know what I mean. (The old man had told me it had a mind of its own.) I couldn't wait until the time came round to get to the café. Morning came and the clock shouted at me. *Go!* it seemed to scream.

I was up, washed, dressed and on my way before my uncles could get there. The last thing I wanted was them behind me taking the piss, they would surely ruin it for me – if I hadn't done so already.

I walked into the café after hanging back for ten minutes until she had served her customers. Both Gina and her mum were serving but I needed her to serve me. I needed that excuse to talk. I surely couldn't just walk straight up to her, could I? Not after making such a fuck-up . . .

Here I go, I thought. It was my turn. She looked straight past me as if I didn't exist. My stomach turned somersaults. I didn't understand, what was going on? I loved her; I knew it from the start. Her lips, her eyes, her hair, I would have died just to bless my lips with hers or to fall into those dark liquid eyes, maybe to feel the softness of her face against my cheek.

The only stirring I had ever had to equal this was when I fought, but this was a different feeling. My bowels heaved, every part of me began to feel uneasy. I loved her. Why wouldn't she look at me?

'Love is a many splendoured thing . . .'

Darkie strode in singing at the top of his quivering voice. 'La-la-la-la-la-la-la-*la* . . .'

He obviously didn't know any more, just enough to make me feel a prat.

By now I was being served by Gina's mother. I stood staring across at my love.

Gina. My beautiful Gina. I'd never get tired of her name.

I bought a tea; I was no longer hungry. I went to sit down. What was this, though? She was coming over. I held my breath, my stomach turned over again. The way my luck was going I would pass wind just as she got to me, I thought.

No . . . she wiped my table over and dropped a note by the side of my cup. I opened it quickly, I couldn't have been less discreet. 'I am sorry about last night,' it read. 'Meet me at 8.30 outside the market square.'

She was sorry? What did she mean?

My mind was turning things over and over all day. I couldn't work, I didn't talk.

'I'll be glad when you've done your business,' said Darkie. 'You're no good to no one the way you are.'

What did he know? He was an old man. He knew nothing of love; nothing of youth. My heart was racing as the time to leave my work came close. I was discovering another me. A nicer me, someone I liked to have inside my soul. I had this weird belief that all of the feelings that I had were different beings. My emotions were so intense I felt they couldn't come from one person alone. When I hated I did so with hell inside me. When I was happy I was unbearable to have around – a complete nuisance, in fact. I would walk into a trailer and leave again like a whirlwind. I had found that I was the same with my love. This was a feeling I liked, one that I could enjoy and never have to question. This person, I thought, could stay with me forever.

I got myself ready as quickly as possible, going through the same ritual of the evening before, except that this time I locked the trailer door so that the uncles couldn't get in and use me for their sport again. This night was going to work if it killed me. I drove quickly but steadily to the meeting place. I jumped from my Ranger and stepped toward Gina who was standing waiting. I could see no one but her as I arrived: although the area was bustling with folk, my eyes were focused on her small figure. I fell backward as Gina threw herself in to my arms, her small body pressing hard against my chest, her arms clinging to my body as she quivered and cried in a way that touched my very soul.

I held her close. Her perfume filled my nostrils and I felt a lightness in my chest. My body became calm; almost spiritual. I felt

TARMAC WARRIOR

59

moved, the way I did when I went into a church. I held her firmly until she stopped her sobbing. 'What's the matter? Have I done something wrong?' I asked.

'Oh, Billy,' she said. 'I can't explain what I feel. As I saw you drive up I was completely overcome by emotion. A sort of wave of sadness ran across my body. I think I love you but dad doesn't want me near you, he said he'll have you beaten up if you come near me again.'

I stood staring at her for a while. She'd said she loved me! I didn't really hear the rest. I was so happy I didn't know what to say or do, I just pulled her towards me slowly, firmly but gently, and kissed her eyes, her nose, her lips, her mouth – soft, warm and full; her olive skin so smooth but cold against my cheek.

'Let's get into the car,' I said. 'You're freezing.' I had suddenly developed this urge to take care of her. We sat in the car and talked until it was almost dawn.

'Christ!' she said. 'I'd better get home. Dad will kill me if he finds I am still out. I have to be at work in an hour.'

I drove the 15 miles back to where Gina lived with her parents. She had her own little flat above the garage. It was a huge house with lights picking out the path leading to her front door. The music sounded distant in the car as we drove; the heater buzzing softly as the warm air surrounded us. Our thoughts seemed to drown out all other sounds.

I parked a few yards from the front of her house, shielded by the ornamental trees that decorated the front garden, giving all who passed a clue to the wealth of the occupants. Gina slid from the car quietly and, looking up and down her road making sure that she hadn't been caught out, brushed my lips with a kiss. She slipped away through the hedge toward her little part of the house. I watched her as long as I could, stretching my neck even to watch the branches of the bushes move as she passed through them.

We arranged regular meetings at the café. It became a sort of ritual, with her passing me little notes trying not to let her father see. She said he was very strict. We met every moment we possibly could night after night and sometimes in the day too. Then arrived the greatest night of all, the night when our emotions ran too high for us to control. I took her – or did she take me? I really can't remember. I just know that my body ached for the fullness of her love; I wanted to enjoy every part of her and for her to share every part of me. We laid down the back seats and curled under the blanket that was always kept for my gran. It somehow seemed like sacrilege to use gran's blanket but my passion soon removed all guilt! I was thinking with my little head instead of my big head. The moment was ours and it fulfilled my every dream. It was my first time and it was everything that I had fantasised it would be. I am sure that I didn't do everything right, but then how could I? I knew nothing except what I had heard around the lads. But I knew it was right for me. I didn't know women made a noise when you did it, it scared me at first. I thought I was hurting her but she explained everything as we went along, she never ridiculed me in any way. I knew it wasn't the first time for her but I didn't care. I just wanted to enjoy the moment, this one moment I would never have shared with anyone else; the one moment in my life that I was never to find again. I loved her so much. I felt a wetness on my cheek. I was crying. Why was I crying? This was the best moment in my life, but I was crying like a baby. She held me and talked to me, telling me to let it go. The emotion had been too much for me, I had waited all these years and finally it was here and with the most wonderful girl I could ever wish to be with. Each night after this, we did nothing else but make love. I found that my imagination was only inhibited by the room in the back of the Range Rover.

We went to a hotel along the A1 and booked in. I had never been in a hotel before, it was strange to have a bathroom, with a shower as well. We had room service, wine, a steak meal. We did it all that night – several times, in fact! It was great. We laid in the big old bed holding each other as close as we could and slipped into a sleep like I had never known before.

We were woken by the telephone. It was the receptionist asking us to vacate the room.

'Fuck!' I shouted. 'It's nearly mid-day!'

Gina panicked and fell out of the bed. 'What am I going to do? My father will kill me!' she said as she floundered trying to get into her clothes.

'Don't worry, I'll come home with you and explain. We love each other. He'll understand. It's not as if I am a stranger. I want to marry you. I will care for you better than any man.'

Gina fell quiet for a while.

'Papa would never let us marry. He does like you but you are a Gypsy boy. In his country *gitano* are seen as thieves and beggars. I am expected to marry someone who is at the very least a Catholic. There has been talk of me going to Spain to live with my grandparents for a while. I think papa believes I will find a husband there. It's so unfair. I don't want to live in Spain. I am English. I don't really know the country.'

I felt then that we were never to go any further than this day. Even in secret. My heart was breaking but I never let her know, perhaps I was wrong. Perhaps I was reading more into her silence than there was. We didn't speak much on the way home except a few comments on how to approach her father when we arrived. I dropped her at her impressive driveway and her parents were standing there, waiting. I went to get out of the car.

'No,' she said, and held her hand on my leg. 'I'll talk to them alone, let me go alone.'

I sat there like a statue – a lifeless, gutless statue watching my little Gina walk away from me – walk away from my arms, my heart, my life. I knew I would never hold her again.

The difference in our cultures wasn't a problem for Gina and me, but her father's prejudice ruled her life and at this moment in time, I thought it had ruined mine. Gina was submissive to her father; that was her culture, their way. I understood that. I could never have blamed her, not my Gina.

I drove home and went to my bed. I locked the door and just lay there. I don't know what I felt. Those past three months had been so wonderful, so full, but now they were gone. I lay in my trailer hating my parents for making me a Gypsy. Why did they do that to me? What had I done to them? I really felt that I would have been better off had I not been born at all. 'Oh God, why did you let me be born a Gypsy?' I yelled.

I locked out the world and stayed in my trailer for days refusing to emerge. The uncles knew me well and they didn't bother me. A Gypsy man knows and respects the value of privacy, especially when it involves one's feelings, and I appreciated their consideration.

There was a loud knock at my trailer door. I heard my father's voice.

'Are you there, boy?' he said. His voice was soft and faltering. I knew there was something wrong immediately. I jumped up, quickly putting dad's needs before my own self-pity.

'It's your granddad,' he said and broke down in tears.

Granddad had died.

We cried together, holding each other for what seemed like hours. We had never held each other before. Why did it have to be on such an occasion that he would share himself with me? I would have dearly loved him to hug me with pride for instance.

Things came together a bit and we wandered up to the uncles' trailer. They had already heard the news from Ruby who had travelled up with dad. Mum and auntie Sylvia had stayed home with gran. We all sat round and talked for a long while, taking turns to cry. The reality of it hadn't yet sunk in. It was Darkie who led the way. He organised for the men to carry on working and told them what had gone on. They would all attend the funeral, of course, but only we were to go home.

Before we set off, I had to see my Gina once more. I walked to the café where she worked and stood in the doorway. We just looked at each other. Her hand rose slowly but dropped as her father appeared. A tear filled my eye. Was it for my grandfather? For my life's love? Or was it because of the racial divide that had treated me so cruelly in my life? I'll never know. I whispered my words to her across the grubby tables. 'Goodbye, my love.'

I turned and walked away slowly, my steps picking up as I took control of myself. I needed to be strong. My family needed me.

We all headed for home, the trailers one behind the other, slowly moving through the traffic until we reached the plots we all shared. Granddad's trailer seemed to look different now. Obviously I knew he wasn't in it any more but it just somehow *looked* different. The whole place did, in fact. Even the chiriklos seemed to be quiet.

Everyone was moping around in the days that led up to the funeral. We all spent hours sharing stories about granddad; we got drunk some nights and we cried. My own memories of that time however are still fresh and full. As I lay on my bed, I began to remember those childhood Sunday mornings when granddad used to take me down to Petticoat Lane (known simply as 'the Lane') and

Club Row in London's East End. As long as we were in reasonable driving distance we would go there. Sundays were a culinary delight for me at the Lane. I recall the vendors scattered around and the smell of the hot chestnuts cooking in the winter months, cracking open on the mobile stove; the hot apple or banana fritters. Then there was the unforgettable taste of the hot sarsaparilla drink sold from the back of a truck. It was like medicine, yet still a treat because we were drinking it in an unusual place. Then along came the summer. The fresh pineapple stalls; herring and onion from the pickle stall; the many foods off the deli bar; fresh salmon and cream cheese in a bagel. I remember the big African that stood in Middlesex street chanting: 'I have anorse . . . anybody wanna buy anorse . . .'. Prince Monolulu was his name and he was not selling 'anorse' at all; he was selling a *tip* for a horse that he thought would win a race that week. He would dress in African tribal dress – big plumes of coloured feathers in his head-dress, a grass skirt with coloured bits all around it and he'd carry a spear. We would see him dressed the same at the big race meets that we attended too.

With Prince Monolulu there would also be a Romani Gypsy man known as 'Marko the Tip'. Not only did we see them at the Lane but they would be at every race track I remember visiting. (I have since found out that his real name was Reg Hancock and he is, in fact, the uncle of the Honourable Ian Hancock, a Romani Professor from Texas University. Ian has written many books and been quoted in many more, he has even acted as an advisor to the President of the United States. His specialist fields are the Holocaust and Romani languages.) Both Monolulu and Marko were real characters, the like of which the modern world appears to be lacking. The Lane wouldn't be the same without these people. Granddad often bought horse tips from these men until he sussed that they would sell the names of several horses to be the winner in the same race. (They had to be right with one of them, didn't they?) So there was always a group who had bought the *right* name that would be very happy with the service they received that day!

In summer months we always had young birds to sell. Granddad and I used to go out birding. Sometimes we would net a bush full of goldfinches. We would load the branches of bushes with a gum so that their feet stuck when they tried to fly away. We would then just pick them off and cage them. We made a good living out of selling British finches – bullfinches, greenfinches, chaffinches and goldfinches. Goldies seemed to be the most popular birds to sell. People would buy the finches to mate with their canaries. That way they would reproduce what is known as a 'mule'. This is probably the best singing bird you will find. The birds would be boxed or caged and taken to the 'the bird pub' at the top of Club Row where we sold them to punters. I loved Club Row. This was a market in Brick Lane, close to Petticoat Lane, always held on a Sunday and was filled with stalls of second-hand stuff. There would be hundreds of stalls and caverns of childhood fantasy, selling army clothes such as tin helmets and hand grenades. I would be lost for hours while granddad would do his business – either selling birds or perhaps a goat or some chickens he had chored. We used to sell those to the Pakistanis for food (alive, of course). I would roam the streets looking through piles of old junk that would be for sale. It was like Aladdin's cave to me. The men with the nicked watches and rings furtively looking for the gavvers as they tried to sell their wares. Then there was row upon row of animals. Puppies, kittens, tropical fish, tortoises, terrapins, rabbits and the like. Yes, my Sundays would be pure fantasy to any child.

I also remember the horse fairs and the October Welsh horse sales in particular. Dad and Bendy would drive their old float up to Wales. I would go with granddad in his motor and listen to his stories, making the time pass so quickly. We would park up there for the three days until the men who were auctioning the ponies would bring them down from the mountains. Between us we would buy as many as 60 ponies and bring them all back in two floats by taking out the partitions. I recall the trouble we had loading those ponies on to the float. There would be men beating the horses to get them up, whipping them ferociously. Granddad used to get really angry with those men. Our family always loved horses. Bendy and granddad had a particular way with them, I remember. Granddad used to spend hour upon hour talking with the ponies. He'd have them penned between the two floats with a barrier at each end to form a corral. He would stand in there with a bit of bread or some hard feed and almost ignore the animal, while talking softly about anything that came in to his head. You would hear him talk about the weather, or the trip up to the sales, anything. He would continue to ignore the pony for ages, having it follow him around. Granddad would walk round and round in the make-shift corral, back and forth across the pony's path until its natural inquisitiveness got the better of it. The pony would now begin to follow granddad. He knew then that he had a 'good un'. Then he would begin to feed it bits of bread or a handful of nuts maybe – never oats, though, that would make it too lively. There was a herbal mixture the old horse men made also. He would feed this mixture to the pony with a piece of bread. It calmed it for the trip home. He would always be thinking of the horse's welfare. A lot can be told of a man's nature by his treatment of animals. Our family were gentle people – although in his day granddad could have a good kor. Granddad's last fight that my dad remembered was with a man called Jack Palmer, a Romani man who came from near Heathrow. He was nicknamed 'Peddlar' Palmer by the gorgio men. 'Peddlar' or 'Tinker' would be the name they gave to 'acceptable' Romanis. Others were just plain old 'Pikeys', or 'Park-where-you-likeys' as my gorgio pal calls them.

Fight nights were real treats to me as a child, something else I shared with my granddad. He took me to the wrestling or the boxing wherever we happened to be stopping. My very favourite venues would always be Poplar Baths or York Hall. Granddad often had the job of being steward there and so I would get well looked after and would get to meet the fighters. He was a well-known figure who stood tall and straight.

As all these memories came flooding back to me I suddenly realised that I had spent more childhood time with granddad than ever I did with my dad. It was almost as if he liked me more than my dad did. Now, obviously, as a man with kids of my own, you know that you are often too busy working to support your family to be able to spend that precious quality time with them. These would be my most treasured and personal memories of a great man with his words of wisdom and whose many stories fell on my immature ears without me even knowing that he was moulding my character all the time. He was quiet, gentle and yet very strong in body and mind.

There were flowers arriving all day. It was a late funeral and as is traditional, we had granddad home for friends and family to pay their respects. We raised a huge wooden shed that we bought from a garden centre. We decked the outside thickly with flowers and inside the walls were lined with lavender linen and the ceiling was lined and ruched in the same colour. It was beautiful. The floral tributes were like I had never seen before. There was a Jack Russell like my old granddad's, Jack; horseshoes; horses; sheaths of flowers – thousands of pounds worth of floral tributes lined the lane and pathways beyond. You could not move on the plot, or up the road leading to it. There was a huge vardo with a pony pulling it. A stream of steady visitors came and then finally the car came to take granddad on his last journey. Gran had to be held up by my father at first, then she insisted he let her go.

'I will make him proud of me,' she said, 'And walk with my head held high, as he always did. It's the last thing I can do for him and I will do it well.'

The procession of cars seemed never-ending. It is a cultural tradition that when a Gypsy dies, Gypsies from all over the country attend the funeral. There were hundreds. We even had a police escort. Granddad would have loved that irony. In the chapel several men got up and sang. Gypsies love a song. When we came back from saying goodbye to granddad we all drank and shared the stories of our memories of him and the man he was. Another part of my life had been taken away. I felt the coldness growing within my heart becoming my only friend. It was the only thing I could rely on.

The next morning we gathered around granddad's trailer in a field at the end of the lane. His possessions were placed carefully and lovingly inside the trailer along with clothes and photographs. The family and very close friends stood solemnly watching as dad and gran put a torch to the trailer. This was our final goodbye. The old way. I stood and watched the trailer roar to life, lighting up the evening sky as granddad would do with his stories on those memorable nights around the yog or over dinner. Suddenly a strange feeling crept over my body, a wave of coldness teased my skin as goosebumps formed over my arms and the small hairs stood on the back of my neck. My eyes were surely playing tricks on me – through the tears that welled in them I could see granddad as plain as day, standing in the middle of the flames. He was standing there, his thumbs in the top of his trousers as always, his shirt with no collar hugging his broad chest as it heaved with laughter, the red braces strapped to his cords, the old trilby tipped over the left eye in a cocky manner. I began to recall the happy times we spent together; his little sayings and teachings, the trips he took me on and the little days out that seemed to mean nothing then but were now my greatest treasures. Then as the roof crumpled with the intense heat, he was gone. I watched the sparks rise into the sky carrying my granddad to Heaven. I stood mesmerised till dawn as the remaining embers just blinked against the early breeze. I suddenly felt the cold and moved towards my own trailer. My life was beginning to change yet again.

'Goodbye, granddad. I love you. And thanks!' I whispered.

SIX

Tarmac Warrior

Darkie and Bendy had to get back to their work but were of course reluctant to leave gran. I told them not to worry and that I would go back and get things moving. We did have some lads on the job keeping it going, but they really needed an eye keeping on them.

Needless to say I no longer ate at the café and became pretty much a recluse while living on the side of the road. I just sat in my trailer reflecting on my life to date, such as it was. I was nearly 19 years old and had done *fuck all* with my life except scam and work.

Early evening came, it was the end of the week and the uncles were back on the job. I was lying on my bed listening to the radio and thinking about the birthday that was chasing me, when a loud thumping rocked my trailer door.

Who the fuck's that? I thought.

I got up and peered into the darkness.

'How's it hanging, son?' came the voice from a figure shrouded by shadows from the passing headlights.

'Who is it?' I asked.

'Your worst nightmare, you tosser.' It was that big ol' boy who'd knocked me on to my back.

'Woah up, Denny mate, come in. Wanna drink?' I offered.

'Nah – I don't touch the stuff.'

'Not even a beer?'

'No,' he said firmly. 'I saw my old man go downhill and saw all the things he did to me mum and me. Booze'll fuck wiv your brain every time.'

I didn't let him put me off, however, and opened a can for myself. 'Sit down, mate.'

'Where?' he said sarcastically.

I looked around the place and suddenly realised I was living in a shit-hole. I was so wrapped up in my self-pity and life's reflections that I had neglected the place completely. If my mum walked in now she'd go mental. 'Now then, little Pickles, there's a mochardi young 'un,' she'd say. 'You was never brung up like this. What's a goin' on?'

I quickly dragged everything around and formed a neat pile ready for sorting later. Denny perched himself on the edge of the seat, you could see he had something on his mind. Almost as soon as he had parked his bum his reason for calling tumbled out of his mouth.

'How would you like to earn some real dough? I don't mean wages. I mean *proper* cash – and regular.'

'Course,' I replied quickly, without even wanting to know how.

'Right, I am going to bring a mate of mine called Benny Harris round to you tomorrow night. He's the best manager I know and he's looking for another fighter.'

'Fighter?' I said, 'Why does a fighter need a manager? To find him fights? I can find my own fights, thanks. In fact, they have a habit of finding me!'

But the next evening came and sure enough Denny turned up with another quietly spoken man. Denny made the necessary introductions and we got down to business.

'Well,' said Benny, 'where do you see yourself in five years time?'

'What do you mean?' I replied.

'Well – do you want to be sitting in this mochardi ol' trailer or do you want to be able to spread out in a 28-footer, pulled by a brand new four-wheel drive?'

'What's on offer?' I asked. 'Talk to me.'

'I know you've been fighting on the circuit and after the fight you had with Denny he thought you would be good for moving into another area where bigger money's involved. You won't just be fighting for pride, you'll fight for something a bit more useful . . . like dosh.'

'How much are we talking?' I asked.

'Well, if I get it right, and I usually do, you'll be taking around three grand a week for yourself. I pick up all the expenses on the trip, take my percentage off the top, and side bets are mine. What do you say?'

'I say let's fucking move. I'll start tomorrow . . . Nah, fuck tomorrow. I'll start tonight.'

'Woah! It's not that easy, I have to get you on the scene first. I'll give you a couple of days to right yourself here and I'll pick you up to hit the road on Sunday. How'll that suit you?' said Benny.

'That'll suit me just fine, cocker!' I shook Benny's hand and he went to the motor. Denny looked at me and smiled – a big, soft smile. How could this mean bastard look so gentle and be so caring?

'You'll do well to listen to Benny, and you'll be all right. All you need is a little more experience and some coaching. The attitude's there,' he said.

'Thanks for everything, Denny,' I said. 'I hear you've a battle coming up Friday with a London boy. I'll be coming along to that with the Rice family and the uncles. I can watch what you're doing this time.'

'I'd sooner you didn't come to this one, boy. It's not going to be right,' he whispered. There was a mixture of shame and disappointment in his voice.

'What's up? Anything I can help with?' I asked.

'Nah! Forget it,' and he walked away with his head hung.

All night I sat wondering what was up with Denny. I had never seen such despondency in anyone before. Had I missed something? Was I letting him down in some way? It sent me mad all night – although mixing with the prospects of my approaching new life and its big money, it really didn't get the consideration it deserved. Perhaps if I had sat longer or talked to the uncles I would have understood what Denny's problem was, but I was so naïve and wrapped up in my own greed I missed it. What was to happen on that day served as a good lesson to me for the rest of my life, and reminded me how I neglected my friend when he had needed me.

Friday came. The uncles and I drove back to dad's together talking excitedly about the coming evening's event. When we arrived we saw the Rice family's screeve in the drive. There was a lot of hugging and back-slapping going on. It was ages since we had last all been together.

'What's going to happen with the fight then? Denny going to do him?' I asked.

The big man looked back at me with a stern face. I watched as the anger washed over it.

'I think it's been fixed,' he said in a deep voice. 'Denny has been set up not to get up.'

I felt a shock. The explanation ran true to me immediately. The shock turned to panic. What was I to do? How could I help? I pulled my dad outside and explained the way Denny had acted that night outside my trailer.

Dad shook his head. 'Dirty bastards. There's nothing we can do, boy, it's out of our way and out of our league. This is a big boys' game that's being played and it's not a way I understand or want anything to do with. Your pal knew what he was getting in to. Let him deal with it in his own way – after all, he's the one who will get hurt if he plays it wrong. Either way he'll get hurt, except maybe if he plays it the wrong way he won't get up after the count. No, son, leave it alone. It's not your day to get involved with.'

No wonder Denny didn't want me to go to the fight. He didn't want me to see what was going to go down, or more importantly he didn't want me to see *him* go down. Poor bastard. I bet he felt gutted.

We drove into London arriving at Wanstead, then up through Forest Gate into Stratford and out toward Silvertown on the back road. We eventually came to a big old building that looked as if it was once part of the Tate & Lyle factory. It smelled inside – a smell I couldn't describe. It was a huge iron-clad building with ample room inside to park the motors. It was perfect, the gavvers would never spot the cars and so not become suspicious of the gathering. To the back of the building there was a ring set up and some chairs to one side of it. Obviously some important people were arriving. Fucked if I was going to sit down, though. If it went off in the crowd I'd want to be on my feet. The Rices and us moved to the ringside, when suddenly Barney Rice walked off alone.

'Where's he gone, dad?' I asked.

'He's gone to challenge the man fighting Denny tonight.'

'Who is he fighting anyways?' I asked.

'He's a good boy out of the East End. I forget his name but he's "The Face" here at the moment.'

Barney came back, he'd had his offer rejected.

'I'll just jump in after the fight ends,' he said. 'Once I've hit him he's got to fight me, ain't he?'

I looked at dad and the uncles.

'Oh shit, it's going to go off ain't it? I've got me good jewellery on too.'

'Best you nip it back to the motor, Billy,' dad said. 'It'll get ripped off your neck, else.'

As I walked back quickly to the motor I saw a couple of huge cars draw into the warehouse. The windows were blacked out so I couldn't peer in. They drove slowly, majestically, almost up to the ringside. From behind I could see a woman with long, blond hair get out, wrapped in fur. She was over six foot. The man with her was much shorter wearing a long, black top coat, slicked-back hair and sunglasses. He must have had dough to be with a sort like that. What was the prat wearing glasses for anyway? It wasn't sunny – we were inside and no one gave a shit who he was.

I forgot my jewellery for a moment. I had just had a glimpse of a world in which I felt I belonged . . . big cars and money. I walked back to where the motors were emptying. The second car was full of men and I mean *men*. These guys were built like the side of a house – all in impeccable Italian suits, highly polished shoes, hankies hanging freely from their top pockets, crisp, white shirts with button collars, and ties with a neat Windsor knot. One had a leather tie, flash git. I wanted what they had.

As the new arrivals took their places, I remembered my errand and ran off quickly. When I returned things were stirring. The betting was furious. I wanted a monkey on Denny. Dad pulled back my hand.

'You fucking mad? You know what's going down,' he whispered. But I still wanted to bet, I just knew Denny wasn't going to lay down for no man.

A cheer went up and Denny came from a room at the top of some iron steps. He walked to the ring quickly with his hands firmly on the back of his seconds. An Asian doctor gave him a quick once-over and walked off. My man stood in his corner quietly. He was not the man I knew. Behind Denny's own seconds stood three other large men. One stood awkwardly with his arm across his stomach. As the villain turned to talk to a pal I got the fleeting glimpse of the barrel of a sawn-off shotgun. Things weren't looking good at all. This wasn't the world I knew and it roused within me an excitement and longing that I didn't understand.

These two other men stood with their hands folded over their privates as if they were guarding the family jewels. This, I learned from Barney, was to hide the bulge inside the breast of their sharply cut jackets. Both had holstered handguns. I felt such an excitement – I couldn't take my eyes off these men, I was more interested in them than the fight that was about to take place. This was nothing like the world of fighting that I had enjoyed. These men meant this stuff for real. It was their business, their life. With all my new knowledge and the information given to me so far, I still couldn't decide whether these men were protecting Denny or threatening him. I was soon to find out.

The man fighting Denny came into the ring. I can't recall his name but I do remember that he sold commercial vehicles in Stepney. He was a terrifying sight. I would have shit myself if I had been standing as his opponent. The crowd roared as the fighter opened his mouth and threw in what I later found out to be amphetamine tablets. This muscle-laden man was obviously already full of something. He was tearing at his clothes, roaring abuse at Denny and the men at his side were using all of their strength to hold him back. This man was an animal and the scene I witnessed was without doubt the scariest thing I had ever seen.

The beautiful woman sat at the ringside. I later found out she was a budding star – and all of you would now know her as a household name in the film industry. She clutched frantically at the arm of her boyfriend, who I did eventually recognise as another American film star. She was clearly excited at the violence and the animal frenzy that this man displayed.

Denny rose from his stool and the two men leaned forward and pulled him back down. This answered my earlier question about whose side they were on: they were obviously not there to cheer him on. The bell went and the big man flew across the ring at break-neck speed. As he ran he tore at his tracksuit, ripping it off his body and spitting abuse. He crashed into Denny who still hadn't risen from the stool. The nut came down and split the top of Denny's forehead. His eyes were filling with blood, the feet were coming up inside one after another. I don't know how he moved so fast. The man's hands pummelled the face and body of the already semi-conscious Denny. The falling figure held pitifully to the sides of his assailant. Denny looked him full in the face. He knew he was going down but he wanted to at least go with some respect. He tried to pull himself to his feet but another astounding downward blow into Denny's upturned face from the fighter's powerful fists finished him off. As the huge deliverance of bare knuckle wrapped only in flimsy cloth hammered viciously into the flesh of my friend, it appeared that the whole face just split open, delivering parts of its flesh and blood sparingly through the ropes and into the crowd. The blood spattered the starlet's face. As it did so it sent her into a childlike hysteria, with squeals of delight as she jumped up and down screaming, 'Kill him . . . kick him!'

What had happened to this woman? She had entered the venue with the deportment of a debutante and the grace of royalty; she had now before my very eyes turned into a rabid animal, reminding me of a vampire in one of those Dracula films, a woman frenzy-feeding on a screaming victim.

As Denny was falling for the final seconds, the feet of his destroyer were still finding their target. Suddenly Barney jumped to the side of the ring, shouting as he went. He was enraged at the bloody battle and needless carnage. As Barney's right foot went under the rope, the three big men pulled him swiftly and efficiently backward and straight to the floor in what appeared to be a well-rehearsed operation. A foot was shoved across his thick neck, pushing his cheek into the gravelled surface and a shotgun was wedged between his shoulder-blades. A second man sat on his legs and grabbed him by the nuts whilst the third pushed a chrome, snub-nosed .38 pistol up his left nostril.

'Stay down, cunt.' He squeezed his words through gritted teeth.

There was no doubt in anyone's mind that this situation was to develop into a bloody battle. My heart was pounding – not with fear but anticipation. The danger excited me and that familiar arousal within my loins visited me as it had done all those years ago at my first fight. I had moved on to another level; a rush I hadn't been able to find in any of the battles I'd seen fought in many fields across the country. I was ready to go – even ready to die. Dad and the uncles were stood at the side of Barney.

Darkie shouted bravely, 'We'll take him back.'

The men just stepped back, their champion had left the ring surrounded by his supporters screaming his name and shouting his praises. They simply allowed the uncles to pick Barney up and walk him away.

'Don't look back, just walk,' Darkie said.

These men had taken control of the situation in an instant. They had floored their man and done what they had to do, what they were employed to do. It was no more than a job to them. Such coolness. I know they would have killed and not felt any remorse because it was what they had been employed for. I could see it in their faces, feel it from the aura they had emitted while their adrenaline was rushing. Everything had gone smoothly for them, they worked so well.

I had learned so much from that day. Apart from learning about a whole new world of excitement and violence that paid more money and fame than I had ever dreamed about, I learned to keep my neck off of someone else's chopping block. I'd learned when to say yes and who to, and most of all how to stay calm and not lose my temper. That's what those men did. They didn't take it personally, it was a job. Because their emotions weren't being fucked with they were able to think clearly and plan quickly. It was so cool.

I did look back (I thought I'd risk one eye!). I caught sight of Denny being dragged to a big old transit van with the Asian doctor walking quickly behind. Benny, my new manager, wasn't far behind the injured fighter. He saw me looking and waved me on quickly. I knew my friend wouldn't have wanted to share this particular moment of his life with me and I am more than sure that I wouldn't have known what to say anyway. I wasn't good at making witty comments, or comments that helped ease a situation.

We all got back into our cars and started to drive off. As we did so big black limousines whooshed past us, ignoring us as if we were dirt. A window opened just enough to throw a bottle out that went spinning across the hard floor and under our wheels.

'I knew he was a prat when I saw him first. Fucking lucky prat though, ain't he,' said dad.

He had a way of shutting me up every time. Our slow trip back home was a quiet one. We were all sickened by what we had seen although I kept my secret yearning about it burning inside me, saving it for my dreams.

My weekend arrived and Benny turned up to collect me on the Sunday afternoon, just as mum laid my dinner out before me. Dad asked him in. I hadn't told them about my new adventure yet. I knew I would get real grief.

'Hello, Benny,' dad greeted my new manager. 'Long time, no see.'

I sat back in my seat astonished. They knew each other, how could that be? This was *my* private world, one that *I* was developing, how did dad get into it?

'Want a bit of dinner?' Dad added.

I jumped up quickly and shouted, 'No! We have to get out. Mum, dad – I'm going to work away with Benny for a while, it's something I have to do – no, I *wanna* do.' And with that I kissed mum, gave her a big hug and slapped dad across the back. I closed the trailer door and I scooped up my ready-packed hold-all.

I didn't care what they felt or what they thought. I didn't care what was going to happen. I was getting a life back and would make some money as I did so. I realised that I had become very insular with my feelings. I really didn't care about what I'd just done to them. They were my own parents and I didn't care! This really wasn't me – but I had to admit the strange absence of my usual pains of remorse was a lovely feeling. I was free!

'How come you know the old man?' I asked Benny.

'Our families grew up together in Cumbria.'

I looked at him in surprise. 'You a Romani then?'

'Well, I wasn't the gavvers' chavvie – twat.' He replied.

'Well, fuck a duck sideways, there's thousands of us, ain't there?' I said.

We drove off slowly. I looked back and saw mum and dad staring down the drive. I waved. They waved. Then I was gone.

'Well, what's the plan, Mr Manager?' I said selfishly (I didn't even think to ask about Denny's well-being).

'Well, we're going to hit a new circuit,' he said. 'We're going on to the motorway service stations and A-road cafés up and down the country. You'll be fighting truckers.'

I laughed.

'What's funny?' said Benny.

'I'll muller the fat fuckers,' I said. 'They just sit behind their wheels and float around all day eating fry-ups, they can't fight.'

He looked at me sideways. 'You thought that about Denny and he done you in seconds. Anyway there's not only truckers – loads of people are getting in on it, and don't forget the overseas truckers too – they bring fighters over. It's a big world out there and you're going to fight it!'

I liked that thought. 'I'm going to fight the world!'

'First thing we gotta find you is a name,' he said. 'I know: Gypsy Joe. Or Romani Pete – how about that?'

'Piss off. I don't wanna be called anything like that. I just want to be a normal bloke with names like the others.' This was the first time I remember denying my culture. I really had become a different man. I felt I was ready to move on into a new life designed by myself. As far as I was concerned I was now almost a gorgio. I was settled. I recall that day with sadness and disappointment that society had made me seek to be someone else by imposing its judgement on me.

'Use your own imagination if you're on my payroll,' I joked.

'Hark at him!' said Benny. 'Okay, your lordship, what do you suggest?'

'Well, you met me on the road and we're going on the road. How about King of the Road?'

Benny laughed his head off. 'Sounds like a cue for a song, you silly bugger. How's this one then: Tarmac Warrior.'

I loved it.

I had a new life, I had a new name, I was born again, with another chance to be an equal amongst men – although even that wouldn't be enough. I needed to be better. I was liking the idea more each moment. I would never have to suffer the indignity of prejudice or racial taunts.

We started on the M1. Benny had already done his work. He knew who was passing through where and when. We sat and waited at the Blue Boar service station near Northampton. Parking in the commercial park, we waited for the right truck to come along and sure enough, along it came – around 3½ hours later. My arse was sore and my legs were dead. 'Fuck this lark,' I thought, 'where's the glamour?'

The driver of the 16-wheeler leaned out of his cab and jumped down in a casual fashion, obviously trying to look cool – after all he did know we were around somewhere.

This was my first glimpse of the man who was contributing to my payroll this week. He was a little under six foot, I guess, with long hair and a 'tash hiding his mouth. But I knew that mouth was behind there somewhere and I wanted some of its teeth as souvenirs of the day. He was very slim and appeared to be quite fit. He'd had the sleeves ripped off of his brown boiler suit, so that his tattoos would show, I suppose. I hoped this was his only weapon – my fear of his tattoos. This was his feeble way of psyching his opponents, apparently: obviously if he had a tattoo he must be hard!

That was enough. I had seen all I wanted. Remembering all I had been taught and all that I had learned from my latest experiences, I moved to the rear of the park right at the back of the services, up a ramp, past some workshops and beyond where the police would park.

I stood and waited while Benny moved in on our target. It wasn't long before about 30 men were gathered around their lorries – a bit suspicious, I thought – if the gavvers drove through they'd know something was going down. I ran up and down the ramp, warming up. It was essential that all the joint fluids were running efficiently and that the muscles were warm so that they would respond in a way that I needed.

Benny came walking briskly out of the service area and found me quickly. 'We were hoping for a long 'un,' he said, 'but he wants to go for two 'cos someone told him it was your first fight.'

'Who the fuck did that?' I said.

'I did,' he replied quickly.

'What did you do that for? He knows that I am a beginner now – he'll try all the tricks that I don't know.'

'You let me do the worrying, boy, it's my money that's up,' he replied.

'Oh right. Silly me. Sorry for caring about my own safety. Tell you what! I'll put up the money and *you* fight him.'

'Look,' he said, 'you don't need any tricks. You're fast, you're fit and you're young. This man's in his late 30s. He'll be a bit slower than you – plus he's just come back from a long haul so he'll be tired too. All you need to do is get in hard and fast, act a bit like a proper boxer – spar up and that. Let him believe you're a novice at bare-fist. 'Cos he thinks you're new he'll be over-confident. He'll let himself down, don't worry.'

I listened to the spiel he was giving me – it all made perfect sense. How did he know about the long haul? Bloody hell, this man knew his stuff, didn't he! I was part of a working team. I was well impressed.

The man walked toward me. He called himself 'Tattoo'. Very imaginative, I thought.

I caught sight of Benny taking money behind a trailer. The betting was going down. Tattoo and I shook hands. The man designated as the ref shouted, 'You're on!'

I squared up and tried to box for a while and then it came – all my fucking breakfast. 'You're late,' I thought, it usually came up *before* I started fighting. I had no fear of being hit while I was heaving. The weedy bastard wouldn't come near the puke. I stood straight and squared up again, this style didn't suit me. My back started to stiffen so I opened up. I swung a right (sod it, I missed) but it appeared that all of these silly mistakes were going my way. The more I fucked up, the more he believed I was crap.

Then it came. He moved in close and I caught him lovely right between the eyes. My aim was perfect. This man led with his right and so squared off leading with his right eye. I worked on that eye hard for about seven or eight minutes until it eventually closed when I brought my nut down just before a clinch.

I was fed up pussying around. I thought: Let's have him. His eye was completely shut now and he had to lead with his other side which meant he was standing awkwardly, leading with his left foot and still trying to hit with his right hand. Prat, I thought. I was going to go to work on him.

I heard Benny, who was stood to my right, softly say: 'Do it slow, son.'

I trusted his judgement. I had to, he had told me right so far. I systematically punished this man for about 12 minutes. I could easily have done it earlier but, like Benny had told me, I worked him and beat him. Sparring and wrestling like this must have been the most boring fight I had ever had. I eventually got fed up with it all and knocked him spark out with a good hook right on the button. He was an open target with no co-ordination and his vision was lost. I've done my job, I thought.

I went up to the man afterwards to shake hands. He looked at me with a destroyed look.

'Never mind, mate, don't fight after a long haul next time, you won't be so tired,' I said.

He looked at me surprised and said, 'Long haul? I've only come from Leighton Buzzard.'

I looked at Benny and he grinned cunningly.

'Worked, though, didn't it?' he said.

'Take me back to the trailer, you crafty bastard,' I replied.

We drove off to Newport Pagnell where we were to stay the night. We sat in the trailer that night chatting, for the very first time really. Every time we had talked before it had been brief meetings or someone had been around.

I said: 'How come you took me on at Denny's say-so? He hadn't seen me fight anyone and he beat me when he fought me.'

'Oh, it wasn't Denny,' he said, 'it was your dad. And anyway I owed him a favour and just took his word for it.'

'Me *dad*?'

I suddenly felt all manner of things – betrayal, relief, anger. 'The old bastard! Does me mum know?'

'What do you think? She'd do him! I believe your dad saw something in you he had suppressed in himself. He wanted you to have the chances he never had. He could see your talent, your spirit and your itchy feet. He thought at least this way he could keep a distant eye on you,' said Benny.

I didn't know what I was feeling. It was a lot to take in. Suddenly a roll of notes landed on my bed with a thud.

'That, my son, is what you've earned today,' said Benny.

I no longer cared nor remembered what I was thinking previously, my mind was on the money. 'How much is there?' I asked.

'A grand,' said Benny.

'Hang on – there was two up on the fight and you had side bets going. You must've cleaned up,' I complained.

'Now then, boy,' said Benny. 'You know the deal, but I will explain it once and once more only. If you don't like it after that then sling your hook. I arrange the fights. I do all the running. I lay on the purse. I do the side bets for myself. I pay all expenses. And I take 50 per cent of all purses. Now – you don't like it?'

'Well, it seems a bit much,' I said.

'How much did you earn last week, son?' said Benny.

'Four hundred and eighty pounds,' I replied.

'How much did you earn tonight?'

'Point taken. Thanks for a great night, Benny!'

With that, I rolled over and went to sleep, forgetting all about the fight, Benny's share of it, and my dad's involvement – except for a little whisper of 'Thanks, dad!' before I dozed off.

We had 18 months together, Benny and I, and by then I had built up quite a reputation without any really bad incidents – until the fight on Manchester's M62, behind the service station.

This time my man was there waiting for me. The service area was crawling with gavvers. There had been a robbery or something in the town and they had road blocks everywhere. We decided to take the next junction off and pick a lay-by. We chose one with a big, old, red trailer on it that had been converted into a café. Benny took the precaution of popping into the café and telling them what was going on, asking them to keep an eye out for the police. There would be a good drink in it for them so everything seemed cool.

We set up the ring with four steel posts that Benny had taken from roadside works, stuck them in the ground and put some rope that he always carried round them. My new opponent was a black fellow from Solihull. He called himself Midnight. This name business was beginning to get to me now, they all seemed so corny. Midnight came out of his corner skipping backwards and sideways, dropping his hands and poking his chin with a dangling tongue. Everyone wants to be fucking Muhammad Ali, I thought.

I bashed the stuffing out of this bloke. As he went backwards I went with him. When he went sideways I went too. He couldn't get away. I was like glue all over him. My eyes never left his and I anticipated his every move; countered almost every punch. He did cop me with a few nice roundhouses, though – he must've trained as a kick boxer or something. People were getting heavily into martial arts at this point in time and it was reflected in the quality and styles of bare-fist.

I was raining hell on the man when the shout came up: 'OLD BILL!'

Everyone scrambled. Midnight and I unfortunately were the last to hear and consequently the last to run – three coppers were among us before we knew it. I got hold of one of them by the visor of his motorbike helmet and spun him stupid. I was laughing my head off. I spun him faster and faster until he lost his footing. As he went down the helmet came off and I stood on his head sharpish like. He wasn't going to get up in a hurry. I turned to see what was going on. The two cops from the car had landed on Midnight although it looked like he had done a job on them first. Someone grabbed one of the steel posts out of the ground and threw it at the gavver with his back to me. I saw it stick firmly between his shoulder blades and he began to run around screaming, trying to reach over and pull it out.

As that bastard let go of Midnight he was able to turn himself round and reach the copper's neck. He lifted him like a baby and pulled the policeman's head sharply toward his own. He must have had a head of steel: the copper just opened up, it was quite a sight. The hot blood pumped from the wound down over Midnight's face.

'Bleed, you fucking pig!' he shouted. 'You won't be calling me a black bastard again!' and with that went down as if to kiss him. When he came up I couldn't believe my eyes. It made me heave: he stood there grinning, his face covered in blood, the gavver's tongue hanging out of his mouth. The dirty rotten bastard had bitten off his tongue. Midnight spat out the fleshy muscle and laughed.

'Nice, mon!' he shouted to me in his West Indian accent. 'We call it square and I'll catch you another day. Good luck, now!'

The gavver missing his tongue passed out, another was running around like a cowboy in the movies with a spear in his back and the other was still sparko – as far as I knew I may have broken his neck. Everyone who was left ran, leaving a scene of carnage that would do any war zone credit.

I jumped into the car with Benny, soaking in blood.

'It's all right,' I said, 'none of it's mine. I'm OK.'

'Fuck you!' he said, 'You've got claret all over me leather, you tosser.' He was so caring – about his car!

We headed off double quick to the motorway, coming off it as soon as possible to the A and B roads. The first thing we did was get a set of plates made. Benny had three sets of number plates in his head – these belonged to cars that were exactly the same make and age as his. We needed anonymity. If he had kept spare plates on board and we ever had a toug, he would have to then explain them, wouldn't he? Clever! He was so clued up, that man, he seemed to know every little trick in the book, but I was learning fast.

SEVEN

On the Run

We headed off south at a leisurely pace on the A roads toward Gloucester, keeping the radio on all the time, catching all the news programmes. We were trying to hear how we'd done. Nothing was mentioned on the news – this was bad. It meant that the police were treating it really personally and wanted their pound of flesh before the courts got us – or at least before we were seen on telly. We swung across to Oxford, then down through Reading towards Brighton, finally picking up the coast road to Dover.

We parked up on the cliffs above the harbour for the night. It was bitterly cold, the wind was blowing a gale and ice had formed over the dew that had settled on the car in the night. The trailer, however, was warm as toast and I woke up to Benny cooking breakfast – he'd make someone a good mum. While he was cooking the gas went off.

'Nip out and change over the new gas bottle,' he asked me.

'Oh Christ, it's always my turn to do the shit jobs.'

'Come on, lazy git. I drove all the way here and cooked breakfast and I've been up an hour making plans. You wait till you hear 'em, you'll love em!'

'Go on then, what've you got in mind?' I said.

'Nah – not till you do the gas . . .'

'You're such a twat.'

Eager to know this new plan I crept from my warm bed, put on my tracksuit and ran to the front of the trailer to change the gas bottle.

'While you're there, adjust the aerial a bit for the telly – I want to keep on top of that news.'

'Bastard,' I whispered under my breath.

I ran round to the back of the trailer and moved the aerial until it suited his lordship, then it jumped at me like black off white. I had seen something that had made my cold errand all worthwhile. I strolled back into the trailer with the biggest grin on my face.

'What you grinning at, dozy-looking git?' he asked.

'You know your last plan for escaping the gavvers by swapping number plates?'

'Yeah,' he said cockily.

'Well, didn't you think they'd notice the one on the back of the trailer?' I burst out laughing. Benny hid his head in his hands.

'Silly, daft twat,' he said to himself. 'I really thought I had it all covered.'

We laughed about that little error for weeks – well, I did anyway.

We sat down to our fry-up.

'Well,' I said with a mouth full of bacon and tinned tomato, 'what's the plan?'

Benny looked smug. 'I've been keeping this one up my sleeve. There is no way we can work the circuits for a while on the roads. Them gavvers will be looking for us everywhere.'

'Oh that's your news, is it, brain of Britain?' I interrupted.

'Hang on, hang on, shit-for-brains. I've booked us on the ferry to Calais this afternoon.'

'What the fuck for?'

'Well, the fight circuit doesn't stop on the tarmac, son, it reaches out across the sea too – well, the channel anyway. We'll have a fight this afternoon for sure.'

'*Yeaaahhh!*' we cried together.

'We're back in business, you cunning old sod, you. I luv ya!' I told him.

'One more thing,' he said.

'What's that, Mr Manager, sir?' I asked.

'We're on the midnight ferry back, so finish the first one quick and save your strength for the second.'

'You greedy git,' I exclaimed.

'I'm only thinking of you, son,' he said – not very convincingly.

Benny had a saver also, well, he always did. We always bought a load of booze and fags back to sell tax-free. That made us good money on its own in case I didn't get a fight. If I lost and we made no money we'd be well covered. We drove down to the ferry terminal. Benny had already got our tickets while I was kipping that morning. There was no one about car-wise really, just a few that looked like businessmen and about 30 lorries.

'Slim pickings,' I said to Ben.

'Listen. This is the way it is this time of year – it's just right. No tourists, so the car decks are empty to fight on; less staff to poke their nose in, and those that do come down are on a back-hander anyway. We got cheap fares and the pick of the drivers. One of 'em will have a go once they're pissed, with a bit of encouragement.'

This worried me a bit.

'You mean I'm going to fight men who are not fighters?' That seemed beneath me somehow.

'Well, you're going to get the odd one or two but give 'em a chance. You had yours and everybody's got to start somewhere.'

He always had a way of justifying what he wanted and I always bought it.

We got on board. I had to leave the car and trailer for a while – it was the rules of the ship apparently, no one was allowed down below once the boat set off.

I went up top for a hot drink then wandered down the stairs slowly and sat in the back of the trailer. I waited. Benny went up top and 'worked' the passengers. Sure enough, an hour had passed and there was a knock on the trailer door. Thank God 'cos I had just began to doze off. I had wrapped myself up in bed, it was fucking freezing down there.

'What you got?' I asked.

'There's a big ol' boy says he can take you big time. I've called it on.'

'Oh, that sounds like shit. You're making excuses for yourself. How much did we get?' I asked.

'A ton,' said Benny.

'How much? A fucking *ton*? You can go fuck yourself – I ain't fighting for that money. I'd piss that against the wall on a Friday night.'

'Listen, it's all we got at the minute. I'll split the side bets with you and take nothing off the top except expenses. How's that?' he said.

'Well, that sounds OK. What's the expenses?' I asked.

'About sixty quid.'

'Sixty quid? Sixty fucking quid? You mean I'm actually going to fight some poor bloke for forty quid? There goes all my hard-earned cred out the window.'

Benny turned a bit funny then; he did sulk at times: 'Listen, I didn't do the coppers. You did. But I stood by you and got you away. I could have just driven off and left you there.'

I glared at him.

'I'm gonna kill him for making me fight him for that money,' I said.

'That's better,' replied Ben. 'We'll pick up some good sides. Don't worry, it'll be worth it.'

I got changed into my tracksuit and jumped from the trailer.

'Take a nip of this,' said Benny handing me some brandy. I drank the warm liquid and started a slow jog around the deck. On my third lap the big metal door to the cargo deck slammed open, a mountain of a man came piling through with 20 or 30 men behind him. The passenger decks must have been left empty. Using the side of the ship as one side of the ring and the enclosed staircase as the other, the few men we had watching were just enough to complete the rest of the square.

Benny shouted the off and away we went. Well, this was hard work. I could barely keep on my feet and as usual up came my food.

We fell about holding on to each other as the ship rose and fell. He had hold of me tightly. He was stepping in my puke, and as the ship lurched, up the big man went, with me in his arms. He landed full on his back with me on top of him and I heard a loud escape of air as he shouted with the pain. Still he wouldn't let go and we rolled over to his right. I was now underneath this poxy mountain of a man with my face pushed hard and firm into my own sick on the deck.

Well, call me weak (and I realise it was my own vomit) but nevertheless up came yet another lot at the feel of the gooey substance on my face and the smell of it up my nostrils – and yet again. I retched three times, spewing vomit from that funnel I used to call my mouth. We were covered.

By this time several of the onlookers began to be affected and they too were retching and spewing as the boat rocked and threw us all over the place. We were slipping and sliding in liquids and foodstuff. Eventually the big man could hold back no more. The smell had got him – plus, I must admit, while he was roaring his abuse at me I'd spewed right into his open mouth. I felt his big chest rise and as he did so he released his grip – just in time for me to crash both hands down on the back of his fat neck, and as I did so his beer and breakfast left his body. As he was retching I bashed fuck out of his roaring face. Between heaves I hit him in the head and afterwards I kicked him in the stomach. This kept the events flowing for a while until he threw his hands up.

He had given in. By now most of the onlookers had disappeared. I left him lying there in his blood and vomit. He no longer had an entourage of friends, they had abandoned him – a loser, a wreck of blubber.

Benny and I went up top to hit the showers; he was laughing like a drain. It was the funniest thing he had ever seen and I can't remember such a fiasco in my whole career. This puking thing could be my greatest asset; my secret weapon!

Once clean I threw my arms round Benny's shoulders.

'Well, how did we do, mate?' I said.

'Better than I'd hoped. We got the hundred pounds from the fighter, four and a half cold cash in bets, a thousand ciggies, ten bottles of booze, two colour portable tellies and a stacker system off the removal lorries. Oh yes, and two sheep from the French freezer truck.'

I just sat and laughed. I laughed like I had never laughed before, my head in my hands. I laughed till I cried. I felt great. There had not been the pressure of the past year's fights. I'd had no level to fight at, it was just like I was a kid again. We got off the ship at the other end. The crew just stared at the amount of sick on the floor wondering how the fuck it all got there.

Benny worked the rest of the day at the docks in Calais getting rid of all the bits we had won on the trip over and as usual he came through. We did all right on that trip but didn't go back that night.

We stopped over in the trailer, parking in the nearest village. It was a long time since we'd just wasted a night on our own. We ate, drank and sang with the locals, and we fell into a deep drunken sleep still laughing. It was a good feeling.

Two more days we stayed over, just chilling. Benny was working the docks. He wanted to do it properly this time. He didn't want to go on a ship hit-or-miss. He got to know what was what with the other drivers: who was on the circuit, their nationality – in fact, everything but their wives' bust size. He was always thorough in his preparation when he put his mind to it.

Benny and I worked the cross-channel ferries from two ports in the winter months, and since we'd created an international reputation we were able to fight in France, Belgium and Germany. We had some great times and it paid well. We didn't know when we set out, that the winter of 1969 would be our last together.

Benny as usual went into the truckers' area. He was known by now and as usual we knew who was on this crossing from Calais. I was to meet a German – the others called him Attila for obvious reasons. He didn't call himself anything. Like all Germans he took the issue seriously and wanted nothing to do with circus names.

Benny had seen this man fight before but failed to tell me about him. He just pretended it was just another fight. He didn't tell me that Attila used to be a pro fighter and had once killed a man in the ring by sheer power. He went on to kill three more on the European circuit through internal injuries.

The time was set and the decks were crowded. Ben had been taking bets heavily, I could see him working the drivers frantically. The appointed ref called it on and away we went. We stood and fought toe-to-toe for around 15 minutes. This man was tough.

Suddenly I felt a surging pain in my right calf. I went down. There was a man in the crowd who apparently worked with the German. He would put a school compass in his shoe, the point sticking out of the end and as I went against him in the crowd he gave a hard kick, pushing the spike in to my calf muscle. The pain was burning me; I had never felt anything like it before. The German grabbed my head and threw it against the side of the iron ring that was used to strap down vehicles on the decking. My blood soaked the deck. I felt a foot come down on my neck hard, then another hit me in the side trying to find my kidneys. I curled in a ball to protect my soft body organs and my face. I knew I was done. The kicks went on and on until I fell unconscious.

I woke up back on British soil with Benny changing a dressing on my face. I sat up slowly and looked in the mirror. I was a mess and every part of my body hurt.

'What the fuck went on there?' I asked painfully. 'I was doing great – working to a plan, I knew I had to fight this man right when suddenly I remember a piercing pain in my leg.'

'That was his partner. He uses that trick a lot,' said Benny.

'You knew. You *knew* and didn't tell me, you bastard!'

'I can't remember everything,' replied Benny.

'What do you mean, you can't remember everything? It's your fucking *job* to remember everything. I rely on you to remember everything, you stupid cunt.'

He knew I meant it when I said that word. I hated it and it rarely came to my lips. I was mad. The argument seemed to go on for hours. I forgot my pain. The only pain I had was that caused by Benny's greed and abandonment. I'd trusted him.

He had won a fortune on the fight. He had bet against me with every man bar none. He knew I was going to lose this one and he could have stopped it. He had bet against me before but that was okay, it was expected. 'A little saver', he'd call it – just to offset any losses. I didn't mind, in fact there were times when he would hand me a little wad and say, 'Not all is lost; I put this on for you.'

He was my best friend – he had become my family. We'd shared our lives for seven years by this point, for Christ's sake. Why had he done this to me? Greed. Money was his only motive – it had finally got the better of him, so much so that he couldn't resist betrayal even at the cost of our friendship.

I packed the small bag I had come with. I left everything I couldn't carry – there were suits, shoes, shirts – all good stuff too, thousands of pounds' worth in fact. I got to the door and looked at him.

'Here's your share,' he said, solemnly holding out a handful of money.

'Shove it up your arse, Judas,' I responded.

I turned and walked away from the trailer, not daring to look back in case I gave in to his gaze which I could feel burning on the back of my neck. I knew it was time – time for us to go our own ways. The friendship had suffered an abuse that I believed we could never put behind us. Things would never be as they were.

I jumped into the cab of one of the regular drivers on our route.

'Where you going, Taff?' I asked.

'Barcelona, Tarmac,' he said.

'Tarmac? Just plain Billy will do now, Taff. There's no more Tarmac Warrior. Want some company?'

'How far?'

'All the way, son. All the way'.

The final tear my body had to offer left my eye. This was the ultimate death of my soul, my final push from getting close to any one ever again.

EIGHT

Viva España

Taffy and I reached Calais around 4 a.m. and decided to drive on into the night towards Spain. Using the motorway systems it wouldn't take too long although the tolls and the eating places were expensive. Still – I had plenty saved and didn't need to worry. I'd treat Taffy to his meals as he was doing me a huge favour taking me as a passenger. I took over the driving for around four hours on the motorways; it was only a straight road and there was no chance of getting pulled over providing I drove in the appropriate manner. Anyway, I thought, if they pull me over I'll just knock 'em out and do a runner – Taffy could say I was a hitchhiker.

The trip through France was uneventful and we finally reached Barcelona on the Thursday – two days' drive almost to the hour. We pulled in to the harbour area and parked up, the air brakes interrupting the silence of the morning air and sending a flurry of seagulls high into the sky from their resting-places.

I got out of the cab and looked around me. I had never seen such beauty; I love old buildings. I really hadn't seen anything much of other countries by this point. When visiting to fight, it was in and out really, and often at night time. The beauty of the city lay in the imagination; architecture reflects the cities, thanks to careful and intricate designers. We got our heads down in the cab until day broke properly and the city became bustling avenues of noisy people and noisy vehicles, the fumes eating away at those beautiful buildings.

Around 10 a.m. we walked up into the labyrinth of tiny streets away from the harbour to find a small café that Taffy 'knew well'. It took us nearly an hour to find the thing, that's how well he knew it.

We sat on the rickety little chairs outside the grubby café window looking out on a small, busy cobbled street. I sat back, looked around me and thought: 'What the fuck's he brought me here for?'

A lovely little girl around eight years old came skipping through the door and greeted us with a *'como estas señor?'* and Taff came back with *'Muy bien, gracias.'* She threw a huge blue-and-white gingham tablecloth down and as she did so her brother placed a vase of fuchsias in the middle, that lit up the air with their perfume. A balding man of around 40 appeared, beaming at the prospect of custom at this time of the day, and placed a bottle of red wine with two glasses down, followed by crusty bread, all cut up. This is more like it, I thought.

The man asked what we would like and Taffy ordered us a whole *pollo* each (whatever that was) and *pomfrites*. I sat waiting for this Spanish delicacy; I could have eaten anything, I was starving.

My eyes lit up when the man placed before me a huge spit-roast chicken and a plate of the finest-looking chips I'd ever laid eyes on. We sat and pigged the lot, drank the wine and ordered another bottle. It was great. The whole lot came to the equivalent of a measly six pounds. I couldn't believe it. I gave them another fiver in Spanish money to cheer them up. Taffy was on a quick turnaround so he couldn't hang around too long. I didn't know what to do, where to go or what to say. I was like a little lost boy.

As we got back to the lorry a small group of youngsters came over to us and asked if we were going to the islands – and if we were could they have a lift, that way they didn't have to pay a fare. Taffy told them he wasn't going anywhere but home, so they walked off.

Hang on, I thought. They seem to know what's what.

'Make your move now, son,' my companion urged.

So I bid Taffy a fond *buenos dias* and went to join the youngsters.

What an adventure to be having at my age! I caught up with the young 'uns who were queuing up for their tickets at the ferry. I paid my fare and boarded the tiny ship that was due to sail at noon.

The trip over was noisy and uncomfortable and took nearly six bloody hours. I was going crazy with boredom. I couldn't sleep. To the left of me I had some French kids playing a poxy guitar and singing songs. And about eight seats behind me I had some hippie twat playing a mouth organ. Noisy bastards. I could feel the blood boiling inside me.

The past years had made me one selfish git; I cared for and feared no man. I realised all of my feelings, my emotions had gone. This was a good thing. It made me mean. It left me hateful. I put up with the noise for about two hours; eventually I stood up, walked over to the lad with the guitar and snatched it from him.

His pal jumped up quickly. I simply rested a hand heavily on his shoulder and pushed him down again. Now I am not a big man and looking at me would not install either fear or caution in anybody's heart – but your face does tell your fortune. When I am angry my face distorts with the passion that drives me to hurt people. My normally bright-blue eyes darken and my lips drain of colour to a deathly grey.

The boy sat down. No one said a word except his trappy little girlfriend but he soon put a stop to that. They just watched as I laid the guitar on the seat and shook my finger. I then walked steadily down the aisle approaching the harmonica player. I fiercely knocked his hands down from his mouth.

'Oi!' he said, 'What's your game?'

'I am trying to get some sleep, mate. Best you either shut it or piss off up top and play,' I warned him.

'Fuck off, I'll do what I like,' he answered foolishly and went to play again.

Just as he got the instrument to his lips I gave him a right-hander, pushing the noisy little machine right up into his teeth. He screamed in pain and fell forward, holding his mouth. No one uttered a sound, they just carried on about their business, reading or chatting. I glanced around to cover my back and simply walked back to my seat.

All was quiet and uneventful for the rest of the trip and the youngsters I came aboard with walked off to another part of the boat.

Fuck 'em, I thought.

We pulled into Palma harbour, Majorca. It was early evening and I remember thinking how warm it was for May. The many private yachts and ships harboured there were just putting on their display of lights as they danced gently at the water's edge. I could just smell the money. This was a good place to be.

I moved through the terminal slowly, keeping a close eye on the kids – they seemed to be clued up. We got outside, though, and I felt lost – completely lost. This was the very first time in my whole life that I had been alone. I saw the kids at a roadside food trailer and walked over to them and spoke to two couples.

'Where you lot off to?'

'Shagalluf,' a tall lad answered reluctantly.

I laughed. 'Where the fuck's that?'

'It's about an hour's drive. It's called Magalluf really but it's got a bit of a reputation for being somewhere it's real easy to get laid.'

'Well, how about I spring for a cab and you show me the way?' I said.

The two couples looked at each other and it was on. We called a cab and set off to 'Shagalluf'.

The car dropped us at the top of the main drag. The shops were buzzing with tourists and it was just beginning to turn to dusk.

'Where you crashing?' the kids asked.

'Dunno. The beach looks okay for tonight,' I said.

'No way, mate – kip down there and you'll get a hiding from the *guardia*. They are real mean bastards and hate us Brits. We're going to just chill for a while. When the bars open we'll look for PR work. You can hang with us till we all get sorted if you want.'

'Guess that's the best offer I got – ta!' I said.

'Well, I reckon we'll go up to the Robin Hood Bar or Mano's. One's a worker's bar and an all-nighter; the other's a right busy little place. Lots of workers go there, so we'll hear of some work maybe,' said my new acquaintance. So off we set.

'Kinda quiet here for a tourist spot,' I observed.

'Well, it's only just May, ain't it. Now's the time to get your job for the season, before it kicks off. You get a better crack at accommodation too.' I looked at these kids in admiration, they were barely 17 and knew everything, it seemed.

I, on the other hand, knew nothing – but I was a fast learner. By the time we left the bar in the early hours, I had a job as doorman at the Underground disco and a room close by the Robin Hood that belonged to the lady who owned the bar. The kids were still looking but I had what I wanted and that was the main thing. My job didn't start for a week so I spent my time driving around the island in a hire car. I also made myself known amongst the workers and various bar owners (mainly ex-pats) in the main area. I was taking control and learning quickly: all about the *guardia*, the *policia* and so on; who does what, and who to grease.

I really got to know how the place worked that summer, including the little earners from the tourists. I started work at last and made sure that I was working legal. (I had my NIF number, which is like social security in the UK.) I was head doorman. Not that it seemed to make any difference. I was still paid only 1 mil (a thousand pesetas) a night, plus all I could drink and shag of course. Oh yes, I could get to like this life, I thought.

The work was quite easy. It was not very busy and I got to bash the Germans when I wanted. I grew to hate those bastards. Strolling round and knocking into people just as they liked, always going to the front of the queue rather than waiting – they really thought they owned the fucking place.

May passed by quietly, and most of June. But then it started. Boy, did it start. By this time I had quite a few acquaintances. I never refer to them as friends – most of them would stab you in the back. You could never tell anyone where you were living, of course; if you did they would know what times you were out at work and rob you.

The two I hung around with most were Scouse (I never did know why they called him that, he came from *Dublin* for Christ's sake) and Makka, a mad Geordie – and I mean mad. He was ex-para and had worked as a mercenary for some time. He had no boundaries in anything he did, and he didn't possess morals, values or principles.

Every now and again we would get into it: drinking contests, strength contests – and then one day Makka came up with a new one: a 'Who Can Do The Most Repulsive Thing' contest and I have to say he won every time.

One night it was 'What Would You Drink?' He won with someone else's urine. I stopped at my own. Another night it was 'What Would You Eat?' I stopped at a slug, he went on to win with some piss-head's hot sick off the club stairs. He scooped it up into his mouth all stringy and bitty. It made me puke. Eventually he devised the all-time winner. He chewed a used tampon. Dirty bastard. I never ever got into a contest with him again from that day. I knew I would never win – except for the scalping game. That was a right crack, and it quickly caught on with all the doormen until it became an inter-club contest thing. If you ever went to Majorca in 1970 and came back either bald or with holes hacked in your hair, then the chances are I owe you an apology.

It started off just me and Makka. The young lads would roll out of the bars out of their heads and crash around being loud and sick – often ending up at the top of our club's staircase, or in the alleyway up the side, sound asleep. The idea of the contest was to collect as much hair as you could by the end of the night. The one with the biggest bag of hair got a free breakfast. We would cut big chunks out of their hair, even huge circles. When we got really good at it, towards the end of the season, I bought some battery clippers and started doing stripes. You got extra marks for being inventive.

This game caught on like wild fire. Behind every doorman's desk or podium lurked a pair of scissors. The best targets for us would be the Germans, Swedes, Dutch or the Danes as they were still into long hair. Most Brits already had skinhead cuts to start with.

After scalping got old-hat we started to take off eyebrows. And the game, of course, got bigger. We started belt and shirt collections, jeans too (designer ones always carried more points, of course) and then we went through the phase of stripping the lads stark-bollock naked, while they were in their drunken stupors.

We used to cry with laughter. Of course we knew we were always covered 'cos the doormen looked after each other. Anyone causing trouble at one club would bring the whole town around their ears. We were like an army really, I guess. I suppose in a way we seemed like cowards or bullies but we really weren't, you know. It was mainly boredom. Both Makka and I were used to having our lives full in similar ways: fighting, planning to fight, or using our inventiveness for an earner. We needed that energy outlet, that release of aggression driven by testosterone and alcohol. Sometimes things we did made us laugh in a hysterical manner. It was all very childlike and harmless to us. And the tourists? Well, they went home with their tales of: 'remember that night . . .'

The only time I ever backed off was when they started doing it to girls. I didn't think that was right. Men are fair game, aren't they? But I would never physically assault a female, that part of my culture was branded into me. When I saw the girl-thing going off I was very angry for several reasons: because of the act itself, because I always deeply respected women and because it began to stir thoughts of my dear sisters. An emotion that I had hidden away deep inside me wrestled its way out. Of course, once I thought of my sisters then mum crept in, with dad, my brothers and the uncles piling in behind them. It was all too much for me. I had grown to like my life – light on emotion and heavy on the aggression. It was easier to understand.

The fighting began to get heavier in the clubs as the summer drew in. Each night we got ready to go to work the adrenaline would start pumping. It was like taking a drink. We'd start getting ready and the conversation would begin to get louder; we'd start talking about the birds and the fighting and you'd notice the difference immediately. The lads grew intoxicated with excitement and anticipation. We would get more and more boisterous, start pushing at each other. We thought we ruled the island and to some extent I suppose we did – at least our little part of it. The power was our nectar and we drank every drop. Young 'uns would point us out in the street as we went to work, like we were pop stars.

Girls would drape themselves across us asking if we could get them into the club later. We always did and often ended up shagging them or getting a blow job in the little cellar by the entrance. We were insatiable. I am sure I became addicted to sex.

I was like a child with too many sweets. You'd unwrap them all and throw most of them away. The girls gradually became uninteresting. I'd start fucking then remember something I had to tell a mate and walk off, leaving the poor girl standing there with her drawers in her hand or bent over the barrels, sometimes both.

Then life all began to get on top of us. The fighting was boring 'cos no one ever had a good go back at us. Makka and I had a couple of goes with each other just to break the monotony. Sometimes we went at it for semi-real. Each time we agreed: no holds barred but no use of weapons. We'd end up black and blue but always mates. It was a man thing, you understand.

Come July we'd really had enough. Makka announced he was off to Gran Canaria and asked if I wanted to go with him.

'Same shit; different place,' said Makka.

What the fuck. I was only drifting anyway. We did the bar that morning – nicked all the fags and two crates of spirit and sold them to Kevin who had an English bar up the hill a bit. We grabbed a ride with one of the holiday reps on their client coach to the airport and bought our tickets back to Barcelona first, then out to Gran Canaria.

The plane landed with a thud as the wheels touched tarmac and the engines raced to pull us to a halt. It seemed like we were back in Majorca – loads of reps and tourists running about like lost souls acting really stupid. We saw a big old bird called Angie who we knew from Majorca. It turned out she was running the show for one of the tour operators in Gran Canaria, so we got a lift into Playa del Inglés with one of her coaches.

We hit the centre of town around 9 p.m. It was rocking. The two of us headed for the Metro centre, first trying to find door work. We tried a couple of bars and talked to some DJs – 'Dodgy' Dave and

'Scouse' Nick. They said that their boss never used security, which we thought was daft, seeing as the place was geared up for footballers with all the pictures on the wall and that.

We made our way downwards; the Metro centre was a converted car park with clubs at all levels and for all nationalities. We got to the bottom, which was scattered with English bars like the Happy Duck and Popeye's. Legends looked the busiest, although the biggest, Revival, was not yet open – it didn't start till 10 p.m. We saved that one till last and called back around 11 p.m., it looked right up our street: big, dark and banging.

I worked in both clubs. We fitted in really well with the other doormen. Every one of us was mental and we all loved to hurt people. We took special pleasure in throwing the 'geezer birds' about; they became our fun targets. They were pre-op transsexuals who preyed on drunken Brits, mostly older men. They would get their tits out and ask for 'fucky-fucky', pretending to be real women. They would even take men into the toilets and give them a blow job for money. Often they worked in groups. They would get their target outside and nick his wallet. They were always tooled up with knives or CS gas, which you could buy in the shops.

We got to know everyone really fast there, mainly through Dodgy and Scouse. They became really close acquaintances and they knew everyone. It was a great island. Our digs were in Puerto Rico about 30 minutes drive away; it was better there. We never got bothered by the tourists 'cos no one knew us in that part of town; we had perfect peace all day.

I thought up a right scam with the car hire there. A lad would rent a car in Playa del Inglés and we rented a car in Puerto Rico. We then swapped cars, and drove them back to our respective towns. The hire companies took months to find them and we'd only paid for a day's hire.

NINE

Timeshare Terrorist

One night we were in a big bar at the top of the Metro and my luck changed from bad to good. It was early evening and a small crowd of eight men walked into the bar – very smart, impeccably dressed – obviously designer gear almost to the man. They stood by themselves, quietly drinking and obviously comfortable with their surroundings.

'Who're them lads?' said Makka to Dodgy.

'Timeshare,' he said quickly.

'What's that?' I asked, and Dodgy began explaining the concept of the timeshare scheme.

While I was being bored to death I heard Makka give a large hoot of delight, and he ran across the room crashing into a huge man, well over six feet in height and almost as broad. The two men ranted off in their own language of gibberish, obviously both Geordies and both as mad as each other. I was called over to meet the big fella. I looked up at his face and saw that half of it was missing. His cheeks, part of his forehead and his chin were caved in and had been poorly repaired.

'Meet John. He's a great mate from back home,' said Makka.

'Alright?' we both said. Makka, enjoying his excitement at meeting his old friend, didn't bother telling him my name. John put his arm round his buddy's shoulders, gripping him tightly, and led him over to the well-dressed crowd we had noticed earlier. Makka turned back and beckoned. I followed like a lost dog. John introduced us to the group one by one and was forced to ask my name which he found a little embarrassing – strange for such a tough lad, I thought. I was pleased to have been included this time, though, and started to get to know the new crowd.

We were drinking one drink after another as quick as you like and talking furiously, our wealthy company taking the odd bit of cocaine. I didn't touch it but this was my first contact with drugs of any kind. I had seen it before when Denny got bashed but this stuff was in my face, almost literally.

Out of the eight men we met, three were salesmen of timeshare apartments. The other five were what I could only describe as 'mercenary bullies'. They worked for the highest payer, which happened to be a man I will just call 'D' (just to avoid a knock on my door followed by a loud 'bang'). 'D' had worked his way to the island from the mainland – and through all of the other islands, doing the same thing. He was a millionaire just through his bullying, maiming and, allegedly, murder. What I was learning about was both shocking yet exciting. I was moving up again. Violence was like a drug. I always needed a bigger fix to get the same high.

Makka and I were invited to meet the lads at their apartment in Paguera. This was a place where all the British boxers went to train. They were given free apartments and the use of a full-size boxing ring in a complex there. The owner, an Englishman, loved boxing. I believe it's still used for that purpose today when our British boxers go the islands to train for a title fight.

This place was pure luxury. There were very few English, who didn't have the sort of money needed. The occupants were mostly Germans. The lads larged it all of the time; they were earning big bucks, that's for sure.

John approached us about having a chat with his boss. There was a place on the team if we wanted it but questions had to be asked on both sides first. And once 'in', there was no 'out'.

We met with 'D' who was 'accompanied' by four other men, two of whom we knew. Our duties were detailed in no uncertain terms. We were told that we just did whatever we were told to do. He had bought and paid for our time to use it as he wished. We were paid monthly up front and no questions asked. No questions, no discussion, and no way out. Things had to be done and even killing was not out of the question; in fact, I was of the opinion that it was an immediate possibility in view of the tasks we were being taken on for.

Our position called for new faces because it involved Spanish officials on the island who happened to be on the payroll as well. That island was so corrupt with its own little Mafia-type organisations running each town and then a bigger one running a principality and so on towards the top.

I overheard a conversation while we were waiting with some of the other guys. A man was to 'fall' – and they didn't mean from grace. They wanted this man over the cliff, where many had gone before him apparently, right at the lower point of Puerto Rico town where we lived. It was to look like an accident: a car going over the cliff at the bend where the road led to Mogan. Makka and I had landed ourselves a job, and what a job. We sat up all night talking about it. I was a novice in all this but Makka, well, he had a sixth sense almost, and he planned every detail of the possible slaying.

Our *real* job was to get some money for the mayor who had insisted that the bars and clubs in the district had to put sound limiters on their PA systems. Those who refused were leant on by 'D's men and ended up paying dearly. By the end of our 'sales pitch', all of the bars would have machines fitted by decree of the mayor – who just happened to be the brother of the man who owned the company manufacturing and fitting the machines. 'D' was to get a profit share after sales and would pick up the maintenance contract. However, once the sales were done the mayor would then repeal the law and the bars would go back to normal trading. 'D' saw this as bad business and quite rightly so. He knew that he had been conned out of his maintenance money. Now he had to make it right. 'D' was fairly new on the island and saw this as a tester, one he welcomed really. He had the opportunity now to really show everyone what he was all about. We were told to collect, maim or kill, but whatever we did it had to be a good show.

Makka and I went to the mayor's brother's house, who 'D' decided owed him the money (after all, why damage the mayor himself, he might need him later for some scam or other). He lived at the top point of the town, overlooking the bay. Since he'd had it all his own way on the island for many years, he was not suspicious of our presence. He thought himself beyond punishment.

We were invited in by a member of staff. We were offered drinks, which we refused of course, and simply stated our business. The man never said 'no', but he did give us the biggest load of shit you have ever heard. He talked about everything but the subject we had called about. In a while Makka had heard enough and kicked a coffee table up in the air. Two bichon frise dogs came yapping full-pelt into the room. Makka kicked them both up in the air, one after the other. We never saw them again. Two Spaniards then came at us from a room annexed to the main lounge area and another bloke ran in through the open patio doors.

The man from outside had a pistol which he began unloading at us furiously. He was a real shit shot though, thank God. Bullets found everything in the room but us. Makka hit one man and I did the other. The man with the gun ran out of bullets without hitting either of us but still he came running at us, screaming in Spanish. He ran so fast he tripped on an ornamental elephant and smashed his face on the marble table knocking himself spark-out. We looked at each other and laughed. This was mad, I thought. I had no fear and my senses had never felt so alert. Maybe it was seeing the gun that woke me up. The gardener came dashing in next, waving a shovel. I started towards him. He swung the shovel, which glanced my head, but I just kept on ploughing into him. I grabbed him with both arms, shut my eyes, took him straight through the window and into the fishpond. It was brilliant – the pond went red with his blood as his skull opened up on the rockery. I left him there lying over the side of the pond, giving him one last kick in the side as I went. Makka grabbed the mayor's brother by the neck and dragged him out of the front door, over to the edge of a hanging garden and just threw him over. He turned to me and just looked. We both burst out laughing again, loudly this time; a sort of frenzied laugh. Those were the craziest few minutes that I had ever experienced – scary, fulfilling, yet they left me wanting more.

We jumped back into the car and reported to 'D'. We didn't know if our man was dead or alive, and we didn't care but word had it that the debt was paid in full, with a settlement for the lost maintenance contract. The new boys had made their mark on the island. From this point on there was the three of us: John, Makka and I. We felt invincible yet never turned our backs to the other lads on the payroll. This game was for real. It was played with respect, caution and loyalty. You were allowed no mistakes. There was no margin for error.

One day the three of us went up to the lakes; there was great carp fishing in the mountains. We were drinking wine there and had the barbecue going ready to cook our catch (providing we didn't get too pissed to catch anything). Luckily we had brought some steak and ready-cooked chicken also. We had done this before and although we still went through all the motions of fishing, we knew that we would only mess about. Suddenly, and for no other reason than being nosey and drunk, I asked John how he damaged his face. Makka went quiet and turned away. I thought 'Oh fuck, here we go,' but John sat and explained exactly how it happened. It may have been the booze, the sun or just the company but he seemed relaxed. As the story unfolded Makka slowly turned to listen. Of course, he knew anyway but he'd apparently never heard John tell the tale himself and he was intrigued.

John had been on a raid, a jewellery shop in Newcastle. They had been inside and closed it down, filled the bags almost at their leisure and were walking quickly to their car which had been parked two streets away to avoid suspicion. I piped up, 'Fuck suspicion, why didn't you . . .' John and Makka both looked at me hard. I backed off and apologised. This was clearly a hard story for him to tell and it was definitely not the right time to offer advice.

'We were walking quickly to get to the car,' he continued. 'My young brother had gone round the block as he was told but came back up by a wrong turning. First we went to the road up the side of the shop. We couldn't see the car. A horn sounded and we could then see him at the next corner which had big iron bollards across the precinct, so he couldn't get through them. There was no time to falter and the decision had to be made to run. As the three of us ran for the car a doorman came out of a large store to see what the hooting was about and bashed into me. I had the shotgun stretched out in front of me to put off any "have-a-goers". The poor doorman didn't want to get involved in it all, he just ran into me by accident. He began to fall over. When you fall over, of course, you grab at anything to help you stay up, don't you? Well, this man in his efforts to stay on his feet had grabbed the barrels of my shotgun. I shook him loose and turned the gun to hit him with the butt. It all happened so fast. As he grabbed the gun again he got hold of my hand which was on the trigger. The gun went off and the shot hit me in the face. The man won a medal for bravery and found himself a local celebrity for a while – until the lads started coming to the store taunting him, call him "grass" and "copper", making his life hell. They even smashed the window until eventually the shop had to let him go. Some reward for a hero, eh?

'I got into the car but the lads had to leave me at the hospital, I was bleeding like a pig, me brother was crying and the old bill was everywhere. I ended up with 18 years and this fucking souvenir to remember the day by.'

'How many did you do?' I asked solemnly.

'Just over 12,' he said. 'But that was another life. Things are going well now, like.'

We all suddenly appeared quite sober – which was just as well because we needed to get back to work that evening.

There were some new touts on the street working for the German timeshare companies who never paid for our . . . let's call it 'attention to detail' (being the careful arrangement of limbs and facial features). The timeshare companies sent kids out on the street with flyers to encourage prospective purchasers back to the developments by offering free tickets to attractions, lucky tickets, and other such freebies. It was our job to make sure the opposition was not represented on the streets and that our PRs were left a free rein.

The two lads and I drove round in a big Mercedes van with 'Time Machine' painted down the side in big red letters. When anyone entered the Time Machine, they never returned.

One evening we were cruising along the Maspolomos area and turned into the square at the beginning of the beach where Playa del Inglés began. There were two sets of PRs on the street that shouldn't have been there (well, not according to our boss anyway). We drove up to the square in the van and parked on the double-yellow lines. The motorbike cop saw what was about to happen and drove off quickly, throwing his cold drink aside, not even having time to put on his helmet. We got out of the van and casually walked over to the kids handing out flyers. Reaching out and taking the flyers from them we pushed them into the back of the van. Those that wouldn't get in we picked up and threw in. John stood at the door of the van with a small cosh in his hand. No one was getting out.

Once in the van we would talk to the kids and tell them the story of 'choices'. This story was about the young adults who came to a hot country and found they were not welcome but if they chose to change their job and not show their face on the timeshare scene again they could continue to live. The words 'and they all lived happily ever after' usually end a story like this. But these kids were content to end the story '. . . and they all lived'.

This was my life. Every day the same. It was easy work, a couple of hours terrorising the streets. The odd leaning on someone and each month a fat pay cheque came my way.

There was one other little job we were employed for that comes to mind: a sort of sub-contract to the local Mafia. We went to a club at one end of del Inglés that was trying to attract the younger holiday clientele. We were told to wait until the groups got into the club and the party was in full swing, then we had to go around picking on little groups of blokes until the whole place was a blood-bath. We did this over and over until the reps stopped taking the groups to the club in question. It got too much trouble for them and the news would get back home to young 'uns coming out on holiday. They were warned by their mates to stay away from that particular trip, which meant no earnings for the tour operators. The reps made their biggest money off of trippers.

It all ended in tears in any case. On the last visit we torched the bar and burned out the club upstairs also. Our firm was the best on the island, and the biggest payers. Most of the officials were on the payroll including the police, and the local Mafia left us alone because we would do work for them on a reciprocal basis as a mark of respect. It worked for us all and I was getting an education that you just couldn't buy anywhere.

The end of the summer season was drawing on but the work was still there. That's the good thing about the Canaries, it was an all-year season. Though the Brits died off about November, for most of the time we still had things to do. I went up to my favourite little hideaway, a town called Mogan. Mogan is a little fishing port not far out of Puerto Rico on the coast road. It's beautiful there. There are avenues of small villas hung with the most colourful flowers and a small square overlooking the harbour with many fine restaurants. I was sitting at one such restaurant when I saw 'D' pull in with his Rolls Royce, carrying a passenger I had never seen before. The two men came towards me in the restaurant and out of respect I rose to move along allowing them their privacy to discuss business. 'D' motioned me to sit and I continued with my meal. As I ate I strained to listen in on the conversation two tables away. I even tried to lip-read but I must have made it so obvious, they both sat there staring at me.

'D' called me over. This was a man you didn't fuck with. I would have him one-on-one but I just knew he wouldn't go away if I did. He would hide in the dark and bash me with a hammer or shoot me, anything to get even. He was dangerous. You would never beat him unless you killed him. 'D' introduced me to his guest.

'Billy,' he said in his calm, deep voice, 'this is Jerry the Yank.'

It turned out that this was not a business colleague at all. He was a friend from the States who lived on the island having jumped a US ship in Morocco some years earlier. Gran Canaria was a magnet to the Moroccans at the end of the year, about August onwards. They would come with their trinkets and drugs, as the Africans did, it turned into a real melting pot.

We chatted all day and got quite merry. People in our business never got drunk in a public place. We had to be in control, respectful. Anyway if you're pissed you make a good mark for the opposition. You begin to make mistakes and you just can't afford to. Your life may depend on it.

When we parted company we arranged to meet that evening for drinks at the fight that was being staged in the new complex outside Puerto Rico on the road to del Inglés. It was a bare-fist fight night put on for some special guests of 'D'. There were to be four fights in all – all Brits with the exception of a Swedish mush, who looked a bit tasty as it happened.

This was a big night for me. I was a guest of the boss; I was mixing with the dosh now, mate – couldn't be bad. I put on my best clothes and really looked the part: designer from head to toe, not a thing out of place. I was a special guest on a mission, just wait till the lads found out!

Suddenly there was a knock at the door. I opened it to find John and Makka standing there as dapper as I was.

'Good, you're ready,' said John. 'We wasn't sure you had heard about the fight, we're all going up on the boss's table tonight.'

I was gutted. I really thought I was special, the chosen one. Turns out these were regular dos and all the lads get to go.

We ate first. The spread was fantastic, the drink was flowing, the conversation was great, and everyone was on their best behaviour. It was really no effort though, because we had our best gear on and we were in a civilised environment. We all acted like real human beings. (Does that sound strange to you?) The air was warm and the sky was clear. The lights dimmed and the ring lit up brightly as the first two men came to the centre.

I sat back, my heart thumping as the adrenaline triggered my instincts. The memories of a not-too-distant past came rushing back, but not to haunt me as memories often do but to whet my appetite, to furnace my need.

I wanted to fight. It had been so long since I had treated myself to a real one-on-one. The past year had been just bullying easy targets and thuggery. This is what I really wanted. The first fight was on. It lasted about 12 minutes, which was quite a long time really. The lads were equally matched and put on a good show, the result was a knockout so no disappointment there. It was always better when it was an outright win like that rather than someone just giving up. I could feel this urge inside me and the old familiar stirring of the loins. An erection was brewing and I was ready to throw up. Lovely! I thought. I'll have to keep it down or I'm going to make a right dick of myself.

The second fight wasn't so good, it lasted about six minutes. Steamer, the bouncer from the club Fantaseas beat shit out of the lad from Paschas bar (I never knew his name, he was new on the island). Then it was the turn of the big Swede. He was fighting Jabo, a big Jamaican who worked all over the town. He was around six feet seven inches and built like a brick shit-house.

This was going to be something to see, I thought. The Swedish guy came out of his corner like a rocket, he was all over the black man who lumbered around slowly, trying to get his opponent in a hold all the time, he obviously thought he could do more damage that way.

The Swede came underneath, round the side, and in the middle. He was like an ant on jam, poor old Jabo didn't know what was happening. All of a sudden the Swede caught a left hook the size of a mountain off Jabo. He went through the ropes and crashed on to 'D's table. He shook himself and wiped the food off his legs. While Jabo was dancing around the ring doing the Ali shuffle the Swede jumped back into the ring, came round in front of him and hit him with a barrage of combinations like you've never seen. It was sweet. Jabo tipped and hit the canvas. It was over this time and he was out!

The lads were well excited by now. It wasn't enough – they wanted more. Fuck it, I thought, I'll give 'em more. I undid my shirt cuffs and took off my coat. I jumped into the ring and ripped off my shirt from the centre upwards as I had been taught. I was back!

'You want more?' I said, 'I'll fight any man for a monkey!'

No one moved. 'D's American pal stood up and shouted, 'I'll add another grand to that, winner takes all. We *are* talking English, not pesetas, ain't we?' he said with a grin, showing his gold tooth.

The prize was set; all I needed was someone to take up my challenge. I saw a movement to my right. It was Makka! My *mate* wanted to fight me?

He jumped into the ring. 'This time it really is for real,' he said and smiled.

We were set. My lunch went all over the ringside and my seconds parted like the Red Sea. Makka and I moved around the ring for about half a minute or so, just getting the feel of each other. When you are fighting you have to develop a sense of your opponent; a 'taste' if you like. It's hard to explain but you really can tell people what he tastes like, you become that close. Although we had fought a couple of times before it had been more on a drunken, boisterous level. Now we had to get the measure right.

Crack! The first one went to Makka; he caught me on the forehead.

Fuck it, I thought, I was slow there. I put together a nice

combination throwing my opponent backward. His head hit the corner with a thud as he toppled.

Makka came back with a flourish of poorly aimed punches. I say 'poorly aimed' because although most of them hit me they did not find a target worthy of the punch; they caught the shoulder or lower arm, nowhere that would do any damage.

I countered and caught him a nice blow to the nose. It exploded like a ripe peach, and claret washed his face and rushed up his cheeks and into his eyes. He came in for another flurry. *Bang. Bang.* One each side of the head – a classic. He was angry and wasn't thinking now, his blows went nowhere. I remained calm and focused. I was enjoying this too much to waste it on rage.

Makka came towards me, I was ready to sidestep and come in with a full-right to the lower body but I must have sent him a signal. He anticipated my move and brought his knee up into my left side. I went down winded. Bastard, I thought, he's going the other way. This was supposed to be a straightener – we were doing this clean and now he was pulling in a few dirty tricks. This dosh must mean something special to him. He had, I knew, developed a coke habit that cost him dearly. I didn't believe he would ever be out of 'D's debt.

I recovered quickly enough to put my hands up and stop Makka's foot from finding the side of my head. This *was* for real. He wasn't joking. I jumped to my feet and went in crouched, ready to work inside.

This man knew it all. He lifted with the inside of his foot and opened my defence. As I came up, he came down with the nut and my head split like an eggshell. I stumbled backward and ripped off some of the tape covering my knuckles. I moved round the ring backwards as I fumbled trying to tie the rag round my head to stop the blood going in to my eyes. I just wanted to re-direct the flow so that I could see long enough to finish this.

Makka walked round the ring following my backward steps. I danced to the right then the left. He faltered and came through the centre at me. I delivered a roundhouse like you've never seen, then another similar move with my fist, the back of my hand catching him good. I did another with the leg and caught his side. As he went down I kicked him in the temple and when he hit the deck I jumped on his head hard with both feet.

Fuck me, I thought swiftly, that came from nowhere. As my feet landed on his head I lost my balance and crashed on to my back. Makka rolled over and threw a fist into my gut. The blow caused me to sit bolt upright, and he followed suit. There we were, sitting on the ground hitting each other blow for blow.

We rose to our knees, still fighting. The blood was everywhere and the screams from our pals were deafening. Fruit started coming in at us – the onlookers were becoming as frenzied as the fighters. Makka lurched forward and sunk his teeth into my shoulder causing a searing pain to go down my arm. I thought I was going to be paralysed. I grabbed his head and pulled it into my face taking off the tip of his nose with my teeth. I don't know why, I just couldn't reach anything else. I didn't know what to do to hurt him most, I even spat at him 'cos I couldn't reach to hit him. It was sheer frustration.

We rose to our feet and still we were fighting. We had gone beyond pain; sheer determination and hatred was driving us now. I cupped my right hand and lifted it smartly under Makka's nose (what was left of it anyway). He brought both his hands over his face in agony. This is it, I thought, I've fucked him. I gave one more hit to the body, a straight fist just under the ribs as hard as I could, right below the heart. He spun in agony not knowing whether to hold his face or clutch his body. As he opened up his hands once more to hold his torso I came up with the left and across with the right. He hit the ground, out cold. Lucky bastard. At least he wouldn't hurt for a while. I, on the other hand, was in extreme pain.

I fell to my knees exhausted. The lads were going wild and three of them were fighting. 'D' jumped into the ring, covering me with adoration. 'That was the bravest fight I have ever seen. We could have made a fortune selling tickets for this,' he said. I put my hands across Makka then fell across his back in pain.

'No more,' I said. 'No fucking more – the man's an animal. The cunt nearly killed me, I still can't breathe!'

And with that I passed out. I woke up in hospital. It turned out that when Makka had pulled his legs up into my side, he had cracked my rib and punctured a lung. I'd been fighting on 50 per cent breathing capacity and pure adrenaline. The lung collapsed at the end there and I just passed out. I hurt, but it was a nice hurt. Know what I mean?

The American came to see me several times while I was in hospital and we became great friends. He introduced himself by saying:

'Hi. Remember me? It's Jerry.'

Nice of him to pop in, I thought. (Little did I know that he had his own agenda.)

At least he paid me his grand during his visit, though, which I split with my opponent. It was well worth it, I thought. I gave Makka his money when he came to see me and he was over the moon. They had sewn his nose back and it was quite a good job.

'D' sent his Rolls round when I got out, with a driver, John, who took me straight back to the complex. He talked non-stop about the fight.

'Everybody's still talking about it, mon,' he said, 'you're fucking famous, like.' I got into my apartment by 1 p.m. The Yank was with me by 2 p.m. – with a proposition that set me alight.

'How would you like to fight bare-fist, full-time in the States?' he said. 'Under my management.'

A dream, I thought. It must be a dream. I had always wanted to go to the States. I loved everything I knew about it. The cars, the weather, the people, the lifestyle. What could I say? It had to be yes!

We planned the trip over the next six weeks of my recovery, which brought us to the end of the summer season. I had to get a passport sorted out. I needed a ten-year one to get to the States. I had the required paperwork okay but we needed to send someone back to the UK to get the passport. Jerry handled all that stuff. It was no problem to him. My little work crew were all round. They were sad to see me go but all wished me well. Makka gave me a big hug (which didn't go down well at all, I was still in pain).

The day came and Jerry called to collect me.

'All packed?' he said

'Yep,' I replied.

This time I had more than a hold-all. I had real clothes and good cases. I was a proper gentleman now with money in my pocket and a career in front of me. On the way to the airport I asked Jerry: 'How come you can go back to the States? I thought you did a runner off the forces.'

'I got a new name now,' he said. 'I bought it from a pal stateside, he works with the police. They find a bum who's overdosed or been killed, then they take the ID and just sell it. The bum gets buried as a John Doe and I go on living in his honour, so to speak. Simply speaking I have a new identity, but to travel home I always take a long route round. We're going to Switzerland first, then to Florida for a while. After that we'll drive up to New York and do our business. The wheels are already turning for you, boy. We have great things in store.'

What I should have asked then was – 'Who is this "we"?'

TEN

Stateside

The flight to the States seemed to take an age. We went business class. I felt like a king – a king with arse-ache and a hangover, but a king nonetheless.

We touched down at Miami airport, Florida. I was so excited I felt I could split. I walked off the plane as if I had landed on the moon. My eyes were all over the place. I knew I was in a country where the people loved life and knew how to encourage the quality of that life too. We collected our bags and the porters swiftly piled them on to their trolley and walked us outside.

That was it. I couldn't breathe, for Christ's sake. I began gasping. 'I think I am going to have a turn,' I said to Jerry.

'Hey. No sweat. Sit here and take it easy. I'll go to the cooler and get you some ice-cold water.'

I sat for a while and tried to relax. The humidity of the place hit me square on. I have never felt so uncomfortable, I was gasping for air. I went back inside the terminal where the air conditioning was blowing full on. That was really nice. Jerry came over with the water, which I drank quickly.

'Right, let's get this show on the road. There's a courtesy bus running to the car hire. We'll jump it and get ourselves some wheels, fellah!'

I braved it outside again. This time I was more prepared and didn't feel so bad. We got on the bus and headed off out. We then hired the most beautiful car for peanuts. I just couldn't get over this place. People were pleasant, even *pleased* to serve you, not like the

British. Shop staff in the UK consider it an extra if they actually have to serve you. They appear to go out of their way to make you feel uncomfortable and if you get a smile you know it's gonna cost you in the long run.

We drove out of the gates and hit the highway. Cruising along, music playing and no pressures . . .

'Where are we going?' I asked.

'I thought you'd like a little break; see a bit of the state while we're here. I've planned a trip down through the Keys, we'll stay at Key West for a couple of days then drive back up to New York. How's that sound?' Jerry answered.

How did it *sound*? I thought. It sounded marvellous, that's how it sounded.

I just laughed and said, 'Let's go!'

I was very tired but couldn't sleep with the excitement. If mum could just have seen me. (Oh fuck yes! Mum! She still thought I was in Spain. I'd call her that night, I thought, just to let the family know where I was . . . well, more to show off really.)

We got to the beginning of the Keys. The Keys are a series of islands linked to the mainland by elaborate bridge work. The bridges seemed to go on for miles although I wasn't complaining, I saw some of the most beautiful sites during those trips. The thing I found most strange about the trip was having the sea on both sides of the road while driving on a major highway.

At last we reached the end of the road: Key West! As we drove around the narrow streets engulfed with shrubbery and filled with the scent of blooms, we came across a huge sign saying CUBA: 90 MILES. Christ, I thought, was it that close? I recalled the memories of my teens when we listened to the moves that J.F. Kennedy was putting on Castro. I was terrified in case there was a nuclear war, but old JFK had it sussed. What a great man: as cool as you like and a brilliant strategist. He would have made a good fighting man!

Jerry stopped the car. 'This will do,' he said.

I looked through the window at a large white palisaded property. There were balconies and verandas all around; extremely impressive.

'Been here before?' I asked.

'Only once a couple of years back with a little honey from

Schenectady. We loved it,' he said as he struggled to carry all three of his bags through the big wrought-iron gate. I really didn't believe him for some reason; not that it mattered anyway, I was just making conversation really, the place seemed so civilised I felt I had to.

Jerry appeared to be trying to avoid getting into conversation about anything during the whole journey. Something was going on and I guessed I would be informed when the time was right. I remembered our working agreement: it was his job to think and my job to fight. That suited me down to the ground. He was a great practitioner of the 'Need to Know' theory. He never wasted information, you only got it if you needed to know it. We settled into our respective rooms and got together over an evening meal that night.

It was during this meal that Jerry began to reveal his plan. There was a man he had to talk to in the Keys who loved to watch bare-knuckle. He was a fanatic and it just so happened that the man also knew a young black fellah who would fight me. Now I knew why we went downstate instead of up to New York.

Over the next few days I saw very little of my American manager. Either he was out early and back late or he sat all day on the telephone.

'I guess he's sketching out our future plans,' I thought.

I began to get really bored. There wasn't much to see tourist-wise and so I hung around a few of the local bars chatting to different people, getting a feel for the place. It was on such a casual day out that I met a most interesting man – a black bloke sat up against a fence with a can of Cola in his hand.

'Hi,' I said.

He nodded and I stopped, leaned against the fence and we started chatting. He never even looked at me really. He just looked straight ahead and went on talking for ages. It turned out he used to be a fighter and he was telling me how he and his boss used to fight in the garden of the house at which he worked.

Another few days went past when Jerry sprung it on me that I was set to fight a fellah on the next island. I wasn't really surprised, I have to say, I knew he was up to something. Luckily I had been keeping in trim. I'd never slackened off, it was part of my life to stay fit, especially during the summer months when we travelled. I never knew when I was going to fight.

The fight day came and we drove up to Key Largo. We found the venue quite quickly. It was an open-air event, at the quayside on a small marina. About 50 or 60 men had turned up, sitting around with obligatory beer cans in hand.

I stripped off my shirt and stood waiting for my man to come along. A big old shooting brake pulled in to the marina and a couple of Hispanic-looking blokes jumped out of the front seats. One opened the rear door for their passenger, obviously the man I was to fight.

I watched as the man in the back pulled himself out of the vehicle, grabbing on to the roof edge, throwing his legs around and heaving as if he was a mountain of a man. I smiled almost with relief as the figure stepped forward – about five foot six and built like a ballerina. His clothes were immaculate and his hair was slicked back – jet black with a red ribbon holding his ponytail in place.

I turned to Jerry laughing and said:

'What the fuck's this, mate? When you told me I'd have him fucked I didn't think you meant literally . . . is he a poof?'

My management assured me that this was a sincere and valued opponent – so I just sat and waited for my instructions and for the betting to finish. There were a lot of sick faces when those who had bet against me saw their man.

A big old bloke came over and called the management to the centre, then the fighters. The Hispanic was dancing around like Sugar Ray Leonard on an 'E' tab. The ref called it on and the man spun around me, dancing and kicking – making funny noises and shaping up like Bruce Lee.

I thought, oops – it looks like I might come unstuck here . . .

I watched him for about 20 seconds. Then I stepped in and knocked him spark-out. I didn't even get a sweat up. I looked to my corner in shock. I thought I had misjudged the man and he was going to come on strong. Obviously I was right the first time. He was shit.

Well, you've never seen anything like it. The men flooded around me like I was a film star. All talking at once, offering me beers. This must have been the first piece of excitement they had had for years,

I guess. It was a sleepy old place. Personally I would have been as mad as hell paying for a fight that lasted less than a minute.

The crowd then parted as this huge bearded figure loomed towards me. Quite smartly dressed although not over-indulgent. He had a young boy with him – about 18 or 20 years old, and a black fellah dressed in scruffs. The big, bearded man held out his hand and talked very profoundly about the fight game and seemed extremely knowledgeable about the emotions felt before, during and after fighting. I was completely taken in by the aura, the very presence of this man. He held my attention without wavering. After first inviting me to dinner that following evening, he turned and strode away followed by his entourage. As the visitor moved off, the crowd surged forward once more. I was led to believe during the drive up to New York some days later that the formidable figure who offered me his hospitality and understanding was Ernest Hemingway – apparently he was a good writer or something, and absolutely loved both wrestling and bare-fist fighting. In fact I remember someone sharing with me the fact that he often fought his own gardener in the grounds of his home on Key West.

We never did take advantage of Hemingway's hospitality – which was just as well since more recently, during the writing of this book, I learned that Hemingway had killed himself in 1961 and I met this man in 1969. Now although I was disappointed to find this truth out, I was not surprised given that it was Jerry who told me it was Hemingway, the lying toe-rag. (However it was true that Hemmingway loved the fight game and did actually wrestle with his gardener.) Jerry had it all organised that we were to leave our accommodation the day following the fight and make our way to New York City.

I was just getting to like the place and we were off. I have to say there are now many places I think of in my life that were memorable or important in many ways, but Key West . . . well, it just had that smack of romanticism; a beauty and peace that is rare. If you ever find yourself in Florida, remember that it's well worth hiring a car and taking a trip to Key West. I promise you that you will be in awe of its beauty. Stay at least one night. Watch the sun set. And then watch it rise again. If you don't like it give me a ring and I'll send you your money back. That's how confident I am.

ELEVEN

New York, New York

We finally arrived in New York City – sprawling buildings disappearing into the clouds, clouds that were at this time spewing snow across the entire state and causing havoc in this bustling city. I saw more people in the streets here than I have ever seen anywhere else before in my life, more than I could even imagine being in one place. Everyone was running about his or her business. No one seemed to have time to just walk, they were almost regimental in their tracks as they filed along the swelling streets, careful not to cross the path of another human being or to make eye contact for fear of confrontation. The people of New York appeared to live in fear of social contact, without a smile to share between them. I think they didn't want to talk to anyone in case it took time from their busy day.

They wanted to use all their time for themselves and didn't want to have to share it. This was not what I expected from the people of the nation with everything. My first experience had been so warm and welcome down in Florida State, I'd thought America was America and that people were the same all over. This was clearly a huge mistake.

As I toured the country a little more I found out that the personalities in different states were similar to those found in different countries of Europe. Each state had its own weather, its own beliefs, architecture, landscape – almost its own language. Something that I found impressive was the architecture in New York City. The engineering was awesome! (See, I even picked up the

TARMAC WARRIOR

lingo!) It was strange for me to notice something like this. My only interests ever seemed to lie in things around myself – stuff that affected *my* life directly. Was I becoming more sensitive? Was I growing up or was I just so bloody bored with the trip I was beginning to find anything to look at interesting? I decided I was bored.

One thing was made absolutely clear to me, though, New York does not like strangers. It is not a welcoming city and a visitor will never be any more than that – unless of course you are with someone like Jerry who happened to know everyone in the whole world!

We edged our way through the impatient traffic, vehicles full of drivers with contorted faces and foul mouths. All I understood was 'motherfucker' this and 'motherfucker' that. The people of New York seem to growl a lot and scream at each other in their very own language, their own version of already bastardised English.

A lone policeman stood in the centre of a busy crossroads, his arms waving white paddles frantically. As we grew closer to the lonely, frozen character I laughed like hell. He was my first sight of humanity in an animal kingdom. The policeman had developed this sort of acrobatic dance routine as he controlled the traffic flow. What had at first appeared to be a lonely man turned out to be the life and soul – the heartbeat of the city traffic. This man truly made my day. My memory of him will stay with me forever.

I soon found we were travelling on a route out of the city. I turned to my companion in surprise. 'Where the fuck're you going?' I asked.

'You didn't expect we were going to stay in that crazy house, did you?' he replied. 'Only the mad, the rich and the lonely live there.'

Now I was confused.

'Well, you said we were going to stay in New York,' I said.

'And so we are, fellah, so we are. We're in New York State. That there was New York City. New York State has some beautiful places and some functional places. We are going for beautiful and travel to functional just when we need to.'

Jerry had a sure-fire way of confusing me almost every time he went into an explanation. He could never just say it as it was, in plain black and white. Perhaps that was why he was so good at his job. Bullshitting.

We drove on for around another 20 agonisingly slow minutes. The snow appeared to be falling faster and thicker as we cleared the protection of the tall buildings. The roads were quite obviously treacherous and had we been allowed to travel any faster I am sure our lives would have been in threat. As it was, though, only my sanity was compromised.

I remember peering through the misted window, pressing my forehead against the cold glass relieving an on-coming headache probably caused by the flame-thrower Jerry described as a heater – and the fact that I had had my arse glued to this seat for what felt like days.

We hit a major road and began to pick up some speed.

'Slow it up, mate, I'm trashed of this,' I said nervously.

I was never a good passenger. As far as I was concerned I was sitting on the right side of the car but with no steering wheel. I never did get used to driving on the right-hand side of the road. He put his foot down a bit just to show me that he was in control and we slid a little to one side.

'You kill me and you're fucking dead!' I shouted.

We both burst out laughing as the stupidity of what I'd said dawned.

'Woah! Stay cool, little cockney, we're nearly there. I know these roads like the back of my hand.'

Suddenly he gave a shout. 'What the hell . . . ?'

As we rounded the bend we saw a pile of twisted metal spread across the carriageways of both lanes. Jerry hit the brakes hard but he may as well have just let go of everything. We were obviously destined to join the carnage. We ploughed through the slush and through the police officers, almost taking some of them with us as they tried to leap aside. Luckily I had been a little on edge with the driving anyway, so my instincts were very sharp.

I leaped into the rear of the skidding car and fell down across the seat. I heard the crunch and grind of metal upon metal as we hit the crash. Jerry sat screaming profanities until we came to a sudden stop. I sat up and dragged Jerry into the back by the scruff of his neck. I don't know why; I thought I was saving him! It's funny the things you do in a crisis, ain't it? He shouted at me 'let me the fuck go' and called me everything under the sun, but I was intent on saving his life.

In reality it was just a silly overreaction, I guess, but I did it with the right intentions. It was probably a fucking stupid thing to do too, he might have hurt himself – internal bleeding, a punctured lung or something. I could have killed the poor bloke. He fought his way out of the car door shouting loudly, 'Shit. Let's move it! Grab everything!'

I moved without question. I had got used to doing that by then. Since I had been with Jerry, he had convinced me that as manager he did the thinking and was *always* acting in my best interest. I believed him and was fast becoming brainwashed, I think.

Too late! The gavvers were closing in fast. We quickly became surrounded. Fortunately they were more interested in getting us out of the crash and moving us to the side of the road set up as a recovery area, where other victims were already limping around and moaning. Women and chavvies, screaming and crying. Mushes running around like chickens with their heads cut off. It was without doubt the worst accident I had ever seen, let alone been involved in.

Jerry was clearly panicking. He was pacing up and down.

He looked at me hard. 'We gotta move,' he said, 'come on.' And he began to make his way back to the car.

'We ain't going nowhere in that shit-heap now, mush,' I said.

'Help me get our bags, man, we can't leave any trace of us in that vehicle,' he replied.

We ran to the car quickly and popped the boot, grabbing everything we could possibly carry. I pulled out a couple of the cases and Jerry got the rest while I rifled the inside of the car, grabbing maps, newspapers – anything that we may have scribbled on. I felt like a fugitive – not an unfamiliar feeling, I have to say. I spent my whole life feeling that way, even as a child.

The gavvers were everywhere. We ran to the roadside and slid quickly down a small bank and off into the fields. I followed the man who had led me to this desperate situation like a little lost puppy – what the fuck for I don't know, he had really messed up this time. Looking back on it now, I suppose I was a little lost puppy in a way. Although I was as streetwise as the next mush, I had very little worldly experience – I was in a strange country with a very strange man, running to God knows where.

I suddenly became aware of how stupid I was beginning to look – I was soaking wet and cold – and very, *very* pissed off. I stopped dead and dropped the luggage I was carrying.

'What the hell are we doing, you fucking dinilo American twat?' I asked. (I had a way with words, didn't I?) 'If we just waited at the roadside with all the other mushes we would get a ride in a warm vehicle to somewhere we could stay for the night.'

'Oh yeah, we'd get a lift all right.' Jerry said. 'Flashing lights and everything – somewhere to stay too – probably for a couple of years if we're lucky. Are you really that stupid? I have a bent passport, I just rented a car with an even more bent driving licence. I've been on the US Navy missing list for eight years and I just smashed through a row of America's finest officers. Now pick up them bags and move it!'

He turned and stormed off through the sludge. Although at the time I couldn't work out just what I might get banged up for, he had put up enough of an argument for me to follow. After all I was a Gypsy. I knew I was going to get banged up just for *being* there. It was part of my heritage.

We made our way back up the bank, struggled past the many police cars lining the carriageway and got back on to the road. Cars approaching had either slowed down or completely stopped to negotiate a diversion set up to take them through the central barrier and back towards the city.

Jerry ran to the centre of the filed trucks, cars and vans, and started banging on the doors of a huge articulated truck.

'Hey, buddy,' he shouted.

The window of the driver's door slowly opened and a bearded face peered down.

'Say – can you give me and my buddy a ride back to the city? Our car has broken down.'

The figure motioned for us to go to the other side of his truck. As we did so he just sounded his horn and drove off, leaving us standing in the mist of exhaust fumes.

'Bastard!' Jerry shouted. 'Fucking sick *bastard*!'

I stood there, soaking wet, cold, pissed off, fucking pissed right fucking *off*. What was I doing here following a foul-mouthed Yank around in the dark with no money, no friends, no car and nowhere to go? Suddenly my whole dream was collapsing before my eyes. I'd have given anything for gran's apple pie and a mug of my mam's tea.

I took the incentive. Fuck this, I thought and walked up to the very next car, opened the driver's door and shouted: 'Give us a lift!'

I frightened the driver – he leaped two feet off his seat. Before he could answer I had leaned across him and opened the catch to the back door. Jerry was in like a flash and I jumped up beside him, bags and all. The poor sod never knew what hit him. I think he spent the rest of the drive in shock. After about three or four miles, we spotted a sign off to the right for a motel. We asked our new driver to drop us off there and he was, of course, very obliging.

As we stepped out and unloaded our bags, Jerry turned to give the fellah 50 dollars but before you could say 'hands-up' he was gone, skidding and slipping into the darkness.

'You crazy bastard, you ain't in Europe now, that guy could have shot you dead,' Jerry said. 'He could have had a pistol in the glove box or anything. You scared the shit out of him. You really must take more care. This isn't England, old boy!' he said in what he thought was a posh English accent.

'Piss-taker,' I said and shrugged my shoulders.

'Come on, let's get booked in here and get drunk, I'm fucking frozen.'

We booked in to the small roadside motel. As I found our cabin, I had immediate visions of Norman Bates dressed up and brandishing a big knife. Sod having a shower, I thought.

We shared a bungalow with single beds (at least they called single but they were the size of the doubles used in England). Jerry got straight on to the telephone. I think he was born with a phone strapped to his ear, that bloke. He had a hurried conversation and dropped the receiver as he turned to look at me.

'Be ready to go by 5 a.m.' he said. 'A car's collecting us.'

'There's no such fucking time,' I said laughing. 'I had better go to bed now, I'll never get up.'

'Don't worry, you'll get up, pal,' he said in a cocky voice. (I have to say it rubbed me up the wrong way a bit, I was only joking.) I didn't need his attitude.

I hit the shower (see, I wasn't scared), it was lovely. Hot and hard, the water pounding at my aching shoulders where I had wrenched them pulling those bags about. After I'd got dressed we wandered down to the little bar in the lounge area for a few drinks and then went to bed. The next thing I knew I felt a heavy hand on my shoulder, shaking me furiously.

'It's 4.30. Get up,' a voice said.

'Oh no, I am bolloxed. Give me 15 minutes,' I replied.

'Get up, the guys collecting us don't wait for nothing or no one.'

We sat on the edge of our beds until about 6 a.m., Jerry jumping up at every set of headlights that hit the window. At last a car swooped in and the driver came to our door tapping gently. When I opened it there was the biggest, fuck-off mush I'd ever seen. The figure blocked the light from the flashing blue motel sign. He had a chest like a battleship and wore this long black Crombie overcoat down to his ankles. I thought it was the angel of death coming for me.

A smile crossed my face as the figure spoke. A small effeminate voice sort of minced its way from his lips asking if we were ready. I felt my smile bursting to turn into laughter as I went to take the piss but I caught Jerry's face which told me that I was about to do the wrong thing. I ignored my urge and instead began to grab at the cases.

We began to walk towards the car when a shock ran through my body as I realised the worst.

'Oh fuck!' I blurted out.

Jerry swung back towards me. 'What's up?' he said.

'My leather jacket and holdall – it's not here, we must have dropped it when we got into that bloke's car.'

He looked relieved at my news.

'We'll get you another tomorrow – or later today if you're that desperate, now let's move it!'

'It's not just the jacket,' I said. 'My passport and everything is inside, you daft twat. I'm knackered now.'

He looked at me in a state of clear panic, then said: 'Forget it. I'll sort everything out later. Right now let's get moving.' This was the very first nail in the coffin of our friendship, or 'partnership' as he preferred to call it. It was my first realisation that Jerry was only here for Jerry. I was just an earner to him – a little scam that he would grow tired of; he didn't give a toss about me. It hurt a bit but the knowledge also fed a driven strength that would end up helping my fighting attitude.

Every pain I had had bestowed upon me, every racially motivated experience that came my way, every gorgio that ever shouted abuse or laughed at me was in the ring when I fought. I remembered their faces as I looked for my target and began to punish it.

I'd had a great teacher in life: my mam! She told me: 'Let the others make the rules, then beat 'em at their own game.' I owed Jerry nothing really, did I? That made life easier. My biggest problem with relationships is that I always give 200 per cent and expect the same in return.

Off we set once more on our journey to fame and fortune. All the discomfort and inconvenience of the past 24 hours had been forgotten. I noticed that we were heading in a completely different direction this time, taking the main drag out of town, heading north.

'Where the fuck you headed now, Jerry?' I asked.

'Somewhere better than where we were headed before,' he answered.

'Well, why didn't we head there in the first place, then?'

'I was trying to save us money, get the best value,' he said. He always had an answer.

'When am I going to work?' I asked after a long silence.

'Christ, let's get a roof over us first! I gotta have a phone and a couple of days space, just be patient,' he said. 'You've been on the road for three days, your muscles need some work and your body will need a tune-up – trust me.'

We were on the road for about two and a half hours. We eventually came to a beautiful hotel, it appeared in the middle of nowhere. Our car swept in and pulled to a halt outside the main doors. Two blokes came running out, one opened our car door and took the keys to undo the boot – which I thought was a bit cheeky, although Jerry seemed to take it all in his stride. As we stepped out of the car, the other fellah jumped in and drove it off while his mate got all our cases inside. It was like a military operation. I felt like a proper lord or something, right posh.

We walked through the doors of the hotel and up to the

reception desk where we were met by a real honey. Immediately thoughts of lust swamped my mind. I distracted myself by looking around at my new surroundings while Jerry booked us in. Everything seemed to be brand spanking new. Kushti! I thought. This'll do me.

Having booked in, the mush took our cases to our room while we had a look around the place. There were a couple of shops with no prices on anything. Mam always said: 'If it don't have a price and you have to ask then you can't afford it.' Uncle Bendy's version was: 'If it don't have a price then how you gonna know what to sell it for once you've chored it!' I liked both versions.

We found a gym, a swimming pool inside and out, a sauna, a jacuzzi, a pool table, a restaurant and a couple of bars – everything you could ever want. I was so excited, I felt like a kid at Christmas time. I had never seen such a place, not even in those American films. I didn't know places like this existed.

We got into the elevator and found our room. My God! This was even better. It was out of this world – I couldn't have dreamed the place up in my wildest imagination. We had a massive lounge area with a TV, bar, dining table and three-piece suite. There were carpets on all the floors, curtains that reached from floor to ceiling and flowers – yeah – *flowers*. What was that all about? The TV was the size of a fucking cinema screen, for Christ's sake. I was running round like a silly boy. Looking, touching, smelling the flowers. I even tried the kettle. And the bathroom, well, the bath was built like a swimming pool and had a jacuzzi in it. Two (*two*, mind you) sinks with a mirror each and loads of stuff in boxes – soap, shampoo, toothpaste, even a little poofy shower cap!

'Christ,' I said, 'I've died and gone to heaven.'

Jerry just laughed, put his feet up on the settee and lit a big old lardy (that's cockney for cigar). Mam would have killed him if she had been there, putting his feet on the furniture like that.

Jerry looked up and said: 'This, my son, is how you will live from now on. Providing, of course, you do your job right. Look at me now.' He went all serious. 'Only *I* can do this for you. I'll make it all happen, there's no one I don't know. I have all the connections to get you on to the right circuit for the right money. Trust me. I'll make you rich.'

Yes, go on, raise your eyebrows. You can see it coming, can't you? I had been sucked right in again. This man had the formula dead right. He was playing on my greed, a trick my family had taught me in my very earliest years. He had played on my need. Another trick I knew well. He had flattered me, then laid out his store and I was buying.

TWELVE

My Time Came

The next few days passed very slowly. I swam, watched TV, walked, jogged, trained, but I had no fights. I didn't even have a sparring partner to keep my moves fresh or work out new ones with. I was growing stale and impatient. Worst of all I was bored shitless and began working out little scams that I could pull in the hotel to earn some cash and relieve the boredom. I didn't need the money but I certainly needed the fun.

Jerry made a thousand phone calls – well, it seemed that many anyway. I was getting fed up with his company. He really gave it large, talking like a big-time Mafia boss. I know he had dealings with gangster types and moved amongst them when doing his little deals but you just knew he was really small-time. But he was all I had at this point. I needed him in the worst way. As soon as I got my feet under the table, I told myself, I would dump him like a piece of shit.

It was a bright, cold Thursday morning when Jerry burst into my room and started to jump up and down on the bed.

'Get the fuck off, you crazy bastard, or I'll knock you the fuck out!' I said – I meant it too. Not only was I fed up with the mush but I hated mornings. I was more a night person. Dad would say I had my head on back to front, my body clock was right off. Granddad always said it was because I was born at midnight on 31 October – Halloween.

I kicked his legs from under him and he fell off the bed. 'You are a miserable fuck,' he said. 'I come here with good news and a smile after working hard for you on that phone.'

I stopped him swinging into another bullshit line.

'Shut up, you hooky little dinilo twat. Just tell me the news and piss off, let me get some sleep. I'm sick to death of hearing about the work you do for me. It's bollocks. Tell me like it is with no shit and we won't fall out. But feed me another line and I'll bash you.'

Oh, he'd really caught me at the wrong time of the day.

'Well, there's gratitude.'

I cut him dead again. 'You're fucking straight at it. Just *tell* me, you thick cunt.'

'Okay, okay. I've just called my man who promotes in Brooklyn. He has a fight meeting fixed next Wednesday and says he has a new fighter they are trying to push. You're on the bill. This'll be your first experience in reality fighting.'

(Extreme Reality fighting is now called 'Ultimate' or 'Total' fighting in the States. It has a huge following and the rules nowadays are about the same they were back then: no gouging, no biting . . . yeah, *right.*)

'Reality? That's where we fight in the 27-foot circle that you were telling me about, right? Will we have ropes?' I asked.

'Well, sort of,' he replied. 'The ring will have a boundary but not ropes as you imagine a boxing ring to have. The crowd are moved tight to the ring in some places, you have to watch your back. There's big money involved at these fights and no one wants to lose theirs. Stuff comes out of the crowd that might hurt you real bad but let me worry about that. I will have some men around the ring,' he assured me.

'Let *you* worry about it?' I shouted. 'Fuck you! How about *I* worry about it and you fight. You're so good to me.' I replied. 'What's my end?'

'A grand,' he replied.

'Dollars or pounds?'

'Dollars, of course. Why would it be in pounds? We're in the USA. You get a grand win or lose.'

'What do you mean, "win or lose"?' I snapped. 'What's the incentive to win if the fighters get the same money either way?'

'Well, you get the grand and, well, the other guy's gonna win – he gets a little extra,' he replied.

He walked to the other side of the room putting a little distance between us.

I stared at him. 'Oh, fucking thanks for the confidence boost – tosser.'

'You ain't got it, have you?' he asked.

'What?'

'This guy you're fighting has to win. That's what the fight's laid on for. The guys are building him a career. He needs a few good wins to get to the right circuit.'

I stood up, stunned at what this man was telling me.

'Sorry, you gotta take this one on the chin,' he said.

'You dirty no-good mother's cunt,' I said, fuming. 'You mean I have to lose on purpose? And what do you mean he has to win to get on the "right circuit"? What happened to all that shit about you getting *me* on the "right circuit"? Are you telling me this ain't it after all your crap? Now you tell me I have to drop to get someone else on the "right circuit". Where's that leave me, then?'

I couldn't believe what was happening. *This* was the good news this twat woke me up for. I swiped my bedside lamp from the chest of drawers and it crashed to the floor.

'I'll come back when you've calmed down,' he said. 'I understand, it's just nerves. You think about it for a few minutes. I'll order breakfast.'

He left the room and I dropped heavily back on to my bed.

I was so angry, my stomach was knotted. I had spit running down my face from shouting at Jerry. I caught sight of my face in the robe mirror, and saw my eyes were bulging. I thought I was going into a fit or something. Suddenly I became calm. A sadness washed over me as I realised what I had to do. I knew I had to swallow. If nothing else I was practical. I needed some money to get out of this place and away from that leech.

My head dropped into my hands. I was gutted. Imagine the worst piece of news you could have, imagine your wife or husband has just told you they are sleeping with someone else. Imagine you have just been told one of your immediate family has a fatal illness. Imagine your daughter has just asked to go on the pill, or you've just got the sack from a job you thought you had for life. Then you will know what I was feeling at that moment. I am feeling it again now as I relive that conversation for you to read. Some things I tell you in this book reach inside me and cause me the same pain as they did then.

TARMAC WARRIOR

I had built up so much around what this man was going to do for me in the US. Big money, big fights, fame and fortune . . . it was all just bollocks. All I'd had so far was deceit and disappointment.

I thought a little longer about the whole thing and made up my mind that I just had to get on with it; come to terms with the fact that I was about to go against all that my parents had taught me. I was raised to be true to myself above all else.

Dad used to say, if you begin to lie to yourself, you are lost forever. 'Be the best you ever can be in whatever you decide to do,' he'd say. 'Work as hard as your body will let you, then push it some more.' All this I remember. These have been the rules of my life. I can remember dad saying: 'Just make me proud, son.' I am not ashamed to say that tears filled my eyes. My dad never once told me that he was proud of me. He'd never once told me that he loved me. Whatever I did to please him, he would always have to spoil by saying something like: 'Well, it's all right, but if you did it like *this* it would look better, or last longer . . .' I know he was just teaching me the best he could but when you are learning you need encouragement as well as correction. It would have been nice to hear him tell me I had done a good job, just once. Instead he just pushed for better. Don't get me wrong. I knew he loved me and I knew he had some pride in things I did. He told others but he never told me! Now perhaps he never would.

I craved my dad's approval all my life and now I was about to do stuff that went against all his principles. Could I keep this secret from him? I didn't have to tell him, and after all what choice did I have? This was not a good day in my life. I had no money, no independence, no passport, no friends, no family. I was stuffed!

I sat and thought for hours about what was being asked of me. I had to accept the deal and live with it but, I decided, this man would pay dearly for my loss of integrity as a fighting man.

I walked from my room and told Jerry to call it on. He now had to arrange the meeting with the other fighter and his management to 'rehearse' the event. The meeting was called at our hotel as it was out of the city. Obviously there should be no risk of us being seen together.

When I met with my young opponent I thought I was going to feel a hate for him but he was a really nice bloke. We got on well.

He was just another muppet like me, being used by men who could never hold their hands up. He was a little taller than me. That was no surprise, most of them were and as we talked I began to feel that a real good straightener between us could be a fantastic fight, great entertainment in fact. But as they say, money talks, and this little pile of greenbacks appeared to be shouting loudly.

I needed my own money. This business is no different to any other really. The man with the dosh in his hand is the stronger to bargain. My opponent and I were just puppets in a strange charade that had to be acted out. The real money was going to the hands that would never be hurt, never feel the pain of bone-on-bone.

A wave of wickedness came over me. That's it, I thought. That's to be my revenge – the leveller with Jerry. He has to feel the pain I feel. I will use him until I have enough dough, then I will demonstrate the pain of punishment on the hands. Until then I will just play the game.

The day of the fight came quickly. We were at least, it seemed, going to do it in style. A big limo turned up at our hotel and Jerry escorted me down, opening the car door, carrying my kit. What's this all about? I thought. I was dressed to kill. I could have been a film star. I have to say the man pulled out all the stops and did that part right.

We drove into the city at a whisper's pace, picking our way through the streets towards Brooklyn. Under archways, passing derelict cars, groups of blacks and Hispanics on the street. I hoped to fuck we didn't break down out here, it was a shit-hole.

Finally we came to a little building on a street corner guarded by two big, black mushes and I mean fucking *big*. Outside the building were posters advertising the fight. I looked eagerly for my name. It was the first time I would see my name on a boxing bill.

'There you are!' said Jerry.

I looked. That isn't me, I thought.

The second fight on the bill hailed the coming of 'The Gypsy Prince' – all the way from Great Britain. Jerry had even denied me the pleasure of seeing my name up there – this, my first fight as a professional.

'That's supposed to be me?'

'Yeah. They hate Gypsies here,' he said eagerly.

'Well, what a surprise,' I said sarcastically. 'That's sure old news. Everyone hates us. If they hate me then why advertise me as Gypsy Man?'

'It sells tickets,' he said. 'They just want you to get the shit kicked out of you. Only trouble is, the betting will be heavy on the other guy and he is set to win. The odds will be crap so I guess the guys will make their money betting against you.'

Jerry gave his last bit of advice: 'When the fight's over, just get back to your corner and we'll get you out quick. Don't hang around or you might get hurt.'

We got out of the car and marched between the towering guards, climbing the steep staircase to find a labyrinth of corridors. Up two steps, down five, round corners, down another flight. Where the fuck was I going? I was going to disappear up my own arsehole in a minute. I was eventually shunted in through another doorway.

This place was to be my changing-room. I recall the extremity of my feeling. It was fucking *freezing* cold! It was like an ice palace. You could see your own breath as you spoke. How was I gonna get ready for a fight in here? I needed to get my muscles warmed up or I would hurt myself – what was I thinking about, though? I was going to get knocked out anyway . . .

'Don't get any clothes off yet, boy,' came a stranger's voice from behind the door. 'You have an hour to kill yet – start getting your gear off in half an hour but meantime you can do a few warm-up exercises.'

I looked for the owner of the voice. It was a little fat mush with one eye up the chimney and one in the fireplace, a face full of tiny cuts as if he had been through a windscreen, and with ears that made his head look like a car with its doors open. One good fart and he'd take right off.

My gaze was fixed on his scars. I didn't even know I was looking.

'Bother you? Sorry,' the fat man said.

'No – no, sorry, mate. What happened?' As my thoughts came out loud I could have bitten off my tongue. Poor sod.

He looked straight at me (well, at least he was facing me so I guess he was looking at me. I couldn't tell with those eyes).

Without any hesitation he said: 'Got caught between the wrong two guys. I just shouldn't have been in the room, they went at it and I got the window. Wrong place, wrong time.'

And that was it. I never asked about the face again, although I must say I was busting to learn the whole story.

The half-hour passed quickly and my princely clothes became suitably sweaty as I warmed up in them. The little fat man bandaged my hands – tight. I'd never been strapped up so well, not before and haven't been since. This man really knew his stuff. It was really tight, but so comfortable. I think I could have punched a wall without discomfort. It was proper.

'That'll hold the little guys together,' he said.

'What little guys?' I asked.

'All the tiny bones in your hands,' he replied. 'You have to look after the bones or the joints'll go when you're older. This way you'll last till you're at least 30,' and he laughed.

We worked together hard for the last 15 minutes. I worked up a good sweat, although it was a waste of time because I wasn't going to have a real fight and by the time I got to the ring it was so far away I was cold again. I was led to the ringside amongst jeering crowds throwing everything that they could lift.

The Fatman said to me: 'You're more likely to get hurt here than in the ring.'

'Thanks for the tip, mate,' I said and tucked my head and hands in.

We had walked for ages to get to the fight arena. I use the term 'arena' very loosely. It was a huge building with a fully glazed roof to it as high as you could see and a maze of pipes woven through the steel structure that supported the glazed panels.

The room was throbbing. I stood in the centre of the ring as the MC called my name to the crowd. All hell broke loose. Coins were thrown, paper cups, cartons, bottles, seat bases. I thought, fuck this, I'm off in a minute. A sea of security men swooped on the offenders who were doing the throwing. Amongst the security men were real police officers. I looked at the Fatman in bewilderment.

'It's okay, Prince,' he said.

I thought, who's this Prince? Oh yeah, it's me!

'They're on the payroll – guns and all,' he said. 'The cops are great supporters of our little shows, best security you can buy.'

My opponent appeared and the crowd rose as one with a huge cheer and the stamping of feet. I thought, I'll show them fuckers! I'll knock the cunt straight off his feet as he comes across the ring. That'll shut them up. Of course, I knew I couldn't do that, not unless I wanted to end up dead.

Jerry pulled me over. He had seen the anger in my eyes and knew what I was capable of. 'You know what you've gotta do. Your turn will come – I promise.' For some reason I believed him, I think I needed to. The Fatman winked and a klaxon sounded. It was the start of the fight.

I met my man in the middle and for a couple of rounds we put on a real display of fighting. Then we leaned on each other and pushed around a bit for the next round, then had another little fight. It got a bit serious at one stage. I think we both would have liked to do it for real. We went blow for blow as we had planned. I was holding back until the time came. It was my turn to go over. A feeling of horror came over me. I realised I didn't know how to fall over! Suddenly it wasn't that I didn't want to, I knew I had to – I just didn't know *how*.

I wasn't an actor. I couldn't pretend to go over, it was bound to look false. I panicked and dropped my hands to look at . . . *bosh!* Darkness fell.

I didn't have to pretend. The fucker knocked me spark-out when I wasn't looking. Shit, it was 45 minutes before I came round. I couldn't walk properly, my legs were like jelly. I had the worst headache . . .

'Well done, kid,' said Jerry when I came to again. 'I've collected the dough. Let's rock!' – and with that I was whisked away back down to all those passageways. Up and down tiny staircases until I was back out in the street and bundled into the warmed-up limo. I hadn't even had time to dress. I was halfway back to the hotel before I realised it was all over. I have to say that I felt like shit. This was firstly because I lost my first professional fight on the circuit. My dream, my great adventure had turned out like this. The second reason was that I had thrown the fight, and compromised my own principles, and the third was because I ached. That boy had a punch. I'd love to fight him for real one day.

We reached the hotel and I could hardly make it to the lift. Jerry half-carried me. This was the strangest feeling I had ever had in my life. He kept apologising. He seemed genuinely concerned about me. He probably thought he was going to lose his meal ticket. He got me up to my bedroom and I managed to get myself into bed and just flopped there. I didn't even take a shower. I just wanted to sleep to get rid of the pain and discomfort I was in.

A few days later Jerry had another 'little job' for me. I had to get into the city and meet another guy to collect a debt. I had done all that shit in Gran Canaria. That's why Jerry had put me up for the job. I had the experience to do it here. I objected loudly.

'Debt collecting and protection is for cowards. I don't want to go along and bully some poor bastard into pulling up money they don't have. It's not a crime to get into debt – we've all been there. Most of these people are only trying to look after their families.' My protests fell on deaf ears, though, and I was in the city within the hour.

I really didn't want to do this. I felt nothing but shame about being a bully. I didn't mind a straightener with anyone but this gave me no satisfaction at all. It was sick as far as I was concerned. I had to go with three other blokes. Two of us were protecting and two collecting. What a game.

The very first place was a small general store with a Pakistani bloke running it. He handed over his money reluctantly complaining that the rate was too high and beyond his reach. He grovelled and almost begged. I felt gutted. His wife had more nerve than him, though, she went off at the collectors. Couldn't understand a bloody word, like, but at least she had a go.

The second visit wasn't so easy. It was a Greek dry cleaners. We entered through the front door (no shame) and asked for our money. The man refused. He was a big, fat guy, adamant that he was not going to pay another penny. The collectors looked at us and I moved in with the other fellah, who was dressed like a businessman. I had jeans and a sweatshirt on (well, I didn't know how it went, did I?). If I was going to have a row I wasn't going to mess up my good gear. My partner grabbed the fat Greek and pushed him back into the rows of racked clothing. Back and back he pushed him as he shouted in Greek and English. I followed through the debris trying to catch up with them. We grabbed the guy between us, a side each. My partner motioned forward and I followed, pushing the debtor's hands into a ringer.

He struggled free, but we caught him in the back shed where there was an industrial towelling section. We gave him a few sharp digs, I held back a bit on the punches but I had to show out. The man buckled a bit and began to cry. This mixed me right up, I didn't like doing this anyway, I felt ashamed but had to keep going. This time we had his hands and the other fellah stuck them in the ringer and shouted for me to turn the handle – which I did. The Greek screamed as his hands went into the rollers and I stopped. I was told to carry on but took the initiative.

'You gonna pay now, ain't ya, mate? No need for any more?' and he nodded.

I reversed the rollers and let him free, then all hell broke loose. The man's sons and some neighbours came flooding in and suddenly we were literally fighting for our lives. One boy brought out a gun which I quickly relieved him of by bringing a broom down across his wrist. I then pushed it hard into his chest. We were giving them what for when the two collectors walked in.

'We've got our money,' they said coolly.

The man's wife had paid up, not wanting any more aggro. I packed the job in after that. I got outside and just walked away. The men shouted but I ignored them and kept walking. Fuck it, I wasn't going to do that stuff any more. It was a shit thing to do to, torture and intimidate a man weaker than yourself and without aggression. Just 'cos he couldn't hold his hands up, why should I take advantage of him? No. Bollocks to it. *And* there was no way a man should be punished in front of his family. I would never take trouble to a man's door. You need to be respectful of families.

THIRTEEN

The Beginning of the End

The morning after my reality fighting debut, I woke up to the phone ringing loudly. I didn't know a phone could ring so loud. My head hurt. I stumbled out of my bed into the lounge and picked up the receiver. It was Jerry.

'I told you!' he said excitedly. 'We are on the circuit. The lads liked what they saw and are setting up some stuff for you – what do you think of that? Did I tell ya? Or did I tell ya?'

'Yeah, you told me all right. No more shit, though. When I fight we do it straight-up, else I'm walking. I ain't taking no more good hidings so that some fat bastard makes a load of dough and a complete stranger gets all the glory. I'd sooner go back on the knocker and hold me 'ead up.'

'Listen, kid, I know what you're feeling.'

I thought: You will one day, you sneaky bastard.

'This is a game you have to play right for a while,' Jerry went on. 'Get to know the moves, become a face. When the guys see what you can do, we'll clean up. Believe me, I'm not lying. There's big bucks to come.'

Well, I listened to his shit as usual. I threw another two fights after that one. And then I had a good win, a straightener. I enjoyed that one. Now, I thought, they'll have to give me a go. It didn't work that way, though, apparently. After that fight I threw one more. That would be the last time I would throw a fight, though, for sure this time! The fight after that, I won. A great Christmas box, I thought.

That same week came my real chance. We were sitting in a small café and Jerry began to tell me he had a fight lined up at a 'really swanky club'. It was a private thing for a group of 'businessmen'. A huge crowd was expected. I asked for the details and Jerry looked down at his beer. I knew he was going to give me some shit 'cos that's what he did when he was going to sell me a line.

I spoke up quickly. 'I'll just tell you this one time, J., I am *not* going down again.' The waitress gave me a strange sideways look. Then I realised what I had said and felt fucking weird 'cos she must have thought I was a poof. I looked back at him and finished: 'If you've fixed this fight for a dive, I will have to do it or I'll get hurt after, I know that, but I'm telling you – I am gonna walk straight out after it. I'll never fight for you again.'

He looked at me, shocked and said, 'Hey! I don't want you to throw it, man. I want you to enjoy yourself . . . go ahead. Do the fucking bloke.'

He was all indignant, as if he would never suggest such a thing as a dive. He made me feel bad for piping up.

'Alright, when's this thing set for, then?' I asked.

'Tomorrow night,' he replied.

I looked at him in disbelief.

'There's no fucking way, mate – my hands are knackered, I've had eight fights in three weeks, I am totally bolloxed, I need to rest my body and my hands are seizing up; the joints are swelling with the constant pounding. I need to rest. I can hardly lift a knife and fork, let alone fight!' I complained.

He looked at me with a sort of funny smirk. I hated his face when he did that. (Do you ever feel that way? You just look at someone and think: 'You know what? I fucking hate you', and feel as if you could just push their face in? Or is it just me?)

'You ain't gotta worry about this one, man, it's your turn for a favour, this next one needs to go down hard – you have to cut him bad,' he said.

'I may not be able to hit him hard enough or catch him right to cut him. I might be able to bring the nut on him, though, if I can drop him a bit.'

'No – I mean *cut* the bastard,' he said and he brought out a Stanley blade. 'Open up his eye. This one's for a favour.'

'I thought it was supposed to be *me* getting the favour, not me doing one. This is one of your shit scams again. I want nothing to do with it,' I said. I looked him straight in the eye. He just looked back and pulled out some money.

'Five big ones,' he said.

'Where do I cut him?' I asked, persuaded. I had never done this move on a man before but I knew roughly how it would be done.

We went and bought the resin to make a new gumshield from a drug store. Then we proceeded to mould the piece by putting it in hot water, until it was about the right shape. They popped it into my mouth and I bit down hard, moulding it firmly into the shape required around my teeth and gums, so that they were protected.

At the bottom front of the shield Jerry moulded a little nick, big enough to house the section of blade. It was fixed there with a small clip of the resin, which acted like a spring. The weapon would be slipped into the shield by Jerry or the Fatman when I was in the ring. To remove the shield afterwards, I simply went to my corner and one of them would reach in quickly and snap the blade downwards which broke the clip and left me with a clean mouth. If there was any suspicion, and the ref wanted to look, I would just complain and go to my corner shouting and protesting innocence. By the time I reached my corner the water boy would have another clean shield ready for me. I would then spit out the adapted shield in protest at the ref's complaint and the water boy would pretend to pick it up and exchange the doctored shield for a clean one. There would, of course, on this occasion be no objection though, because everyone had fixed it for me to win. This was a real fix set by the men with the money. They always got what they wanted. There was no point in arguing, but it did scare me. How far down the road was my turn? I wondered.

I tried my new weapon. It was a great fit. I looked into the mirror and could see no sign of the blade as I brought my lips over the top of it. We spent some time practising the 'stripe' and the movement afterwards that would remove the evidence. Six months earlier I would have played right up about this dirty little trick but I found myself in a circuit where everything was fair. Winning was the only aim here. If I didn't do it to him, he could be doing it to me and I had a strong sense of survival. Secretly I had a sense of excitement about the whole thing, and I knew any complaint would fall on deaf ears.

'It's you or him, kid,' Jerry said. 'You're in too deep to cry now. The big boys are playing and someone's going down. Is it you? I don't think so!'

We continued to practise the move. I had to get it right. I had only one stripe, maybe two if the opponent didn't notice the first straight away. If he did then he'd scream up.

'Right,' Jerry said. 'Let your man come to you. In the second, go head-to-head for a while, then start moving back slowly, drawing him with you. Let him get you backed on to the ropes, but when you get there start a little flurry to the head. Not hard; you don't want to hurt him yet. Don't forget to shut your mouth over the blade when it's there. The lights will pick it up like a diamond in a black man's ear. As he crouches, you go tall, up on your toes and lean as far back on those ropes as you can. As he comes up again, put your hands up by your head to hide the blade from the side view, and keep your elbows tight in to the chest as he attacks your open body. Don't forget to tighten those body muscles – you're an open target and he'll take advantage of that. When he goes on the attack, lift your foot and drag it down his shin. As he looks up to scream to the ref, bring that blade down, clean through his brow. If you get it right it should open up like a peach. And don't forget to get straight to your corner so we can get the blade out your mouth *quick*. And stand fucking still when you do, I don't want my fingers cut off taking the thing out.'

This was all too much to remember at once. It had to be an act of precision, everything had to be done smoothly and at the right time. Jerry continued his lecture.

'Now don't forget, cut above his leading eye so that he has to change position of his fighting leg and fist. And most important of all, *don't* forget to bring your lips back when you go in for the cut or you'll be whistling when you breathe with a big slice in your lip! Once he is blinded with the claret he'll be fucked, he'll be leading left instead of right, on the wrong foot and off balance. You will have him completely ruined. Do him quick and clean, boy.

'As soon as the ref calls the fight, get out and into the dressing-room. Make sure you get out my side and we'll shield you through the crowd. If anyone guesses what you've done in there, you are going to get hurt and it's odds-on he'll have a man at our side. They ain't daft.'

I suppose there are many of you reading this thinking how sick I must have been getting. Well, you're right. I was pissed off with being shoved around – I was pissed off with having no dosh and I wanted my life back. If I had to hurt someone to do it then I would. It was sick and I was probably preparing to ruin the career of someone I don't even know; someone who may have had children to care for. I may have been about to ruin a man's life – or at the very least his life as a fighter if he didn't heal too well. This was the point I had come to in my life. A million miles from the man I used to be, to a puppet controlled by men and their money.

I didn't care though, and I dare say the man wouldn't really blame me either. This is a life you choose to lead, with its ups and its downs. You have to stand in line and take your turn of both. It was my turn to go up this time. The fight was scheduled to be in Brooklyn, New York. It was just another night in a shit-hole to me but the money was good. We drove to a quayside in the old dock area and pulled up outside a big old warehouse.

The place stank of fish. The faces on security and in the crowds didn't seem to have changed since the last time I was in the area – the smell, the atmosphere, it always seemed the same. It was always pumping – and I was still bringing up the contents of my stomach before each and every event, except that by now I had it a bit more controlled: I never puked in the ring any more, I kept it for the changing-room!

My opponent was a man who had been around for some time. He was very well known in the industry but was disliked intensely by other fighters because of his practice of using foul techniques. He was an instrument of the syndicate who controlled the fighting scene, just a pawn in their money-making machine. They had made him and now they wanted him gone. These were the people I was involved with. I should have woken up at this point and moved on, but those dollar bills kept screaming at me: 'Billy . . . Billy . . .'

I don't recall the name of the fighter I was facing but I won't forget his gnarled features and the smell of his body. (Phew! Man, he was rancid!) Even though he was disliked by fighters, many of the crowd liked him – after all they had come to see blood, hadn't they? And this man always showed them what they wanted. The fight was top of the bill. It was the first time I had been top of the card since I'd been fighting.

It was the last fight of the evening, the one they were all waiting for. Betting was heavy, and my opponent was tipped favourite. After all, I was a relative new boy on the block and a foreigner at that. This was where the money was going to be made and lost; big money that the syndicate had marked as its own. Anyone betting on the other man had lost before they even got their dollars from their pockets.

A strong Irish contingent was present here in New York. Probably as powerful as the Italians, I felt. Just a hint of the Irish in my name or publicity and the betting would have fallen my way. The promoters stuck to the Gypsy thing even though I didn't feel or act like one. I was so far removed from that culture now and in any case I considered myself to be settled, only a part Gypsy in real terms. I knew I was getting five large in dollars but I still couldn't work out how much that was in English money.

Fight time came and the Fatman had me ready. My muscles were oiled, my hands ragged up and the shield ready in the bucket, wrapped in a towel. I was escorted to the ring, the first man in and I was dancing around making the crowd go wild. I taunted them, pointing to the opponent's corner and giving the 'wanker' sign with my hand. I gulped water and spat it over the men in the first few rows. The betting picked up furiously. I was giving them what they wanted.

I had seen all this stuff when I was a kid and granddad took me to the halls in East London to watch the wrestling – Les Kellet, the Royal Brothers, Mick McManus, Jackie Pallo. They were my teachers and they taught me how to work the crowd. I was an entertainer now, not just a fighter. These WWF boys think they're the first, but they come nowhere near those old fellahs. I wonder where they all are now?

My man joined me in the ring and looked at me with daggers and contempt in his eyes. He slid his finger across his throat. I just laughed, knowing this man was going to make a serious donation tonight – to the blood bank!

I moved in to attack. Taking my normal stance, low and tucked in, making myself as small as I could, the way I'd been taught to do if I knew I might be in for a long haul. My opponent came crashing down across my neck, delivering a double-handed blow that pushed me to my knees. I rose quickly. There was no count in the reality circuit, just fighting. I was steady on my feet. He hadn't hurt me, it was just the power of the man's body falling across my neck. As I rose I felt a foot across my back. He spun me round and brought his knee into my side as he did so. Thanks for that, mush, I thought. You have made my job fucking easy for me now. Once you are hurt the chemicals pump you right up.

I feigned pain and the man tried to roundhouse me. As he spun I moved down under his arm then rose as it skimmed over my head, catching him with his own momentum and the fury of my own backhand.

Jerry screamed from the side, 'Don't hurt him yet, we need time!'

The fight went on like this for several minutes. I inflicted so much punishment on this man and he stood there a sad and beaten figure. As he moved in again, bravely but foolishly, for more punishment, I side-stepped him and brought my forearm up against his throat, dropping him to the floor as he struggled for breath. Then I backed off a little, letting him come back again; to gain confidence. Gradually he built himself up, taking energy from his sudden victorious onslaught. I was on my back foot and the crowd were going wild for my opponent's victory. They wanted blood and chanted, 'Finish the dirty Gypsy bastard! Hurt him bad!'

Those racial chants that used to heat my blood became fuel for my determination. These gorgios didn't know what they were buying into when they took on a Gypsy heart. Our memories are long and our revenge terminal.

Suddenly the man caught me with a good straight right in the mui as my mind was distracted by both the crowd's anger and the rehearsal in my mind of all the bodily manoeuvres that I needed to deliver my bloody message.

The man's blow flung pain throughout my body like a bolt of electricity. My head jerked backwards. He had given me the wake-up call I needed. I drew him to the ropes to prepare him for the kill. He attacked my body as I sacrificed it to get him into position. I tensed every muscle in my lower body, protecting my top half with my elbows. My hands came up to the side of my face – I drew back my lips like a vampire baring his teeth, put my boot under his knee and dragged it sharply down his shin, opening the flesh. His head came up as he let out a shout and I brought my head sharply down – swift, sure and without remorse, gashing that man's eye, allowing his life's blood to gush. He screamed, motioned clash of heads and went to move away. As I did so I saw the carnage I had caused – blood filled the man's face. As fast as he wiped it, the eyes and mouth filled again. He spat blood, he cried blood. I must have opened an artery, I thought. Christ, he's gonna bleed to death right here in front of me.

My legs froze as I watched the man. I felt no shame, just excitement at how well I had done my job. At least we didn't have to carry on fighting afterwards, I didn't want to keep hitting him. I just stood there looking on as the blood pumped and I noticed men turn away in the crowd. The fighter didn't stop screaming, he was running around the ring with his seconds chasing him telling him to stop so that they could stop the blood. The ring was covered in claret, lumpy claret, not just like when you bleed normally, this stuff had clotted bits in it.

I was awakened from my voyeuristic pleasure by a chair hitting me in the back. The voice of the Fatman broke through my temporary deafness.

'*Get fucking here!*' he bellowed.

I ran to the corner.

'Give me the blade.' I reached to my mouth.

'Fucking *open*,' he said in sheer panic. 'Don't *you* do it . . . '

We were in real danger of getting caught here. By taking my pleasure in what I had done, time had been wasted. As both the Fatman and Jerry reached into my mouth to take the blade and snap the clip, the blade came upward and caught my nose, giving me a half-inch gash clean through the nostril opening it right up. I thought you would be able to see my brains – if I could be credited with having brains during that time of my life. Now I was oozing blood too. This was mad!

The Fatman grabbed me and dragged me through the ropes and on to the floor. I tripped on the seating and stumbled as he carried me through the crowd. People were going mad, shouting, screaming, grabbing and throwing punches. Our walk turned into a trot and the trot to a run. Claret was spouting everywhere. The Fatman and my seconds shielded me back to the dressing-room. Jerry, of course, was nowhere to be seen while there was a threat of danger. He was such a shitter. I got back to the dressing-room. I could still hear the crowd and still feel the excitement. My anger had taken me to a new level. I knew there was to be no going back now. This was my new fix. This was a higher level of pain to inflict on those fighters. They would inherit the punishment for the years of abuse, pain and humiliation inflicted on myself, my family and the Romani people. Jerry came bursting into the dressing-room and threw his arms around me, he was grinning from ear to ear.

'You gave it to 'em tonight, kid – this is the man I have been looking for. You were in charge straight away from the moment you went in to the ring. What's happened to you? You are another man!'

He was right. I had a new cockiness to me, a wave of confidence I had never felt before. When I went into that ring that night I knew I was there for *me*. I took the crowd and played with them; I took my man and destroyed him. I had them all in the palm of my hand, taking control. This was my world, I thought . . .

Suddenly the door to the changing-room burst open and several heavily guarded men filed in. Hands were shaken feverishly. Someone had died and made me king! I was getting hugged, pulled, shaken and even kissed. I was a star! The Fatman, however, kept as cool as ice. He had seen it all before and all he wanted to do was work on my nose. This cut was bad and needed several stitches which he proceeded to do without any further thought, or consent. Just straight in there with the needle. Fucking butcher. He used *yellow* thread. I remember shouting at him as he put the roll down to use the black thread.

'By the time the blood dries into it, you'll never know what colour it is,' he said.

He was right, too. And it held together.

We celebrated all night. I was pissed as you like for the first time in ages. My benefactors were buzzing and showing off their new boy although not one of them introduced himself to me or took time to talk to me. It was definitely an 'us and them' situation. I was clearly the hired help and they were the cream. Still, I didn't give a fuck. I had five grand on the hip, women everywhere and some good sounds going on. This was my night and those stuck-up bastards couldn't have spoiled it if they'd tried.

I loved being at the centre of it all, cracking jokes, making people laugh. I thought that if I ever packed this game up I'd go and be a comedian or a clown or something – someone who makes people laugh and is always the centre of attention. 'I wanna be on stage,' I thought. 'I wanna be famous!'

I woke the next morning with a serious headache – I had two black eyes and the biggest nose you've ever seen.

I saw Jerry creeping out of his room and creeping back in again, never saying a word. Then a girl came out and crept back again, then another – skipping back in with a bottle of massage oil that was kept in the bathroom to keep my joints supple and warm. What the fuck was that all about then? I thought. But never ventured to have a look although I was dying to. The sight may have turned my stomach at this early hour! I was hungry and reached for the menu for room service.

Looking back on it now, I can see that I had turned into an animal; a hateful, wicked bastard with no emotions and no feelings for anyone. I only felt revenge. I didn't even feel hate really. I didn't have a woman that night. I only had time for me, nobody else mattered any more. What a sad and lonely man I had become. A pitiful sight of emptiness.

I walked to the bathroom to wash up and see if I could clean some blood off me snout. As I was working on the old mui I caught sight of a stranger in the mirror, someone I didn't recognise. The scary thing was that they had their head on my shoulders. The eyes were not those that I had often seen staring back at me. These eyes were treacherous, full of anger and greed. They were different, empty and detached. I could see that I had somehow obtained the ability to kill or maim with no guilt or remorse. Who *was* this man?

I got really cocky after this fight. I was in demand. I laid back and let the offers pour in. Jerry was going frantic 'cos I just kept turning the fights down. He was losing face and became really angry. This carried on for weeks. I wanted to rest, knowing that I could just pick up the phone and get on any card that was already arranged.

They all wanted the Gypsy Prince in their ring. My, how things change when you're a winner! One afternoon Jerry exploded with anger over something silly, and I had had just about enough of him showing off. I got really adventurous and gave him a long overdue bollocking.

'I'm calling the shots now, J. If you don't like it then fuck off. I'm taking two more weeks, then I'll fight. Call your Mafia mates – call the army, call who you fucking like. I ain't gonna fight till my hands and body are rested and that's that.'

Jerry walked off with the right hump. I saw him drive off with a wheel spin. I was watching the TV when he came back again a couple of hours later to deliver a message from some 'associates'.

'You got two weeks,' he said.

I must be worth money to these men, I thought. They had given way to me and they don't do that easily. Anyway I sure wasn't going to leave – I needed more money.

I worked hard after that. I knew they would have a fight ready. I rested my hands and worked on my stamina, agility and body tone. I also knew that I still had to dance to a tune if I wanted to fight. I wasn't that cocky about myself. I never lost the reality of the situation in that respect. I just thought I had became invincible in the ring, not outside it – the foolishness of youth!

I gave my hands ice packs and warm dips. I had oil rubs and went to the gym daily. I stretched and exercised my fingers slowly. I felt a marked difference, they had become supple again and didn't feel like pork sausages when I picked stuff up. The swelling had gone.

My two weeks were soon up and I was ready – no, more than ready – eager. Just as I had thought, a fight came up within 48 hours of the deadline. It was to be a straightener, no more messing. Proper fighting at last. I had made it. The purse was ten grand. I would end up with about five of that and I was well up for it. I planned to leave New York after this one, with the cash in my pocket and the satisfaction of giving Jerry back every ounce of pain and discomfort my hands had suffered. The last one and I'm out of this shit-hole, I thought. A short holiday and home . . . a winner.

Fittingly this fight was at the place where I had started out in New

York. There was a huge mirror, a bag for warm-up, a radio playing, and the ever-faithful Fatman sat poised to get me ready.

The time went quickly. It was the last fight of the night and as I left my room for the ring I could hear a fighter apologising, whinging to his mother.

'I'm sorry, ma! Yes, ma . . . ! It wasn't my fault, ma! Don't tell me like that, ma! You know I love you.'

It was then the anger within me subsided. I pictured my old mam sitting mending the kid's clothes, a big smile on her face and love in her eyes. 'I love you, mam,' I thought and tears filled my eyes. I suddenly became very sad. We came to the door that led us to the arena.

The Fatman said, 'Hang on, li'l guy, the security will be here in a minute.'

'Fuck em!' I said. 'They should be here waiting. Come on, let's go in.'

Jerry and the Fatman stood each side of me as I walked, swaggering and dancing towards the ring. Men were cheering me from all sides. I felt great and had the biggest grin on my face, when – *bosh*!

I was blinded by a thud as my forehead burst open and gushed blood. A man had jumped the rope and caught me square on the nut, smashing down on it with a claw-hammer!

The security were apparently on the man in seconds and I heard he got a severe beating but that didn't do me any good. The Fatman and Jerry bundled me back to the dressing-room. I was semi-conscious and could barely stand without help and I struggled to hold up the flap of flesh that didn't feel like mine, hanging from my head. There was no feeling in it. I was blinded by my own blood as it flooded my eyes. This was reminiscent of my cutting that man with the blade. Was this God's retribution? Payback time, maybe. Who knows?

I lay in the room for minutes or hours, I really didn't know. Men were running in and out, salts were stuffed up my nose and stung my eyes, cold water was thrown on me and all manner of rags and cloths covered my face mopping up the blood.

Eventually I became quite lucid and began to speak to the Fatman who never left my side the whole time. He took away all the sodden material from my face and my chest and held a gauze pad to the flap, washing carefully around the damage with a warm, clean flannel. After I was cleaned up and felt that I could stand I took the pad and walked towards the mirror to have a look. I removed the pad and saw a flap of flesh about three inches long and about one-and-a-half inches wide fall down my face and instantly blood pumped again. I quickly put the pad back on the wound. The claw must have ripped down my face, tearing the skin. The Fatman called out to me,

'Hold that pad tight, for Christ's sake.'

It was the first time I saw him panic. I was in no pain. There was just blood – loads of it. Several people were rushing around the room, including Jerry. I was then rushed quickly to the hospital in the limousine. I guess that was the only place for me, really. This was too much patching up even for the Fatman!

I didn't go through the front door in the hospital, we went in the side way. The place was a private establishment, very clean and organised. I remember how 'homey' it was too, not like real hospitals. (Funny, the things you remember – there was me with a hole in my head and I was taking in the décor.) An Asian doctor came into assess the situation and he asked what the problem was.

I said: 'I've got an in-grown toenail, you silly, daft twat. *Look!*' And with that I lifted my hand to expose the damage. I was stripped and laid out on a trolley in seconds, all my arse was hanging out the back of this gown. I remember thinking what kind of a man would invent such an undignified garment? This ain't right! I was pushed into a small side room with a huge light over it – not an operating theatre, but I could see that it was set up for some serious work. It took two nurses and a doctor over one and a half hours to stop the bleeding and sew me up. Every time the wound was stitched it just filled with blood and came up like a bubble. The doctor kept pushing down on it with a huge stainless steel thing that looked like a spoon. As he pushed the warm blood flowed out and ran down the back of my head on to the trolley, leaving a pool of blood under my head. Eventually they got it to stop after stitching (and unstitching) a couple of times. I was quite a sight. I had two beautiful black eyes, a swollen face and a lump on the head like you've never seen. I looked like Quasimodo, and that gave me the hump.

I walked out of the hospital like a proper div – bandaged head, a rainbow across the mui and the hump up to my eyebrows 'cos I didn't win the money that I needed to get out of this hellhole. I wouldn't have cared about the damage if I had got my money. Jerry and the Fatman took me back to my hotel. Jerry let me out of the car and said, 'Guess you'll be laid up for a while, kid. I'm going back to the city – probably stay a few days over, maybe a week.'

The Fatman winked and said he'd call me, then he waved and they drove off. I was back on my own. I wasn't king for long, I thought. The reality of life is scary sometimes. I came down with a huge bump. My true value had been revealed, I found that I was only good for sacrifice. I guess I knew that all along but I did think I was set for a bit of a good ride.

I went up to our suite and of course went straight to my bed. I was hurting a little now and wanted to get to sleep before it came on fully. My eyes were shut from the swelling anyway so I couldn't have done anything if I wanted to. The next day I just kicked around. I went for a walk, had a nice meal and just hung around listening to music. By day two I was getting bored although the pain gave me something to think about, and by day three I was climbing the walls. I couldn't train because of the pain and I couldn't swim, sauna or have a jacuzzi because of the bandages. I thought, I know, I'll play patience. I used to love that when I was a kid. Granddad taught me loads of card games I could play on my own.

I knew they were there somewhere. Jerry had them last. I looked through the cupboards, rummaged through the drawers under books and down the sides of the chairs but couldn't find them. I thought perhaps they were in his room. I hesitated to go in but it was just a hotel – it wasn't like it was his house or anything, and I wasn't choring. I tried to justify my trespassing.

I walked in and began to look through the dresser. I felt awkward in someone's room like this but I only wanted cards. I searched from top to bottom but they were nowhere to be found. I had one place left to look – his bedside cupboard and drawer. I walked over and slid the drawer open slowly. I started to move stuff, and there I spotted something that was immediately familiar to me.

'It's my fucking passport!' I said out loud.

I continued my search even more frantically. There was my driver's licence – and some letters. They were all there.

'That snaky, shit, fuck, *bastard*!' I shouted. I couldn't believe my eyes. I rushed to the wardrobe throwing aside the sliding doors. I kicked the stuff around on the floor. There was my hold-all and leather jacket thrown in the corner. He had had it all the time – from when we did the runner from the accident. I'd been held prisoner. I had been held to ransom in this fucking place because of him, he had done this on purpose. I felt abused.

I now began to become even more curious. I searched the room again, I didn't know what I was looking for, I had everything that was mine. I found a book, opened it and read the lists inside with interest and growing hatred. He had been stitching me up on every fight. He'd been robbing me blind, the thieving, no-good mother's cunt!

The 'five grand' fights had been eight grand; the 'ten grand' one was actually fifteen grand. He'd been skimming me and taking a cut as well. Bastard. I was so angry.

I wrecked his room completely. I filled the bath with water and put all of his clothes in it, shoes and all – jewellery, Rolex Oyster watch, bags, everything. I walked from the room laughing. What was I laughing at? I thought. I had just been tucked up. I was acting like a wife who had been cheated on. Looking back on it, I reckon the laughter was relief. I was out of the trap. I hadn't been happy at all and now I could go. I am beginning to understand myself quite well now as I write these thoughts. Shame it's come two decades too late!

I went to my room and packed very calmly. I turned and called a cab. I felt so relieved. I didn't know where I was going and didn't care. I had a couple of grand. 'That'll do,' I thought. It was more than I came with anyhow. I had a call from reception that my cab was ready and so made my way down in the elevator with all my belongings. I still looked a sorry sight but there was a happy face under all that damage.

As the porter helped me with my cases through the lobby and down the steps to the waiting car I saw Jerry's car sweeping up the drive with the Fatman sat beside him. I had calmed down a lot by now and I was quite pleased to have the opportunity of having a word . . . They pulled up behind my cab. Jerry obviously knew I was off; my cases were standing there for all to see. They pulled closer to me and Jerry got out of the car. We began to talk, then the talking turned to shouting and shouting turned to rage.

The Fatman sat quietly listening and looking – in fact half the hotel was looking, and realising this Jerry quietened down. The last thing he wanted was for the gavvers to be called. I sent my cab off, it was just costing me money sitting there.

'Right, you tosser,' I said. 'You can take me to the airport now. I've let the cab go and I ain't calling another one.'

'Where're you going?' he said.

'Fuck all to do with you.'

I didn't want anyone knowing, in case there was some sort of price to pay 'The Man'. You don't just walk out on this kind of people without some sort of penalty.

'Just get the trunk of the car open,' I said.

The Fatman popped the trunk from inside the car and I threw all of my bags into it. I casually dropped my old leather jacket carefully on top of the luggage and watched his face. The colour drained and his mouth fell open. He just looked. He went to say something and thought better of it.

'Go on,' I said, 'explain that then, you snake.'

He leaned heavily on the rear of the car with both hands across the edge of the open trunk. I saw my move instantly and before he could open his lying mouth I slammed the trunk lid shut, hard down across his knuckles. He bellowed in agony. As his mouth opened I filled it with my fist, his lip split wide and I felt the crunch of his teeth against my knuckles – it was great. I hit him again causing his nose to burst open. It felt fantastic. The Fatman saw what had happened and he popped the trunk lid open again, letting Jerry fall to the floor.

As Jerry hit the deck, I stood on his face and walked over him, just like he had been walking over me. He wouldn't do that again, would he? Certainly not to me and maybe he'll think twice when he gets some other poor mug to work for him. I jumped into the passenger's seat.

'Take me to the airport.' I said and laughed. It hurt my head to laugh out loud. I had forgotten about the pain for those few special minutes but it soon came rushing back.

As we drove to the airport the Fatman, whose name turned out to be Julian (no wonder he preferred to be called Fatman!) wised me up on a new circuit that was developing in California. He gave me some phone numbers and names.

He said: 'If you want to make big money and still have the heart for it, this is the place to be right now. But believe me, it's not for the faint-hearted. This is serious stuff that could break a man's heart or even his soul.'

'Mate, I have no idea where I'm going at the minute,' I replied. 'I plan on getting to the airport, sitting at the bar and just chilling until I have an idea.'

We reached the airport and I got out. Julian gave me a big hug. For the first time in my adult life I didn't feel silly about hugging another man. I don't know if that's a good or bad thing for a man to say but I only know it didn't make me feel bad. I thanked him for his help and friendship, then he drove off – I guess to collect the man we left bleeding on the floor. I guess that's someone I won't see again. Fuck his eyes!

Well – that was my experience of the Big Apple. I have to say I grew to like the New Yorkers tremendously. Not the men in the fight business, I mean the real people. They displayed a coldness and detachment and yet in a funny sort of way they were some of the greatest people I have ever met. They had obviously seen hard times and learned to rise above them. I felt at home there. They certainly seemed to stick together when the time was right and their humour was very much like Londoners' – sarcasm and cynicism reigned. *New York, New York* – they must have named it after the two-faced bastards I was working for.

FOURTEEN

Now What Do I Do?

Well! I thought. You're on your own again, my son. Right where you should have stayed. Another adventure starts – as soon as you decide what it's going to be, and where.

I made for the nearest bar in the terminal. I didn't know where I was heading to, what trouble I was going to find myself in, or anything. One thing I was sure about, however – I couldn't go home yet. I did keep sending a bit of money back home so they knew I was all right. I phoned of course too, but I knew that if I sent money that would be proper proof that I was doing okay.

I was sat there in the bar for hours – three parts pissed and happy as a pig in shit. I started having one of those drunken arguments with myself, not out loud you understand, just in my mind.

'Well, you're a travelling man,' I said to myself, 'let's see you travel. You're still sitting here like a constipated dog. Right then. Where shall I go? Fucked if I know, and fucked if I care. I know. I'll write "California", "England" and "Florida" on a piece of paper, lay out the three names and spin a bottle in the middle. Wherever the neck points, that'll be it.'

I borrowed a pen and paper from the bartender and wrote out the three destinations. Then I spun the beer bottle in the middle of the table. The bottle spun too fast and shot off the table and shattered on the floor. I was asked to leave by security about three minutes later. I must say I didn't argue the point – they had guns strapped to their sides. I moved to the lobby where I sat grinning like an idiot.

I was a sad-looking sod. I had two black eyes, I was pissed, I had a headache, I was lost and I'd been evicted from an airport bar. What else could happen to me? I thought.

Anyway, having had my explanation accepted and having received a suitable bollocking, I was once again left alone to decide my destination.

I know, I thought, I'll sit and listen to people and the first mention I hear of a destination will be the place I go. I sat for an hour and 40 minutes, became completely pissed off and eventually fell asleep with the effects of the beer. When I eventually woke up, I was freezing cold. It was now just after 3 a.m. and I was so angry at this waste of time I told myself out loud:

'Sort your fucking self out, you waster. Get off your arse and make your move.'

This time I worked out a foolproof method of deciding on my destination. I would walk around the flight monitors to see what the next flights out were. It took less than 15 minutes to find my new adventure playground – California.

There were four flights there, and one to Gatwick so the odds were stacked, weren't they? If I had been honest with myself I would have just chosen California anyway. The fight scene that Julian had described did tease my new-found pleasures in punishment. I went to the North West Airline desk and bought my ticket, one-way. I was off to sunny California – at least I was hoping it would be sunny. It was shit weather in New York, after all it was winter once again.

I sat and waited for my plane in the departure lounge. I was daydreaming, just killing time. As kids played around me and Christmas songs came over the loudspeaker, my mind wandered back home to where the family would be settled for the winter months, preparing for Christmas. I missed my family so much. The first thing I'd do when I got to California was call them. I'd wait till I got digs first because they would ask for my new address and I didn't want to worry mum.

I fought the pull to head homeward, though. I hadn't made my mark yet. I wasn't rich enough to enjoy the luxury of choices. Go for the gold, I urged myself. That's what you came for, that's what you want and that's what you deserve. I settled back and waited to board my flight. I began to feel the excitement welling in my stomach again. Sun, sand, dosh, and maybe a little bird to cuddle up to. Who knows? Whatever was waiting there, bring it on.

It was soon time to board my plane and I just settled into my seat for the duration. I had a couple of drinks then slept most of the journey to California. It was longer than I thought – like flying from England to Africa, for Christ's sake, I couldn't believe it. Still, it was a great flight. I was well cared for – drinks were free if I wanted one. I needed to be fresh when I landed in California so I didn't have too much, just enough to make me sleepy. Also if I was looking for accommodation and a hire car, I didn't want alcohol on my breath. No way did I want to get a tug by the gavvers on the road and be over the limit, they'd have locked me straight up then – and they would find I had overstayed my visa.

California is the land of the gods. After looking quickly around Hollywood and Beverley Hills I knew I wasn't going to find anything in my price range and so headed south toward San Diego. I stopped on my way at a place called Laguna Beach. It was beautiful, very English – but with sun and happy people. There was even an English pub called the Red Lion. Ain't it funny – us Brits go thousands of miles away and pay hundreds of pounds for a holiday overseas and then head for an English pub with Fosters or Watneys Red Barrel beer and a café that sells egg, chips and beans. We may just as well stay at home! I loved the place so much, I decided to make Laguna Beach my base for a while and just drove out from there to see where I had to be to earn some money – sort of get the lie of the land before I made a final decision.

Then – Venice Beach . . . I found it, loved it and moved directly to it. It was fantastic. If you're going to the West Coast of America for a holiday, you've gotta give it a visit – just sit in the beach's front bar, buy a jug of Marguerita or a beer and watch the action. There's the hippy market – the dukkerers along the front, and a man playing a grand piano *on the beach*, for Christ's sake. It's a mad place, you'd love it. And girls, don't forget to pop into the gym area on Muscle Beach with all those big guys working out (there are girls too, fellahs!).

I began looking for accommodation here straight away. It took me only a short while because it was out of season and so more vacancies were available. I had a good list to choose from. As I moved around, I found a maze of streets both river-fronted and inland a bit. There were also shacks and a trailer park – a real haven from the law – if that's what you were needing.

Looking at the people inhabiting the place I realised I would be able to get lost amongst them. There were some strange ones about – strange but happy. This was a town for crazies, rejects and those who wanted to be themselves without judgement. Everyone was a character and I loved it there. This became home for me. I was really comfortable with it all.

FIFTEEN

Land of Milk and Honey

I truly believed I had died and found Heaven. California was everything I had heard about it and more. The beaches were beautiful, the cars and the bikes were mad, there was sun by the truckload, the people were wonderful to be with – there was food, booze, everything!

How gullible am I, though? I always think I have made it, don't I? The one place I thought was so right was the place that nearly killed me. It was so good in the beginning then it slowly began to fall apart. So slowly in fact that I didn't see it happening. It wasn't the place, you understand, it was more the opportunities. I never knew where to stop. I over-indulged in everything in California – but then that's me. I want whatever life has to offer and I have to say at this point that I am no different now in that respect than I ever was. I still live life in excess.

Let me tell you the rest of the story and you'll see what I mean.

Here I am on Venice Beach, getting a great tan and chilling out, dozing in and out of sleep. Suddenly these two big old boys came running past. All that time I'd spent prepping myself to make the most of the sun and these two selfish gits spray me with sand! I had just got all oiled up – you know how that feels, when the grains of sand stick all over your body – you can't just brush them off, it stings the sunburn, doesn't it? Now I had to get up and go into the sea to get clean, then oil up all over again. I was *well* pissed off. I hate the sea.

I sat bolt upright.

'Oi, cunt, wot's-your-game, pig-ignorant, selfish bastard!' (I hadn't lost my knack of the English language, had I?) The two men stopped dead in their tracks, turned slowly, looked at one another and started to walk back towards me. As they got closer, I became consumed by their shadows, they were fucking enormous.

'What's up, li'l guy?' one said.

That was it. I was off. I am little, I know, and I guess only little blokes will relate to what I'm saying here – but all the time, you are half-expecting some brainless bully to try to prove himself or boost his own self-esteem by picking on you, so when they do you are already down their throat. You spend your life waiting for it. Every bully loves to flop on a little bloke to put him down, so as soon as anything a bit 'iffy' happens, the little fellah is in battle-mode waiting, where a lot of normal blokes would probably just ignore a similar scenario.

I was on my feet and squaring off now. Steam was coming out of my ears, the lot. I was ready to go. The other giant then piped up and stepped between us.

'Hey, man,' he said, 'we didn't mean to disturb you, it was thoughtless of us, we just got lost in our training schedules.'

He held his hand out to shake. Right – now I was fucked. This bloke was making me look a bigger prat than I already was by wanting to apologise. It did my head in. I didn't know how to deal with this stuff. All I knew was how to go to war. Was it a con? I thought. Was he going to grab my hand and pull me to him to stick the nut on me? There didn't seem to be any moves going on, they looked completely calm and non-aggressive.

I guessed that if I stood square and to one side, he wouldn't be able to pull me to him. I took a chance and held my hand out to meet his, then the other mush shook too. A thought ran through my head. They were poofs, I thought. I was, I admit, homophobic at that time of my life (although I didn't know such a word or really recognise such things existed then). The Romanis did not accept that gays existed – or we'd turn a blind eye.

This was all wrong to me. I wasn't used to people being nice like this. Not gorgio people. Still, they never knew that I was a Gypsy, did they? It wasn't as if I had a row of pegs on my collar or danced round a campfire with my violin and lucky heather in my pocket.

I must admit I was more than a little grateful that these blokes weren't unhappy – getting filled in by this pair would be quite messy, although I think I still had the advantage – with those big old bodies they would be very slow (cocky little fucker, ain't I? Let's just call it confidence).

'Alright, mate.' I said. 'No sweat.'

I sat down. The two men sat down too.

'So, what you doing all this way from Australia?' one said.

'Australia? I'm from England,' I replied.

'Wow – you sound so Australian, have you picked up the accent from a visit?'

This was pissing me off now.

'Well, I suppose I might sound Australian to you – I'm a cockney. We cleared out all our prisons and sent them to Australia years ago – I suppose they kept the accent.'

That was the best I could come up with. The two men laughed.

'What's "cockney"?' the blond fellah said.

I couldn't be bothered to tell him the Bow Bells thing and anyway I think that's bollocks myself – it's just a dialect relative to London.

We chatted for a while and the fellahs ended up asking me to a beach party that night.

'Will there be women there?' I asked.

'Hell, yeah! What's the point of partying if ya can't get laid, man? Just bring a six-pack and any food for the barbecue. We'll bring the music and the girls.'

Sounded good to me. True heterosexuals with shagging on their minds!

That evening I headed to the beach towards the party. The night was really warm with a gentle breeze off the sea. When I pulled up in the car I could see that this was going to be some party. It wasn't a party like you're used to – it was really open-house. Anyone and everyone could go. There were motorbikes, buggies, big cars, little cars – even push-bikes, scattered around everywhere. People were all over the place, some playing guitars. Big oil drums with grills on top of them were burning. I hate to say it, but it was like something out of the movies. Now I was right there in the middle of it all.

I was so excited. I wanted to find my new acquaintances so I sort of wandered between the groups of young people until I came across them. They were amongst a group of well-muscled men and a bevy of beautiful women. I looked at the big guys and then looked at myself – I came up to their chest standing on tiptoe. I must say, I felt a bit out of place.

My body was toned and fit of course, but I wasn't what you'd call muscle-bound. There was one black bloke there whose stomach looked like a corrugated cocoa tin. I just sat back quietly and took it all in but I was enjoying myself. Those two big lumps came over to me with a lovely little sort, introduced us and then went off again. Talk about awkward. I never was good with women, I became very shy around them. This was obviously an attempt to pair us off – nice going, lads. I didn't know what to say. She broke the silence.

'What you doing all the way out here in the States? The guys tell me you're from London.'

Well, that sure opened a can of worms. Being a bit thick I went through the whole story right up to how I ended up at the party. I think she expected a slightly shorter explanation but she was very polite and listened. I do think, however, she was a bit shocked, even frightened, at my recent activities and I did still have my black eyes from the hammering I took in New York. If I had told her I was a professional boxer putting on shows for the Freemasons, she would perhaps have been okay but to be doing bare-fist with the Mafia appeared unacceptable. However, amongst her fear I could sense a suppressed excitement. A sudden cool breeze whipped up the shore and across our bodies.

I noticed her nipples harden against the chill, proudly highlighting her breasts through the tight cotton blouse she wore. I felt myself become aroused instantly and with that arousal came a flood of confidence, a strength drawn from an animal need. I suddenly became chatty – sparkling almost, but definitely 'windswept and thoroughly interesting', as Jerry would have said.

Although the girl shuffled nervously as my story unfolded, she hung on every word. Being a man, of course I began to embellish the events (well, all right, I *lied*!). The hire cars taking us to the fights became bigger and better than they were. The sleazy gangsters became top mobsters. I suddenly acquired a Maserati in my boasts and I told her about all my showbiz friends. She loved it. She had already told me who her favourite stars were, so I obviously had to know them, didn't I? Then I came unstuck as she asked me about individual members of a band and I had to confess that I couldn't remember their names. I felt myself colouring up. I was no good at lying, I always got caught. That was mum's influence. She detested lies. If I ever told her one, even the smallest fib, it would hurt her so much. I could picture the hurt in her face. I couldn't stand it.

Suddenly I broke into a laugh and the girl leaned backwards, looking at me as if I was crazy.

'I *am* a fighter,' I said, 'but all the rest was a story. I really had you going there, didn't I?'

'Phew!' I thought. 'That takes the pressure off – but I bet I don't get a shag now.'

'Oh *you!*' she said, hitting my arm and jumping on top of me laughing.

We rolled about and wrestled a bit then lay quietly staring up at the sky. I suddenly had to kiss her. I was as horny as hell and her tight little body was calling. I rolled over and took a chance, kissing her softly – then when I felt there was no resistance I kissed her again, harder. That's how we were for about an hour.

The beach party ended about 11 p.m. which by California standards seemed late. Everywhere there closed early, all the clubs and bars. They are morning people, sun worshippers. The dark was for sleep and the daylight was for playing.

I took my new friend, Clari, back to her parents' home and they welcomed me into their house. They lived on the edge of Venice Beach and had a really nice home, with a pool and sun-deck. I felt a bit gutted when I saw them all together – her young brother, mum and dad, all sitting around on their chairs out on the deck, eating, drinking and talking together. It reminded me so much of the nights we spent fruit picking and showed how these people were not so far removed from my own in what they enjoyed.

Soon the time came for mum and dad to do their disappearing trick and the whole family went to bed. The air was warm and I remember the Stylistics were being played on the hi-fi. The mood was set and I had an erection that King Kong would have boasted about, I tell you! I was bursting at the seams. We laid kissing for a long while – at least it seemed a long while to me. I just wanted a shag but I was patient, if nothing else. I had my timing right, I wasn't blowing this opportunity.

The time came. I suggested moving from the grass to under the awning from the house. Having already done a quick recce and found out that we couldn't be seen there from any of the windows of the house, we moved, turned the patio lights off and got back to where we'd left off. We just had the glow of the barbecue and the flicker of the flames from the torches they burned.

Now put your dicks away lads, this ain't turning into a wank-mag! I ain't going to share any of my intimate moments here. First of all it's not the Romani way. Both love-making and a man's woman are sacred and taboo. We don't discuss those moments – well not about women for whom we care, anyway. I will say, though, that American women are not as inhibited as the English girls I dated!

Life just seemed to carry on this way for a while: parties, sex, eating, drinking, sun and all the other good things life could offer me. My days were full, my stomach was full, and my nuts were empty. However, in my over-indulgence I became lazy. I grew slow and podgy. I grew this little pot belly that I hugged at night, a double-chin you could carry your shopping in, and I began to stop bothering to get dressed properly. I became a beach bum in essence. I just bummed around in shorts, trainers or sandals and a T-shirt. Although my days were full, my cash box was not. I didn't have a bank account or plastic. I never knew how to open a bank account and I was also well beyond my work visa limit. I had to pull myself together fast. I looked in the full-length mirror of my wardrobe.

'Fat bastard!' I said out loud. 'Sort your fucking self out!'

I showered, put some proper clothes on and decided I had better find myself some work. I wasn't trashed of grafting. I was brought up on work and although I had drifted into a gorgio lifestyle, I never lost my genetic heritage.

I decided to go door-to-door for work, or 'on the knockers' as we used to call it at home. Although I knew I wasn't going to get any tree-lopping work, most of the gardens in the area were untidy, in fact they were shit-heaps, some of them. I put a good pair of shoes on my feet, a skip in my step and determination in my heart. What more did I need to succeed?

Up and down the streets I called, knocking on door after door. Most of the folk were out – either at work or at the beach and I had no calling cards to remind them that I would drop back. There were several older folk at home and I managed to get a bit of work from them, and a few said they would talk to their neighbours. They had never had anyone do this before, it was quite a novelty to them. I swept yards, cleared away straggling or dead bushes, cut some lawns. In all I had a fair day considering, but I had to admit I was well and truly bolloxed. I lay on my bed aching from head to toe from my work. I was burning from exposure to the sun all day and looked in my hands at the crumpled notes amounting to 68 dollars, the result of my long, hard day. It was a sad sum compared to the money I made within a few minutes on the fight circuit but I had to admit also that I felt great about it. I loved the ache I had, it was a good ache, some of you will know what I mean. When you have worked hard and look back on it with a cigarette in one hand and a cup of tea in the other. Complete satisfaction! Only a worker could appreciate what I am saying. The satisfaction of earning that money outweighed the disappointment of the meagre sum.

The next morning was spent getting better organised. I bought a sheet of card and some coloured pens from the stationers. I got black, red and green pens (I couldn't get a gold one) – just what I needed to decorate a business card in true Romani fashion. I sat down and divided the large white card into oblong shapes and wrote on each in an identical way, making myself calling cards for the next morning's work. Around the card I drew designs that are traditional to Romani

ENGLISH GARDENER
WORKING IN YOUR AREA
NOW!
LANDSCAPE AND DESIGN OR JUST
A GOOD TIDY UP
LOW RATES FOR QUALITY WORK

You were out when I called. I will
call again _____ between 8am & 4pm
THANK YOU.

and river people – flower designs. Both cultures used flower designs to decorate water buckets, pots, brooms or the old vardo (the traditional horse-drawn carriage used by European Gypsies years ago). River people did the same with their canal boats.

Now I was armed for action. I went out every day on the knocker. Soon I had a thriving business going. If people were out, I would pop a card through their door telling them I would be back. Sometimes I would leave a message with a neighbour, sometimes a note. I persevered until I had spoken to everyone. I went back in the evenings or at the weekend, I would not give up on a house. I needed as much work as possible in a very local area to avoid carrying tools a long way. I tried to keep it compact but sometimes had to drift out of my catchment. When the job was done and the client was not at home, I would collect from a neighbour or go back. I always insisted on cash on the day. If you leave it too long to collect your money, it becomes their money again and they don't want to part with it – then you lose your money and your client.

The whole thing was working well until one of my clients insisted on paying me by cheque. He got really nosey and I had to explain that it was nothing personal, I just didn't run a bank account. I had never had a bank account in my life. I didn't even know how to open one or write a cheque. We always dealt in cash. To many a Gypsy this would be the norm (and also to many people in the UK). It wasn't considered essential to have a bank account. But in the States they would consider you a complete alien if you didn't have a bank account and three tons of plastic to go with it. My not having an account aroused suspicion in this man. I already knew that he worked with the department of employment and I guess to someone of his background a man working only for cash appeared suspicious, especially a foreigner. I began to worry about this fellah. It was time to work some Gypsy magic and move on, I thought. Sadly, this seemed my only way forward. At least I had some money again and a new way to earn it. I spoke to all my customers, who had become friends rather than clients by this time. I saw most of them daily, by popping in or even in passing on the street.

I told them I was going back to England for a short while and that I would be back later. This, I hoped, would keep the department of employment man off guard for a while. I didn't tell him what I was doing. I just up and left as far as he was concerned. It was a shame to lie to my friends, but I couldn't afford to get caught. I could tell them everything later when things had settled.

Clari wanted to come with me but she was still in college and thankfully her parents put their foot down. I didn't want to hurt her. I hadn't wanted a relationship. I had left one in the UK and would go back to that. Clari had just satisfied a need. Someone to share and enjoy stuff with.

The more I talked about going home the better it sounded. I decided to overcome the passport problem by flying to Canada first. I was told their control was slack and I could sneak through the net. As it happened, no one even looked at the thing – oh, sure, they glanced – but they didn't really check it out. I stayed for about five months but then decided I'd had enough. I felt I had grown away from what was happening in the UK. I loved the States. It wasn't long before I was heading back across, after having time to sow an oat or two with someone I cared for. I enjoyed seeing everyone for a while but the novelty of being back soon wore off. I did need to get back to my work – to my *other* life. The UK made me claustrophobic. It seemed I had changed my life drastically.

SIXTEEN

Scam the Brits

Having arrived back in the States, I set to work to try and prove myself and earn enough money to take home when I eventually returned there for good. I wanted to build a pot of gold to settle down with and there was no work going in England. It was harder to make a living there as unemployment bit. The gorgios were doing all our traditional work – scrapping iron, ragging, paper collecting, tree-lopping, gardening, and carpet selling. Everyone was trying to carve a living out of that little island. They were also getting flooded with migrating travelling groups from Ireland with their tarmac-laying gangs, so it really was getting tough. The UK was going through a depression. A man had to go where the work was and I knew I could make a living in the USA.

When I arrived back the sun was shining as it was when I had left, it was like it had stayed up waiting for me. I decided I would try my luck in Anaheim. This was a town I got to know well during my extended visit. It was buzzing with tourists. It was commercial and there were possibly more opportunities for me to earn some money. I was definitely home. I felt it.

I booked in to Raffles Hotel, right there on South Harbor Boulevard for a few days to let me get my bearings, giving me time to find somewhere more permanent, then I could have a nose around to spot where I could earn a couple of quid.

Now, I thought, let's work out some little ways of helping them spend their holiday money! I was about to show the Gypsy in me at work: that knack of making money by sheer cunning. I worked out my first little earner: The Magic Man. (Go on then, laugh. I don't care.) This was a good move and it brought other scams with it. You only need one to get you rolling, then you diversify. There was a really great magic shop in Anaheim. I had visited it before. They sold everything from stuff for small 'self-working' magic tricks to the skilful larger ones. I went for the self-working; I didn't have time to get clever.

I bought ten good tricks: 'the thumb tip' (which anyone interested in magic will confirm can be used for a variety of very impressive tricks); four trick decks of cards, all great little self-workers ('the rising deck', 'the spooked deck', 'the taper deck' and that other deck with every other card the same); and some coin tricks (including 'the whiskey and soda', my favourite – and 'the coin in the bottle' – I love coins for close-up magic). All these were simple but impressive if done cleanly and with enough patter. I got to know many of these gags from the street performers on Venice Beach and having worked the fight booth for a while, I picked up some of the old 'carni' chat. I was ready to entertain!

It wasn't easy to perform on the streets of Anaheim and I couldn't afford to get my collar felt by the gavvers. I would be deported for working black, so I chose to work hotels and restaurants. I paid the manager, concierge or maître de – anyone in fact who happened to be able to let me in and let me perform without hassle.

I worked around the swimming pools in the hotels doing close-up magic and around the tables in restaurants and bars. I even tried to work it in a McDonalds but got asked to leave. I thought I enhanced their service! The best pitches were the queues where people were waiting to go into attractions like Knott's Berry Farm and the like. I tried Disney but nearly got shot, they were so touchy that you might get your hands on some of their money. The cash the visitors went in with was considered theirs. The queues there were so tiring. The pubic needed entertaining, that's one thing Disney didn't think of – the crowds outside waiting to get in, at the bus queues. (Sort it out, Walt!) I offered to work inside but they didn't want to know. I also sold a few of my easier self-working tricks to the waiting crowds. I'd buy them from the shop and just add a couple of bucks to the price – mainly for the kids, but a lot of dads went for them too, especially the coin tricks. I wouldn't come up with them until the last day, though – if they showed everyone how easy it was, I wouldn't get any dough when I did my work around the pools.

I worked another great scam at Disney. You can buy five-day passes to visit Disney. If you only use three of those days (enough, believe me), then you are stuck with two days left on the card. I just monged these cards off the punters and sold them again. Disney ain't what it's cracked up to be in my opinion, I found it disappointing really. But the punters bought my tickets at the hotels. I did really well out of that one. I didn't just do Disney tickets, I did all sorts: Knottsberry Farm, Universal Studios, Wild Bill's, Six Flags. You name it, I could get you the tickets.

I went on timeshare tours to get most of these tickets – plus I had some other young couples helping on the scam. They would sell me their tickets cheaply or else they just did it for the free breakfast. What I did was just go to the timeshare sales, sign up for a tour, complete the tour and then receive a breakfast and two free tickets to any show you chose. You had to go as a couple, but that was cool, I always had someone who wanted a free breakfast who would go with me. I went on tour after tour and of course had no intention of buying. I told the sales staff straight that I was only doing it for the free tickets. They didn't care, they still got their flat fee.

At the end of the tour I would always get stuck with another sales person trying to sell a second-hand unit at a third of the cost – but I just stood firm and showed them some magic until they gave up and gave me my tickets. Those timeshare scams were quite nice days out, really. I enjoyed most of them. I was fed, had a chat, some coffee, got my tickets and was back on the street by noon usually. I could do two visits a day sometimes. That was as good as any job, and I paid no tax. I also met some great people to deal with. Those salespeople usually had more than one string to their bow.

The magic was going well too. I had my patter down to a tee. As I got to know the tour guides better, I was whisked through the system and often got through three tours on a good day. That was real dough. The Americans loved my English cockney and the comedy I did with the magic. The Yanks were also better payers than the British. Although the Brits were the ones to snap up the bargain tickets, the Americans preferred to pay the right money. (Face it, you

UK tourists, you are real tight-lunch bastards!) When I did the magic the Yanks would tip me five dollars or so. The Brits would just give me loose change if they gave anything at all. They were always frightened to put their hands in their pockets.

Another little scam that worked for me was taking deposits on hotel sunbeds. I loved the cheek of that one. I would wait until the beds were full and then go around and get a dollar off each occupant as a deposit for the bed for the day. This was so funny because, of course, the beds were free to the hotel guests. At the end of the day I would go back with the dollar. Mostly, though, the Americans would just tell me to keep it. Often they were a family of at least four. The Brits would hold their hands out, though. A lousy buck and they took it back off me! The only time I ever won them over was if they had to leave early for their evening meal which had been paid for in the holiday – they wouldn't miss that, the tight gits. So they had to choose: their dollar or their meal.

Another way I managed to keep the Brits' money was to say that they could either have the dollar back or go into a draw. Lots of them went for the draw – for a free holiday. I would give them their draw ticket and ask them to put their hotel name and room number on the stub. When they asked, 'What if we win and have already gone home?' I told them not to worry as the hotel would forward any winning vouchers to them in the UK! That worked a treat, that one did.

Selling maps for movie stars' homes was a good earner but too many people got on that. Then there were my tours of Hollywood and Beverley Hills. I would do personal trips in my hire car. Sometimes I pretended a star lived in a house when they didn't. If there was someone in a garden I would swear it was them or their wife or something. It made their holiday; a white lie that made people happy *and* earned me money.

I would also spend days hanging around the big parks and pools. I would go around bathers asking if they would like a drink brought to them. The queues were always massive and the holidaymakers were happy as hell to think they didn't have to line up. I had several people working for me in some parks because they were so busy. The management never caught on to that one. Eventually I would get to know the staff at these places, they were on crap money and

TARMAC WARRIOR

176

gratitude from me at the end of the day was appreciated. It was the least they could do for me to let me go to the back door to get served. I always paid the right money for the drinks I was going to sell. I would never take less; I didn't want to compromise the scam for the sake of a couple of cents. When I came to sell the drinks, I'd always put 50 cents on everything and usually got a tip bigger than that.

I'd come out of there with 1500 dollars easy some days. I would make as much as 500 dollars clear after having paid the staff. If a manager came in on the scam they would get 15 per cent of the day's takings. I always played it straight. That's one thing my granddad taught me to do: play it straight rather than mess up the pitch.

My easiest earner was my airport scam. I bought a large plastic bucket and taped a piece of card on the top painted with the British flag, then I'd go to the airport and ask Brits for their change, explaining that I worked for a repatriation unit. I told people there were lots of UK youngsters stranded in the States having gone there with the promise of a job only to find that none existed; they then fell into the trap of staying to find work, spending all the money they had and going into prostitution to earn money to get home. I claimed that the unit for repatriation needed money to keep the hostel going, to feed the kids and buy tickets home for them.

I would say: 'Now these kids can't claim benefit here. I won't ask you for notes, in fact I insist you don't give me any. I would however like to take your spare change from you. You can't change it up for English and you can't spend it at home and it would help us to get these kids back to their families – or even to make a phone call to let their mums know they are okay.'

This scam was the big one, but I couldn't work it too often 'cos if security saw me about too much they would throw me out and then I'd never get back in. Some days on this scam I would earn up to 2,000 dollars. I thought that insisting they should not give me notes made me seem more genuine. Each passenger would have more than two dollars. I'd get as much as 300 dollars per flight out. Doesn't take much working out, does it?

The women were the best to hit. They would picture their own kids stranded abroad and empathise with the mothers back home in England. This worked sometimes at the hotels too but it was always dodgy as you couldn't do the hotels where you worked other scams and you had to keep on top of your own rota. It was no good to be greedy. That was part of the art of keeping in front. I could have made a living on that last scam alone here. I wished I had come to Anaheim earlier. A good man can make a living anywhere. Just give him time to think for a minute.

To all of you who are reading this book and recognise my scams, and who remember the dark-skinned little bloke with the big smile and cockney accent, I am sorry! But after all it was part of your holiday. It could even have been one of the favourite stories you tell your friends . . .

SEVENTEEN

Ebony and Ivory

This time in the States I wanted to do it right so that I could stay and work. I was going home every five months and renewed my visa properly. I was still putting on weight. I became described as 'the little chubby bloke who was always laughing'. I didn't like that. 'Chubby' was never a description I liked for myself. I thought 'stocky' was kinder. It was a fact, however, that I had become over-indulgent. I was earning well and was eating better and bigger than ever and I did like a beer. But the day came when I dragged my fat arse off the bed and into some shorts and a new pair of trainers. I had my head shaved close and I told myself I was going to get back into shape or die trying (and I nearly did)!

I jogged in the morning and in the evening when it was cool. I stopped the booze and entered a self-imposed diet of fruit one day, chicken and steak the next. I don't know what made me do such a diet but it started working. By the third week, though, I was very ill. I couldn't get out of bed. I was weak and faint. I knew I had overdone it. Eventually I phoned a pizza delivery and had the local store deliver energy drinks full of sugar. The very next day I felt a lot better and went for a walk that evening where recently I'd been jogging. A big black fellah came running past me, stopped and then ran back.

'Hey, guy, you okay?' he said in a wonderful rich Jamaican accent.

'Yeah, why?' I replied.

'I've seen you jogging here for weeks, then you went missing for a day or so and now you're here walking. I thought maybe you had pulled something.'

I began to explain what happened. We walked together talking, stopping outside a bar.

'Buy you a beer?' he offered.

'Nah. I'm still trying to lose weight.'

'Fuck, man, you'll die. Listen to me – I'll show you right.'

'Go on then, fuck it,' I conceded.

We sat in the bar chatting for a couple of hours. The man introduced himself as Berry (strange names these Americans have, don't they?)

He was full of knowledge about nutrition, training, bodily needs, all that. He said he was going to design a diet for me, suitable for my height, normal weight and lifestyle.

He lectured me heavily on the dangers of improperly designed diets – and he was right. If you want to diet go to a doctor first. Check your health, then go to a nutritionist and they'll put you right. Our bodies *are* what we eat. I learned that each body requires different things. There's no such thing as a diet for everyone.

I began the diet set for me by Berry but my appetite was big. I loved food and found the hunger hard to resist so he got me these yellow pills. Dexedrine they were called, and he told me to take one about an hour after I woke up. I started off okay, but soon it was one in the morning, and one at noon. One afternoon I was working the airport scam and left home without a pill. I got home about 7 p.m. and then took the pill and found I couldn't sleep all that night. I was wide awake pacing up and down. I just couldn't sit still. When I told Berry he just roared laughing.

'They're uppers, little man!' he chuckled. (He always called me that, he was about six foot six.) 'Ten of them will make you as high as a kite all day!'

'Drugs, you cunt? You gave me drugs? You fucking no good *bastard*!' I screamed.

I went raving mad. I was always against drugs. Drugs were never a part of the Romani culture, they were seen as a gorgio disease. He calmed me down eventually.

'Don't fall off your chair, little man,' he said, 'every medicine you take is a drug – even aspirin. It's how you use that drug that makes the difference. You misused it. You just took it at the wrong time of day.'

I couldn't argue. He was absolutely right. I felt a total prick.

'Sorry, mate. I'm just a bit edgy and tired,' I said.

'They'll do that to you, man. We lived on that kind of shit in 'Nam – uppers, downers, charlie, weed . . . I was well fucked up when I came back. In fact that's why I came back. I became unstable mentally through the drugs we used. That Asian stuff is better than ours for kicks but it sure messes with the grey stuff, man.' A sort of sick look came over his face.

''Nam?' I asked.

'Vietnam,' he explained.

'Oh, right,' I said. 'I've seen some good films about it.'

'Fuck the films, man, the real thing was a shambles. Everyone was killing anyone. Gooks killing gooks. Americans killing Americans. It was a war with no leaders. You sort of made a little battle plan of your own, carried it out and came back if you were lucky. I saw stuff that even your worst nightmares couldn't do credit to.' The sickness in his face turned to sadness.

'Tell me,' I said eagerly.

'One day when I'm drunk, maybe. It's a strange part of my life I don't like to visit.'

'I'll hold you to that,' I said insensitively. He absolutely didn't want to talk about it but my own selfish, ghoulish needs wanted all the details.

Berry and I began to form a firm acquaintance. We'd had similar experiences and thoughts, although he was quite obviously more educated than I was and his war experience was far more intense than any experience I had ever had. We were both involved in the fight world and both of us were 'aliens'. Berry came from New Hampshire. In California everyone not a Californian was seen as an alien; it was a strange and wonderful land. Berry had been a 'pro' boxer under contract before he was called up for the war. Apparently he turned pro at 16 years old and was promised great things (that sounded familiar . . .)

During our many chats, he began describing a circuit to me that had grown strong in California called cult fighting.

'It's awesome money, man, but heavy, heavy stuff. I'm going to try and get into it. I have a couple of buddies who work the crowds – they're up-market security. Even they get 300 a fight,' he said.

'Fuck!' I replied. 'What do the fighters get, mushy?'

He looked at me with a raised eyebrow, leaning back on the stool with a tight-lipped smile.

'What the fuck did you just say?' he said. 'I didn't understand – that sounded like one huge long word.'

And so then I explained to him that I grew up in a Romani Gypsy family and that I sometimes spoke bits of Pogardi Jib when I got excited – and money made me excited. He was intrigued to learn about my identity. It was a culture he knew nothing about really although there are in fact many Romani Gypsy groups in the USA. They sort of disappear into the melting pot and are treated with little importance or interest except when one of them gets caught up to some skulduggery – pretty much the same as in the UK, really. Berry was now full of questions about the Romani. He loved knowledge. But all I wanted to talk about was cult fighting and so we spent an hour having cross-conversations. Eventually my perseverance got him back on track and we delved into the world of cult fighting. It seemed we'd be looking at purses of 2,000 dollars for competing and an average of 10,000 dollars for a win.

'Sometimes they pay up to 20,000 dollars,' he said.

This was music to my ears. After all, the fight world was my first love.

EIGHTEEN

Circus of Horrors

Eventually I got the hang of those slimming pills and began to use them not only to lose weight but as a livener when I was a bit tired. But then I discovered speed, angel dust and all sorts – although I stayed away from heroin, probably because I hated injections. Anything that came from a needle didn't go near me.

Motivated by my constant pestering, Berry got us into a fight meeting. It was all very secretive and we drove for what seemed like hours to get there. We went to the meet with his two giant security men friends whose names I forgot as soon as I was told them. They were religious names, Muslim I was told. They did have real names but had found Allah and got new ones.

I was bombarded with stuff about slavery all during the journey to the fight, they were well on the attack: white-man-this and white-man-that, until I had the ache of all that crap and I began with stories of the Gypsy, our slavery and racial attacks and so on. They didn't know how to answer me. The lads had been so brainwashed they didn't know how to argue the point properly. They were both clearly fucked with my argument and just started their sales pitch all over again about the white devils and so on. I looked at Berry and grinned. I think he was just as bored with it all as I was and had probably heard it many times before. We just shut up and looked out of the windows.

Eventually we arrived at a huge farm. It was fantastic. Big, open spaces surrounded by snow-capped mountains. Beautiful. We drove to the back of a massive grain store, a metal-clad building of about

4,000 square feet. Although we were clearly in the back of beyond, half the country seemed to be there.

There was a sea of vehicles: buses, four-wheel drives, trucks, bikes and the huge, flash coaches belonging to the fighters. There was one bus for each stable of fighters. These were real luxury vehicles – blackened windows of course, but clearly fitted with every luxury: TV aerials on top, the lot. There were five fights on the first half of the bill that night, all reality fighting (I heard someone call it 'extreme fighting'). Then there was to be a break for around forty minutes.

Beer was free out of the ice-filled baths lying around the hall; I guess at 200 dollars a ticket it was expected. All the fellahs were pissing their free beer up their cars or behind bushes. There were a few men fighting where someone was caught pissing up someone else's car. I was laughing like a drain. There was as much entertainment out of the ring as in. Most of the men there couldn't even hold their hands up. Big fat blokes pushing each other around, they all seemed suitably pissed.

A huge klaxon sounded and the men started filing back inside. I say 'men', but there appeared to be an extraordinary amount of women in the crowd – not just 'tits-and-arse' types. Most were very respectably dressed; city types.

The second half of the bill was 'cult fighting.' The 27-foot circle that had been used before had been made smaller and squared. It was now about 20 foot square, I'd guess, with sides about six or seven feet high made out of large gauge mesh. I don't know whether this was to stop missiles from outside or escape by the fighters inside. It was, however, extremely daunting.

The atmosphere was electric. I even had a semi-erection in anticipation of what I was about to see. The adrenaline was pumping now. I had been suitably impressed by the previous 'reality' display but this – *this* was what I had come for.

There were to be three of these fights. I didn't know quite what to expect although I knew it was 'anything goes'. Men had died here and blood was cheap. Just outside the fight area and close to the crowd of spectators, by the exit, there was a mobile cabin set up like a hospital room and an ambulance alongside of it. The crowd was shifting restlessly. Fights were breaking out all over the room.

Security moved in quickly, all of them armed. Every effort had been taken to ensure audience members were not armed, though. They had to pass through an electronic arch like the ones in airports.

Anyone fighting was offered the chance to air differences after the main events had ended in the reality ring. Some refused and quietened down instantly, although several agreed. These small fights were to be used as light relief to take the edge off the evening. They finished on a laugh as inexperienced men of all shapes and sizes floundered in the ring, wearing oversized gloves and long, baggy shorts. This way everyone went home on a happy note. Good bit of psychology really, wasn't it? Better than sending them away pumping for a war with someone.

From above the arena a huge, square Perspex box was lowered in. It had no bottom and the top was fitted with a steel barred grill.

'What the fucking hell's that?' I asked.

'Woah, man! That's the *tank*,' said Berry.

'What they gonna do now then – swim?' I asked.

(Well you never knew with this stuff, perhaps they were going to have someone fight a shark or something. Wouldn't fucking surprise me.)

'No, man. The men will fight inside the tank. It's a bit like cage fighting, you know? Only what goes on in there is a little bit more frightening.'

The tank continued its descent until firmly on the ground and six of the stewards ran around chaining it to the floor.

The lights in the arena dimmed. A silence went around the room for a few seconds. The first fighters were coming in. The crowd wanted to see what the style of fight was to be. Apparently there were many styles of fighting – and I'll explain them as we go here. This was the ultimate fantasy of the fight world.

The first fight was called 'glass fists'. As the presenter of the day made his announcement the silence gave way to a roar as deafening as a jet plane. The heat was getting to me despite the huge fans built within the building. The two men were led into the ring as their names were called out.

I expected to see mountainous oafs with beards – Grizzly Adams or an old Hillbilly, but these fighters were slim men of about five feet nine inches, very agile and obviously fit. Both had shaven heads.

I turned to Berry and remarked, 'Not big blokes, are they?'

'No, man,' he replied. 'They come in all shapes and sizes on the cult circuit – as little as you and as big as me.'

I was getting a bit fed up with the references to my height, I have to say. I was always pretty touchy about it. Couldn't give a fuck now like, but then it seemed so important to me. Any reference to it appeared to be a challenge. Berry sometimes referred to me as 'pocket size'. I used to hate that one.

Outside the Perspex tank there were two deep stainless-steel containers on two small tables. One of the containers contained a heavy grease, the other a mixture of crushed glass and grit. The glass was not just broken. A lot of trouble seemed to have been taken to prepare the size; it was in approximately 8–10 mm pieces. The combatants were led to their respective tables flanked by two of their own men. The hands of each fighter had been tightly taped in the usual manner to give their bones some support during the fight. As each fighter reached their table, they were given what I can only describe as a pair of elasticised mittens. The mittens were put on over the top of the tape. They were not padded mittens, although they did have some sort of heavily woven material sewn in to them. They were firstly to protect the support tapes from damage from the effects of glass and grease and also to protect the hands from any glass penetration through the tape when striking an opponent. The mittens had been put on to the hands in a ceremonious manner. Both men now stood there, mittens in place. Each of them formed their fists and rolled them front and backs in the grease – one at a time, of course, to drag the time out, making it more entertaining and exciting for the crowd. Speaking as a true Brit, and not being used to this kind of entertainment at a fight, I just wanted them to get stuck in and start bashing the fuck out of each other.

Once both men had covered their hands with grease, they were then asked to do the same with the crushed glass and grit. This was again done making a similar fuss over the action. It must have worked – the crowd was going wild and working themselves into a frenzy. Both fighters stood in the spotlights. The crowd was deafening. I couldn't even hear the compère with his microphone. It was electrifying. They raised their hands high above their heads. They each now effectively possessed extremely lethal weapons.

Berry was explaining each move as if I was a complete novice. There were some things that didn't register straight away and I was grateful for his commentary.

'When fighting in this particular style,' he said, 'the fighters aim for head shots. The whole purpose is to draw blood rather than knock out their man. The fists are like double-edged swords. Their owners could deliver equally damaging blows with either the front or the back of each hand.'

He explained that while the fighters were punching, most of the glass was lost from the fist, either it fell to the ground or stuck into the opponent. The application of glass to the back of the hand is a saver. The fighter would spin so fast you would hardly see him do it and strike with a skilfully delivered backhand move.

I have to say, while I find this particular style exciting to watch and can understand that it would be a real buzz to fight in this way – the danger, the tension, the anticipation – I also realised it was a sickeningly cruel and vicious form of entertainment, seeing both the organisers and those thousands attending as either perverse or cowardly men. The excitement, though, was getting to me now and I was reminded of how many bottles of beer I had swallowed by the uncomfortable swelling of my bladder. I quickly ran up a couple of steps and just pissed over the back of the stand. I had already tried to piss in a beer bottle earlier to save a walk out into the parking lot but ended up with most of it over my hands and Berry's trousers. He was *not* a happy man. I wasn't going anywhere now, though, in case I missed something.

Next the men were led to the tank, and the stands where we were began to move slightly with the chanting and rocking of everyone. I could feel my adrenaline surge as I imagined what those fighters must have been feeling as they approached each other, knowing that they would soon be in severe pain and would be sharing their blood with thousands of spectators.

A spotlight shone, hitting the roof lining and searching downward through the girders to find two oiled black bodies pushing a huge gong in to the arena. I remember thinking quickly how pathetically contrived it all seemed as the men walked in with this thing but I have to say that generally by now I was wrapped up in this American entertainment. I think the Yanks must have invented the word 'presentation'. I knew these fights had to have 70 per cent bullshit to drag the evening out; the fights themselves can't last long because of the damage these men inflict on each other, so the entertainment package had to be filled somehow.

You know Americans have that knack of being able to change a whole industry. Take boxing for instance, and that giant amongst men who not only changed the face of boxing but had an effect on all sport generally – Muhammad Ali. Before Ali came along, boxers were not paid a lot of money at all and if there was a good purse it would only be for the heavyweights. With Ali's vision there was born a whole new era of sportsmen. The entertainer. And now the string of boxing personalities that followed Ali have money to burn. (And of course Don King helped, God bless him.)

One of the black men lifted the hammer from its position. The crowd grew almost silent as the other man gave the signal. The gong resonated throughout the building but the sound was soon lost as the baying crowd rose as one. The men ran towards each other, the pace was being set. The two men were obviously going to make this a war. There were no rounds in cult fighting. The men just kept going till the end. The end came when only one man was left standing.

The taller of the two men, a dark-skinned fighter, claimed the first blow, delivering a head-butt in a way that I have never seen before. It came down at a slight angle and landed square in the middle of the other fighter's temple. The noise of the crowd became unbearable and the movement of the stand caused Berry and I to look at each other quickly but we soon forgot about the possible danger and jumped up and down with all the other lunatics, grabbing at each other's arms like two silly teenagers at a pop concert. The excitement was tremendous. I found myself laughing and shouting in an uncontrollable, manic fashion. It was like being amongst all the kids at the circus. In fact that was really it – I was at the circus. That described the whole thing. A circus of horrors.

The blond man receiving the head blow tumbled sideways but came back with a skilful roundhouse kick to the abdomen, followed by a combination of punches, causing the other man's ear to flow with blood. Although these blows were fierce and well-placed the recipient seemed unmoved. He bent his body with the roundhouse, absorbing the power. That punch to the ear spoke for itself, though, and another punch glanced across the top of the head and lost all its power but it left a graze caused by the glass fist that surely left glass embedded in the skull. Having cleverly survived this attack, the fighter took his gloves away from his face, opening them up like a door. He adopted the old Sugar Ray Leonard trick: dancing backwards, smiling and poking out his tongue.

What he wasn't expecting was his opponent's ability to regain his composure instantly and deliver another blow, this time a straight one, finding the full centre of the face. The man's head snapped backward and the body followed, smashing into the side panels of the tank, leaving his blood smeared up the sides of the walls.

The crowd loved this mural of claret on the screen and began their vampiric baying at this display of what was on their 'menu'. The two fighters now moved in close, fists delivering their bead-like deposits to every naked centimetre of each other's flesh. The bleeding man instinctively wiped the blood from his eyes and in doing so inflicted even more damage to his face by grinding in the glass and grit from his own gloves. Blood was everywhere.

The referee came in to the centre and gestured to the crowd with his arms outstretched, asking them if he should stop the fight at this stage. The crowd, of course, didn't want this and became enraged at such a suggestion so early on in the fight. The security staff were working their damnedest to maintain control. I could see now why everyone involved earned so much from this one gig.

The blond fighter who had been doing all the damage was clearly in control here. He put his right hand behind the dark-skinned fighter's neck, snapping the whole body downwards and slammed the face of his opponent into his knee. A huge split appeared in the middle of the damaged face of the blood-drenched man. He went down.

As the blond fighter lifted a leg to stamp on the floored fighter he was knocked down by a leg sweep. Now both men were down. I had never seen anything so exciting. I wanted to be in there. The bloodied fighter rose to his knees and brought a double-fisted blow downwards hard and sharp fully into the other's face. Both men were now covered in blood, their heads and faces soaked, and the

TARMAC WARRIOR

blond fighter now became a red head with the bloody dye.

I was screaming as loud as every other person in the place; we were all screaming our instructions, everybody suddenly became expert fighters and knew exactly what should be done. Obviously the two men couldn't hear a word and anyway probably couldn't give a fuck by now.

One man rose to his feet. I couldn't recognise who it was at first. It was getting difficult to see the fighters as the Perspex was smearing up with blood and the men now began to look alike – like walking carcasses. Another leg sweep brought him down, I just didn't know who was who now, I was just screaming anyway. I really didn't care who was winning.

One fighter landed on his back and bounced with the force of his weight crashing down. The other got to his knees again and frantically delivered blow after blow to the face of the man on the floor. He kicked him hard in the side and the man on the floor rolled over with the force. Then the standing fighter went down on one knee and pushed the floored man's face into the ground, lifting the head by its hair and forcing it downwards. The mutilated body lay still except for one last movement of the head as it took a final punch. The attacker seemed to become possessed and wanted to kill the man and grabbed him by the neck. Three men came rushing in from outside the tank to pull him off.

The victor jumped up and leapt high into the air, roaring with the energy and pain that he felt. He left the tank like an escaped animal and came to the side of the ring, running around and throwing his hands high as he did so. The face was not recognisable but I saw a patch of blond hair sticking out the back and of course knew then who the victor was. He clearly felt no pain. The body's special chemistry was protecting him from that. I remember saying out loud, 'He'll fucking ache tomorrow!'

The crowd was, of course, still going crazy. Money was being thrown into the ring, men were running at the victor and hugging him, getting their handkerchiefs 'blooded' as a souvenir as they did so, by pressing them to his face. Some even wiped the blood across their foreheads. This was a sickness that I had never witnessed before in my entire life. I never imagined such behaviour from human beings. I was shocked – and I became even more shocked to realise that I was one of them. I didn't even notice the loser leave the tank. It's true that no one wants to know a loser. He had nothing more to offer us. This business is all about heart, courage and determination. That's what will see you through where sometimes skill may let you down.

I ran to get some more beers ready for the next fight. I got four this time as those bottled ones don't seem to last five minutes. I became a fully-fledged vampire now. I wanted more blood, more excitement. My heart was pumping as fast as fuck, my eyes were open wide, pupils dilated and my mouth was as dry as a bone. By the way I couldn't stop talking you would have thought I had done a gram of speed. The whole crowd were blood junkies.

A man came into the ring wearing a bright orange boiler suit pulling a hosepipe behind him. He walked in to the tank and turned on the powerful jet, washing down the blood-smeared Perspex. He then carefully rolled the hose up again and returned with a rubber blade, like a car window wiper, to clear away the water from the sides to give the audience a clear view once more.

The crowd seemed to be holding their breath to find out what the next fight would be (although several were still watching the nearby topless knife throwers). The compère walked to the middle of the ring as the lights dimmed and a spotlight fell on the figure who held the secret we all wanted to hear. He stood still, looked around the room and announced: 'The Yard!'

Everyone again went wild. I think by now, though, they were so wired they would have screamed if Humpty Dumpty had walked out. I turned to Berry for an explanation and he began to explain.

'The two fighters will have leather shackles fitted to their ankles, each of which has a steel ring. When both fighters are in the tank the ref fixes a piece of rope between the shackles. Then they fight – neither of them can run.'

I looked back and began to feel goosebumps creep over my body. This was without doubt the most exciting experience of my entire life. These different fight styles were amazing and gave me a real rush.

Berry continued explaining. 'You see, the match's gotta be good. Each man must fight in the same style – either both orthodox or both southpaw. They'll be similar height, and weight. Good matching is essential in this style. It's a tough fight, man. You have to stand and slog it out. No wrestling, no holding, but anything goes. It's just brute force with a lot of cunning. This style would kill you, man. I've seen you spar, you move around a lot.'

I guess he was right. I would love to try it, though. I would stick to a style that suited my most natural way of fighting. To do anything else would be poor tactics. But I just knew I would have to try anyway.

A huge drum started beating somewhere, regular beats like when slaves used to row the big battle ships to war. As the beat caught the imagination of the crowd, the two fighters walked in side-by-side, filling the already electric atmosphere with their presence. These men were bigger than the last we saw fighting. There was a bearded fighter with his head shaved which made me laugh. I turned to Berry and said, 'Looks like he's put his head on upside down!'

The other man looked Hispanic. He had his hair tied in a small ponytail and shaven up to the ears. Both men were, I guess, about six feet tall and probably weighed around seventeen stone. Their bodies looked fit, and yet didn't show very much muscle, although their legs had clearly been given a lot of attention in the gym –those muscles even had muscles. These were strong, determined fighters. Neither looked nor spoke to the other. Instead they moved quietly into the tank. Once inside the referee linked them together with a short length of rope. The rope, I guess, was about two centimetres in circumference and appeared slightly stretchy. On each end of the rope there was a clip shackle to fix to the clips on the ankle straps.

I asked Berry about a difference I'd noticed between the cult fights as opposed to the reality fights on the same bill. Reality fighters came up to the side of the ring, sometimes even going into the crowd to get them going. The cult fighters never did, they always seemed better protected.

Berry explained: 'Money, man! These fighters are worth thousands of dollars to their management. See out there? The betting is frantic, the guys over the other side have thousands bet on each fight. If anything happens to a fighter, they could lose plenty.'

'Happen? What the fuck can happen in here? There's security everywhere,' I said.

'The security have to have eyes up their arse, man – all through the crowd there are lightweight hit men. They use catapults with ball bearings, peashooters with small darts, and little air pistols – even bottles and stuff will fly. Anything they can do to stop the fight if they have to, they'll do. They're paid well to do it. They wait until the crowd surge forward and take their best shot without hesitation,' he explained. I had already been told that the Mafia and some local organisations took huge kickbacks from these promotions. I wasn't sure if the Mafia actually got involved in the promotion, but I am sure they handled the betting one way or another.

The fights were used to entertain big clients and stars. You would always be guaranteed to see someone, occasionally Frank Sinatra, Sammy Davis or Jack Nicholson. These were all regular names for the VIP lists, as well as famed politicians and some of the biggest gangster names. I could see as I looked across the arena that there was a special area elevated and guarded by the biggest fuck-off blokes you have ever seen in your life – stereotypical of what you would expect from the land of gangsters: smart black suits, dark glasses and bulging jackets (not from muscle). Very smart, big men. Inside the guarded area there were buckets of champagne, all kinds of spirits and a huge buffet. There were several pretty girls darting around too, all about 20 years old with everything on show. Towards the end of the arena there was the Chinese contingent. The Chinese were always well represented at fight events of this kind and their betting was ferocious.

The gong sounded and the spotlights fell on the tank. The men began to fight at great speed. The shaven-headed man reached down quickly to take hold of the rope on the Hispanic's ankle. He pulled upwards on it, hard and swift, dragging his opponent's leg with it, sending him crashing to the floor. The aggressor took the opportunity to jump hard on the leg with both knees, hoping to cause severe damage. As he did so his hands landed straight in the other bloke's gonads. He took this chance to give them a quick twist with the dexterity of a Ninja.

The Hispanic screamed like a Banshee. He didn't know whether to grab his nuts or his leg. The crowd was howling with laughter but I felt an anger surge inside me for some reason. I suppose my natural emotion was to despise such a dirty trick but my fighter's instinct told me it was a part of the job. While the man lay clutching at himself and struggling to get up, he caught several good full-fist blows from the shaven-headed guy around the eyes and ears. He was well winded. You could see him trying to get himself together again. Both men rose to their feet. They knew if they didn't get up, start to fight and give the crowd their money's worth, they would get a bollocking from their respective managements (mainly because they in turn would have had one from the promoters!).

If a fighter didn't do as he was told he would suffer a financial penalty. That was the only way to hurt them. They would either have money taken from their pay from that night or they would be left off the next bill (and they didn't want that).

The two men again began to trade punches: head, body, anywhere they could make contact. They were short, sharp blows that had to be powerful and were probably learned from some form of martial art to have their most damaging effect. The more I watched the more I believed I could adapt my style of fighting to do this. All I had to do was get the dancing around out of my head – and that shouldn't be hard.

Suddenly the Hispanic fighter got hold of the other man's head and twisted it sideways, taking a lump out of his ear. (Tyson was never the first to pull that trick!) He chewed off the man's earlobe. I was waiting to see him spit out the fleshy lump but instead the sick bastard swallowed it. The dirty rotten fucker chewed and swallowed a piece of another human being. I couldn't believe my eyes. The ear-donor was holding the guy by the throat now, trying to get his fingers down his neck to retrieve his ear.

'You're going to lose your fucking fingers as well in a minute, mate!' I shouted. The fellah was screaming for his ear but it was well gone! He suddenly realised he was getting nowhere and began to nut the Hispanic fighter repeatedly, splitting his face wide open, eye-to-eye and down to the nose. He gashed his own head with the powerful blows but he didn't care.

Now there was blood, snot and tears pouring down their faces. The Hispanic got hold of his opponent's beard and held it high in the air so that he couldn't see what was going on. Then he hit him across the windpipe hard. He then brought his hand back quickly and did it again, this time holding on, gripping the windpipe hard, waiting for it to give. The pressure eventually displaced the cartilage.

The man was choking on blood, his breathing obviously restricted. He dropped to his knees, desperately struggling to survive.

As he went down the Hispanic slammed several swift, hard, straight punches into the pathetic upturned face that was begging for air. The face had already yielded its supply of blood, though, and appeared to have no more to give. Eventually the attacker must have felt the energy of his own body giving way and needed to finish the fight off. He looked down at the poor fucker by his feet, lifted his hands high and gave out a battle cry – a sound that contained anguish, grief and fury; a scream with as much emotion and electricity as any woman in full orgasmic flow.

The fight was over. The Hispanic fighter had defeated his opponent skilfully and with the greatest of courage, having recovered from his first few minutes of torture. However, the victor didn't appear to be impressed by his win and somehow looked sickened. I think I understood, though, as I stood and looked at them both. I felt a sort of empathy that only another fighter could feel. Such a complete defeat is not always gratifying, and when you look at the carnage you have caused there is that small spark of humanity in you that stares back and makes you feel sick with your own actions.

The last event was announced. This time there was no build-up. The crowd didn't even care what style it was by now, they were buzzing. So long as the blood kept pumping they were happy.

'Gladiators,' I heard the compère scream. I waited in wonder to find out what treat we had in store next.

Now for those of you who have watched the *Gladiators* programme on TV, let me tell you now this is nothing like that at all. This one is for real and there is absolutely no sportsmanship or goodwill going round. The tank was lifted high above and six-foot mesh barriers went up around the arena. I had to admit, a lot of work went into the running of this thing. Now I don't know if the barrier was there to keep the fighters in or the crowd out, but all these cages and barriers did make me feel that the promoters were underlining the fact that these men were animals and that they were being treated as such. It added to the entertainment value but I found it a bit demeaning.

Two huge panels of wood and steel were wheeled into the arena, one placed at each end about 25 feet apart. On the racks there was placed an eight-foot wooden pole, a club fashioned like a baseball bat and a chain and mace. A mace? I looked again. Where the fuck did that come from?

This is getting too clowny now, I thought. I began to lose a bit of interest. I thought this one was going to be total bollocks; a farce. I looked at Berry and he was rocking. He was even more excited than he was at the last event.

'Watch this fucker, man,' he screeched. 'These guys are trained to use all these weapons for real!'

'Yeah, right' I said in disbelief. I had enjoyed the evening so far and really didn't want to be let down with this last style of fighting. I thought it was going to be like a carnival performance.

At the beginning of this fight the men were brought into the arena on a chariot – a fucking *chariot*, how naff is that? Can you believe it? I remembered once again watching the old wrestlers and the spoofy fighting they did. You young readers won't remember Jackie Pallo and his like but nowadays there is WWF and it's all the same: a crowd-pleaser, not a real fight.

The men jumped from their chariot and stood with their arms in the air. They each had a net draped over their arm, gladiator-style. The fighters walked to the ringside where the Mafia group sat and they took their bow. They then walked around the perimeter of the arena. The gong sounded and the men walked slowly to the centre of the ring. They shook hands, turned, then ran like fuck to grab a weapon. Perhaps it wasn't going to be that bad after all, I thought.

The fighter could grab hold of any weapon he wanted, apparently – the only disadvantage being that when you took your weapon, you couldn't see what your opponent had grabbed. The rule was that once you had been disarmed, you must go for your next weapon but the opponent could continue bashing shit out of you while you were trying to get to it.

These fighters wore long shorts made from heavy cloth, cut off between the ankle and the knee. One was dressed in red and the other in green. The fighter in red went for the eight-foot pole, the other went for the club (I bet he was gutted). They rushed across the arena at each other and immediately I realised that this was for real! There was no holding back – the fighter in green swung his club at the red, who immediately countered with his pole. They were going blow for blow and fighting hard and skilfully.

The red gladiator with the pole was in front by the number of strikes but then he had the reach, didn't he? He gave some nice jabs with the end of the pole – in the stomach, the ribs, the nuts and across the back. Every time the red fighter tried a swing of the pole he missed. It was like slow-motion, it was so long. He then came in straight but by now the green fighter had obviously got his measure. He stepped aside and spun his net around the end, then brought the club crashing across the pole, splintering it and making it useless.

The red fighter dropped the weapon quickly as the blow trembled through the pole and hurt his hands. He ran for his battle board. Green was already on his trail, though, and had cleared the pole from his net. He chased Red and threw his net like a bolas, wrapping it around Red's ankles, bringing the man down in full flight. As he went down he quickly rolled from the net's grip just as Green's club came down hard. Missing Red's back, the club hit the floor hard and spun from Green's hand. Now he had to run for another weapon. In one gamble he had lost his club and his net.

Red picked himself up again and ran for all he was worth to get his new weapon. This was really beginning to get me excited now. I saw Green go for the mace and as it happened Red came out with the same weapon, but he still had his net also.

They rushed toward each other screaming, their maces flying above their heads. As they swung at each other their chains interlocked. They began to pull, trying to wrench the weapons from each other's hands. Red swung again, but low. Green misjudged the swing and didn't jump high enough. The mace caught his leg and tore the muscle open.

How can these men have careers? I thought. They can't fight like this for very many years. It was obviously a hit-and-run game, a 'get your money and leave' situation. As Green went down, Red slammed the mace downward, catching Green across the right shoulder. I thought that this would have surely broken something, but no – as he went down he swung upwards towards his opponent. This was amazing, and obviously for real just as Berry had said.

'How do they stand the pain?' I asked.

'Chasing the dragon, man,' he replied. 'Or snorting cocaine.' I didn't understand so just ignored him. I didn't want to look stupid. But I learned later that chasing the dragon was the euphemism for burning off heroin and sucking in the fumes.

Green swapped the mace to his left hand. As Red began another swing, they found themselves very close to the barrier. Red brought the mace down in a sort of roundhouse style but caught the barrier, fully misjudging the position (excitement and the sight of victory does that to you sometimes).

As he hit the barrier the mace left his hand and spun round to hit him behind the right ear. He was stunned for a minute and Green quickly tried to take advantage of the situation. Red now had no weapon and ran for his third and final chance – the club. He turned and had taken one step when Green spun on his good leg and brought his mace firmly up the side of Red's face. His jaw dropped loose and numb, broken by the blow.

The jaw just hung, open and shattered. I believed I heard the crack even above the scream of the crowd. An ambulance spun to life at the call of the ref. The makeshift hospital there obviously wasn't equipped for this sort of damage. It would have been okay for stitches and blood transfusions, but was more of a patching-up station than a hospital.

Well, that was the end of the fights for us. The cheering died down and some of the men started to make their way home. We didn't stop to watch the fun fights at the end, we just grabbed a couple more beers and went to the parking lot to look at the cars. We walked and talked excitedly, both of us were buzzing and couldn't stop talking with the excitement. This had been without any shadow of a doubt the most outstanding night of my life. I had never felt such excitement at any event that I wasn't competing in.

I had seen some great fights in my lifetime but none that displayed such courage and determination as these men that night. They had become heroes in my eyes. We hung around for our lift home, while the two guys who got us in did their business, of course: seeing everyone off the premises and getting their pay.

I had certainly had my eyes opened. This was something completely new that had filled the void in my life. My excitement had been reborn and Berry had told me that I hadn't even seen it all yet. There were more fights, more bizarre and perverse than those I had witnessed that day. I wanted to see them, to feel them, to taste them – but for now I was happy!

NINETEEN

Off to Join the Circus

Well, I had seen enough to know that this cult fighting was right up my street. All I had to do now was find a way in. I'd have to get an introduction from Berry's two Muslim warriors. The alternative was to get into the next meet and just walk straight up to 'The Man' and ask him outright. That way I owed no favours. I reckon I would probably be under all sorts of suspicion and it would take ages to get where I wanted to be in the organisation but I wanted the big money and *fast*.

I was really pining for the family at this point. I missed them all so much. All I had to keep me going was the odd telephone call and they cost the earth. I had to judge them just right, when I knew that someone was going to be staying with a relative who had settled, or else in the winter when mum and dad were on the plot. Jed and Lolly were both settled on their own plots now, raising their families. I was missing all this. Of course, there were no such things as mobile phones in those days.

I talked to Berry who arranged a meet at Franklin's bar. This was where we all hung out, just drinking and talking. Drugs would change hands as freely as cigarettes there and we all got to hear about jobs that were going down and all the little scams. I asked Berry to invite his Muslim pals but they were reluctant to be with a lot of white people so we got them to choose another bar.

Berry was late and I was pestering him to shake off the little bird he was with and get his arse in gear. He wanted this bad but obviously not as much as me. Eventually, walking to the meeting, we chatted generally, taking in the sun, and I told Berry of my intentions.

'I just wanna get in and fight until I drop, just to earn the dosh. Then when I think I have enough I am going home – for good,' I said.

'Well, man, I am thinking along the same lines, you know? Except I won't be going home. There's nothing there for me any more. My parents are dead and the wife won't let me see my son. I only get into trouble with the police trying.'

'A son? You have a son? I didn't know!'

'Well, I don't want to get into a big discussion but I send him letters, money and things, I don't even know if he gets them,' he said sadly.

Berry did the business with the Muslims and in less than a week we had a meeting set up in San Francisco (which Berry used to call 'Sam Plank's Disco!'). We parked the car at the edge of town and got the tram. It was so much easier. We had to make our way to a place called Roc Morais.

We had the cabbie drop us off right outside the hotel where The Man had a suite on permanent reservation. We went to the reception and announced ourselves and were taken to the room we wanted. The staff out there were just great. Such service. I really miss it, you know?

The bell hop knocked on the door and then waited. I thought he was waiting for an answer but Berry wised up and gave him a five dollar bill and he quickly scampered away.

The Man answered the door himself. I imagined that he would have maids or a butler or something. He was a short, fat, balding guy, more like a banker or a store keeper you would think. He was smoking a long coloured cigarette in a holder. I saw the box on the side table, a carved walnut cigarette box with the lid open. It looked like a pack of crayons, full of different colours.

We were shown into a huge sitting room, really impressive. There were two young men just flitting around making themselves look busy. They were wearing very tight sleeveless vests. I began to get a little uncomfortable. Poofs, I thought. What the fuck are they doing here? Then Berry put me straight. The Man was queer as you like and the boys were his playthings. I thought, fuck this, let me out. Sod the fighting. My lust for money fought my homophobia, though, and won. I stayed and sat, just where I was told.

The Man took Berry into another room. We were to be split up so that he could check our pedigree better. Berry soon came out of the room and I went in. As I passed Berry I cracked a line, 'You've started walking funny! What you been up to?'

We both laughed out loud. That didn't go down too well. The Man just walked away and didn't even hold the door open for me, he just let it go in my face. Good job he's a poof, I thought. You can't hit them, can you, it'd be like hitting a woman.

I am now ashamed of the prejudice I displayed at that time. My mother would have drawn me one off if she had heard my thoughts. I was acting like one of those mindless skinheads that used to brick our trailers or chase us when we were kids. I had become one of them.

After my little interview he called Berry back in. Now we got a pep talk on general matters: money splits, hotels, expenses, what was expected of us and what we could expect from them – whoever the fuck 'they' were.

We were on the Firm's books. It was explained to us that we would first enter the circuit as 'extreme combatants', not fighters. I felt like a better person immediately now that I had a title. The reason we had to fight extreme first was to get known on the circuit, create a history and a following.

Once we had made our mark we would go full combat on the cult circuit. However, we first had to get a minimum of five good wins behind us. That would be our goal, our history. But The Man added that even if we got three or four wins, providing the other two were good strong fights, he would consider it.

Now to me that last admission showed his hand. He had made the target of five fights, then backed off to make sure we came on board as cult fighters. It had become obvious by that compromise that the 'businessmen' we were working for were struggling for good cult fighters. This was to be our strength. I knew now that I could hold out for a bit more money and push for my fights. I also knew, though, that I couldn't push my luck. These men were no pussies. They were holding my future in their hands. I just needed to work out exactly how much control I had over it!

Berry and I walked from the hotel on air, our strides proud and firm (although I was taking more proud steps than that lanky bastard on account of him having such long legs – I couldn't keep up with him!). Our drive home was full of excited chatter – mostly about what we would do with the money rather than about the dangers of the fights. I don't think I ever considered the dangers for one minute. I was going to like this circuit. I could feel it in my wallet. It was a great start just being able to use my own name. That Gypsy Prince bollocks was just embarrassing.

I spent the next six months training hard. I was out running carrying a weight pack, up hills, in the sea, on the sand, anything to build strength in my legs and back. The key to success was strength. You need strong arms, back and legs for this game. Stamina was important also but not as necessary as the fights didn't last long – not as long as in gloved fighting where you can bash a man forever with all that padding around your hands.

For Berry and me, fights came and went fast and fierce but at least this time the management were being sensible. They were giving us time to recover between them. Each time I fought, the compère introduced me:

'Gentlemen. Brought to the USA at the cost of our promoters, all the way from London, England.'

The crowd must have thought I was on a piece of elastic if they believed I was being 'brought to the USA' as much as the promoter said I was!

Berry and I were keeping tally, a sort of contest on wins. He was well in front, though. I wasn't doing badly but needed to do a lot better to make sure I got into bigger money. During the time we were in training, we also had to fight, though. We had to earn our keep as we were only on a basic wage – a retainer, you might say. Within eight months Berry had fought seven times, winning six of his fights, all by knock out. I had fought six times and won three of them, two by knock out and one by a TKO (Technical Knock Out). In the last one, my opponent's eye was popped out of his head. I was bashing fuck out of him in a corner (not using the best style, I might add). I was like a windmill, arms everywhere, but they were all hitting home. As the man went down, I kicked him across the face to make sure he stayed there. Unfortunately a lower cleat on the corner post had not been covered properly and his head spun round, hitting it, catching him just up the side of his nose, pushing upwards into the eye. It was hanging out. I had to look away. It was so weird. The man just couldn't shut his eye. As I looked across the ring all I could see was this fucking great big eye looking back at me. I started laughing. Not because I was pleased or wanted this to happen, but because this eye was like something from a cartoon. The seconds and the referee were trying to poke it back in; the doctor couldn't get a look in. You gotta laugh, ain't you?

Soon our trial period was over at last and we were ready to join the cult circuit. I suddenly became a bit apprehensive. I don't know if it was fear of failure, fear of getting hurt or fear of the unknown. Although I did know a bit about it all, I didn't know what it was like to face this kind of real danger, *real* pain. My experience up until that time was only to have a few minutes' battle with someone, not to stand and battle it out with weapons or handicaps. Was I going to like this after all my efforts? Had I done the right thing?

Our time came in August 1975, and our first cult fight happened to be on the same card – which was great for me, I valued my friend's support. The venue was an old commercial unit in San Francisco, about an hour's drive from where we were then living, just on the border of Modesto.

I didn't mind the drive down, that was one thing. I got to ride in the big RV our stable had. Even if I ended up getting a good hiding it would have been worth it just to ride in this thing. The seats were all white leather with navy blue piping around the edges. There was a television, a full kitchen, a bar and a full shower unit. It was crazy, I couldn't believe I had landed in such luxury. I would have loved one of these to take home.

When we got there, I remember the pungent odour of fish and the coldness of the building. It obviously used to be some sort of fish canning or gutting place. We went straight to our positions in the dock area and parked. My stomach was doing somersaults and the excitement was tearing me apart inside my head. We were all talking like schoolchildren on a day's outing. One of the crew came to the trailer with the plans for the fight modes of the evening. This was what we were anxious to find out: not so much who we were fighting but how we had to fight them. One of the choices of that evening was Hang Fighting. Both fighters would hang from a long piece of strengthened rope, a bit like a bungee but without the elastication. The fighters would have leather straps around their ankles (trimmed with sheepskin to avoid abrasions) and between the straps were small shackles. The fighters were placed under the huge chrome-plated, crane-like gantry that stood over the arena and the machinery was switched on, unwinding a rope and shackle that came down toward the fighters. Both lay in the arms of their seconds while the technicians secured all the shackles and signalled for the rope to be taken upwards, leaving the fighters hanging in mid-air. I remember thinking: that'll do me. I really didn't fancy the Glass Fist, or the Yard, which were the other options. There was no way my face was going to look into someone's fist of glass, mate. I liked the way I looked . . . well, my mum thought I was handsome anyway.

The Glass Fist just did nothing for me – the thought of someone pushing glass in my face made me feel sick and I really didn't fancy the Yard. Berry had put me off that really when he told me that I would be no good at it. I let his judgement rule my own – a bad thing for a fighter to do, but as it happens he was right, really. I am a mover and jabber, I work my opponent because I don't have a big punch, but I am very fast, and have to take advantage of my best assets.

The allocation of styles came and I got the Hang Fighting. Berry got the Yard (tough luck) and a guy called Mano got the Glass Fist. Mano was a Puerto Rican just fighting to get his family out of the shit-hole they lived in. Although he was a very quiet man and rarely mixed at all with any of us, I had listened to the stories of the poverty he suffered while he lived in his own country. He banked almost every penny that he earned and lived on almost nothing. When we went clubbing he stayed home, when we went drinking he stayed home, when we went shopping he stayed home. He wouldn't celebrate Christmas unless it was forced on him. He was a very sad man but to think of your family living as they were, while you were in the land of opportunity would be depressing, wouldn't it?

I was up first tonight. My stomach was turning like a cement mixer and I felt my throat filling as I ran instinctively for the toilet. *Whup!* Up it came. I gave it to the floor, the walls and the window. This was a real spouter. I spewed everywhere. I just began to get my breath back when up it came again – where had I been keeping it all? It looked like everything I had eaten that week. Berry fell about laughing every time I went through this nightmare. He was always so cool.

I had just done a gram of speed and was beginning to get the prickles up the back of my neck. I used to do speed-balls as I hated the taste and that way I could just drop them straight down my neck without the bitterness. The amphetamine was kicking in well now, I was really chewing tongue and talking the arse of any poor sod who stood still long enough. I had to get some gum quick, my mouth was so dry.

As I stood outside our RV, my opponent came from his trailer parked just a few yards away. There were three stables of fighters there that night, all parked beside one another. He glanced across at me and nodded. I just turned away and went to gob on the floor, trying to looking right hard, but the speed had made my mouth so dry it was like spitting feathers. I felt a right tit.

The time to go to the fight area came and I dropped my gum shield in early, it helped keep my mouth moist. I had a black gumshield with red zig-zags like pointed teeth (scary, huh? I don't think so!) Entering the arena both fighters did their individual displays – shadow boxing, back skipping and general showing off. The man I was to fight did a full back flip. Cocky cunt, I thought. I wanted to do one too, but I couldn't, I knew I would have gone flat on my arse. I just wanted to fight. We stepped up side-by-side, blanking each other completely as we strode solemnly across the fight area.

Our respective seconds lifted us off of the ground and laid us on marble slabs that were supposed to represent gravestones. I mumbled to my second, 'Lovely, innit? Very encouraging!' I don't think he understood a word, however – after all, I was mumbling in cockney with a mouth full of resin.

By now I was speeding like a maniac. I had the prickles all over my body. My legs were desperate to get going, what with the speed

TARMAC WARRIOR

and the natural chemicals in my body being released with anticipation, the heat and all the excitement. This really was 'the nuts' – the best feeling in the whole fucking world, mate.

The chrome-rigged gantry slowly came over my head and the huge spotlights from the back of the venue burst open on to us. The crowd was electric, the atmosphere was second to nothing you would ever feel. As I write I have that whole euphoria welling up inside me. The crank began to buzz behind me as the ropes descended slowly towards me. My heart was pumping madly. The buzzing stopped and the ropes hung with their bronze shackles about two feet above me.

My seconds whispered, 'Do him good, cockney', as they lifted my ankles toward the shackles while supporting my back carefully. The buzzing started again and I was hoisted into the air about six feet above my marble slab, in all I guess we were about ten feet off the ground. It seemed miles away, especially from upside down.

There we were, suspended about two feet apart. I could smell his sweat as he grinned at me. I felt so vulnerable, I'll tell you. I was trussed up for the slaughter. If I hadn't been stoned on amphetamines I would have laughed but I never could raise a smile when I was on that stuff – in fact, there was very little I *could* raise. It put an end to my fight-time erections, that's for sure!

We hung there for what seemed like ages but in reality must have been only seconds. We probably looked really stupid. I began to get angry at being put in such a position. I spotted the huge black man who was to tell us when to begin. He raised the weighty hammer with a slow, deliberate swing up and back, then forward sharply across the huge Chinese-looking gong. As the hammer hit home my opponent caught me on both sides of my head, straight across the ears. It hurt like hell and I was completely disorientated. I was so angry I forgot where I was and tried to knee him, which of course didn't work because my legs were bound together. I went mental. I lashed out at the man. The humiliation of everything was probably the best thing that could have happened to me at this time. I was so bloody angry. I wasn't thinking straight and the first rule of having a kor was to get your mind round it all. Anger was a weakness I couldn't afford. I wasn't powerful enough and had to rely on my cunning.

It took a minute or so to get used to the swinging bit – he kept dodging every attempt I made to hit him just by moving from the waist, this man was well-practised. I swung toward him and grabbed him by the band of his shorts and swung him outwards, he didn't expect that. As he swung back toward me I dipped my head and smacked him square in the face. But I misjudged and hit him with the top of my head. The crowd went wild and I saw stars. It hurt me more than it did him, I think. I was dazed. When I saw the state of his face, though, I felt more assured of my skills. He was covered in claret. I had split something good anyway. I saw his lips move but could hear nothing. I still had a ringing in my head.

From that point the fight was well and truly on. There was no real up-and-down movement in the suspension cord. We fought hard for three-and-a-half minutes until everything went black for me. One minute I was hanging upside down to the roar of a crowd, the next I was back in my RV with the spouts of bottles of smelling salts up each nostril.

I sat bolt upright and began immediately to bollock my seconds. I really didn't know what had happened to me. I shouted loudly at the young one of my trainers, Izzy. He was a Jewish lad of about 20, very slim, tall and slippery as hell. He had thick, dark, curly hair, saucer-sized, deep-brown eyes, was sallow-skinned and had a very gentle nature, although you just knew there was something brewing behind this façade. He got the name Izzy on account of his country of origin, Israel. I blamed him then for not teaching me the right techniques for this style of fighting, but of course it was my own fault and I did apologise later. He never argued, though, he was so placid. I really don't know why he was in this business – a real fish out of water if ever I saw one.

I knew I was going to ache the next day but fortunately the speed was still banging away at me so I felt nothing at that time. I had been out for a while and had missed the next fight which was Mano and the Glass Fist. He had won it, although you would never have guessed if you had seen his face. I looked out of the RV doors in time to watch Berry make his way to the arena, cool and confident as ever, he strode slowly across, nothing fazed him.

I wasn't allowed to watch the fight, I had to go to the doctors and get checked out. The boss wasn't about to let one of his fighters get sick. He looked after us well, I will give him that – although for his own reasons. He had given us a great apartment to live in too. There were four of us: myself, Berry and the two trainers, Kieran and Izzy. Kieran was as tall and skinny as Izzy. It must go with the job or something. He moved like a giraffe and was about six feet eight. He was getting on a bit – about forty, I guessed. He knew the fight game inside out.

I had a lot of respect for both of my trainers I had to say, but was particularly fond of Kieran. He really wanted to be out there but his height seemed to be a handicap and he had no co-ordination whatsoever. We used to laugh at him.

He'd say: 'I'd be out there myself if I could hold my hands up, but with the length of my neck I'd get it broke and knock myself out walking down the stairs!'

Berry was back before I could see the doctor. He had won his fight too. I was the only man to let the stable down. As he walked into the surgery trailer I could see Berry was in a lot of pain but he tried to hide it. I felt really gutted about being the only loser but all the lads gave me lots of support, even the boss was okay. He was like that, though. Even if you got a shit result he would give you a bit of a boost – not enough for you to think it was okay to lose, but enough to let you know he appreciated you doing your best.

My purse for the evening was two thousand dollars which at that time equated to around one thousand pounds. I wasn't unhappy with those wages, how could I be, although I did keep thinking that I could have walked away with closer to five thousand pounds, had I won. I remember sharing that thought with Berry. He said in an encouraging manner:

'Hold on to that thought, man, she will drive you to your next win.'

He was so cool – and right, of course. I had to use the cash prize as my motivation rather than the fear of losing face. Berry's words always made sense to me, it was like he had everything together so well in his head – yet you knew of course that he didn't, there was always something burning at his soul. To anyone who knew him well he was clearly a tortured man.

The drive back was as mad as always – adrenaline still pumping through the veins of the battered bodies, cold beers flowing from the cooler box and cocaine still controlling the old brain-box, not to mention the mouth. Everyone was talking over each other with excitement. It was as noisy as a school bus on a day trip. I had found one common denominator between us all – we played hard! I guess that was our escape from the reality of the world we had joined. Pre-fight weeks were gruelling. Training till our lungs were bursting in our chests, we would be falling through the door in the evenings – but hey – a bit of 'billy' or a line of 'charlie', just as a livener of course, and we would be up there again. When we wanted to sleep it was time for downers we called DF's

We partied hard that night. God knows how much powder was consumed but some Bolivians must have eaten well as a consequence of our appetites for their produce! We were always wild, there were no boundaries. Semi-dressed girls were on tap. They were stepping out of their clothes as they walked through the door. We were at The Man's house, of course. He never joined in with us but he was the perfect host, and anyway he was into men and would never have flaunted that in front of us. He kept his own social life and sexual preferences private from everyone.

The Man was not descended from Italians in any way, but he had adopted the Mafia style. He would use all the little phrases that you would imagine the Godfather would come out with and talked in that respectful, yet intimidating manner to everyone. His house was filled with classical music (when we weren't in it). I guess it was the people he did business with who made him into this character. I just laughed quietly when he became like this. As long as the money kept rolling in, who was I to judge? And why should I even care? I was very happy.

We had three weeks off before we got down to train for the next wave of fights, so Berry and I decided to drive to Lake Tahoe for some ski fun. This was new to me but I was right up for it, I was well excited. I felt like I was living the high life. It was quite a long drive but never boring; we chatted away and took in some of the most beautiful scenery. We started our drive from the centre of San Francisco and went over the Golden Gate Bridge. In the middle of the bay was the infamous Alcatraz Prison sitting there alone on a rocky cradle, and soon after the bay we hit the San Quentin area with its threatening signs telling people not to stop and pick up hikers . . .

We drove for about three hours, I guess, climbing slowly upward through the pine trees, the clean air rushing through our lungs. Although it was June there was a little snow still lying in small heaps on the roadsides. We reached the lake area at around 8.30 a.m. and booked ourselves into a really nice hotel called Harrahs. It was one of the best places I had ever stayed apart from my first New York experience. We were starving and dumped our bags quickly to catch breakfast. There was masses of food and it was so varied. The whole place was exceptionally clean. People were buzzing over the slot machines even at that time of the morning and I have to admit they held my attention for a lot of the time we stayed!

The ski slopes were around the other side of the lake and after an early night we set off there at 6.30 a.m., missing our breakfast and planning to eat when we got there. The drive on its own was awesome, the lake was so beautiful. 'I could live here, mate,' I said to Berry. We got to the slopes and parked the car. I jumped out of the vehicle and ran to look at the snow, so excited. Berry was his usual slow self.

I shouted, 'Come on – before it melts!'

Well, two weeks had passed and I had never worked so hard – I ached all over my body. Each night we went back to the hotel we just crashed for a couple of hours. It was great exercise. I always had a full body massage too at the hotel. The girl there was so good, she never quite took all the pain away, but relaxed the muscles so they at least had a chance. I lost a fortune on the machines at the hotel and decided I would never actually *win* money, I would always have to fight for it! Our final day came and we phoned The Man to tell him we were coming home (we always had to check in with him daily). We had contracted our soul to him and were under his control at all times. He knew more about us than we could remember about ourselves.

Our next fight date had been brought forward, so we only had nine days left to prepare, which meant that we had to cut short our trip and go into intensive training, and that meant almost living in the gym. Our gym was a purpose-built, private building within an old fruit-packing factory. When we got back, we were impressed to see that every discipline of fighting had been catered for inside. Every style known to us on the cult circuit was catered for and so it allowed us to train properly. Little were we to know at that time, though, that some sick mind in Nevada had devised yet another weird and wonderful style of fighting . . .

This time round, most of the squad was off to the San Diego area to fight, they often had Mexicans to fight down there and it was a great place to break a new fighter in. Although the Mexicans had great stamina, they were often undernourished and not very experienced, they were just desperate to earn some money, often impoverished illegal immigrants. So these were easy fights but not big money, so they were no good to me, of course. As for me, I was off to Nevada – to find the most horrific and hellish fight experience imaginable to anyone who was even slightly claustrophobic. The Sand Box.

The Man picked me up from my place that morning and we headed out to the small airstrip south of Modesto. The Man had his plane there. It was a small one with six seats, very flash. But it was also very uncomfortable. The seats were little bucket seats with canvas strung across two metal poles, like the little camping chairs you use for fishing. All over the instrument panel were little notes scribbled on paper and stuck down with Sellotape, like the pilot didn't know how to fly and needed directions. The Man stepped in to the back of the plane and I sat up front with the pilot. I was crapping myself. I wasn't a great flyer and hated heights. This thing didn't seem like it should be in the air to me.

We were all strapped in and the engines fired up. The whole thing shook, including me, and we began to taxi down the runway and had to park to wait for our orders. We sat there dwarfed against a jet plane. We barely came to the top of his wheels. The signal came over the radio and we were off.

The little plane ran along faster and faster until I thought the sound would make my eardrums burst, the nose lifted and seemed to be aimed straight up at one point. I was looking at the clouds and didn't know what to do. My arse seemed to grow fingers and gripped the seat as my knuckles went white against the handle in front of me. I couldn't hold on with enough parts of my anatomy to feel safe!

Once we were in the air, apart from being completely deafened by the engines I was much better. The Man and I just looked at each other and signalled a lot, shouting words that no one could really hear. I began reading every little note fixed in front of me. I watched the pilot's every move. I was thinking that if he died, I could at least attempt to take over. Who was I kidding? But at least it took my mind off things.

Suddenly the plane dropped, it seemed to go flat – straight down for about 50 feet or so. I screamed like a little girl and The Man grabbed me around the face from behind, his hands pressing against my eyes and nose. I felt a warm wetness propelled against my neck and a familiar smell. He had spewed. Now I was heaving heavily, smelling the pungent aroma and at the thought of someone's regurgitated food on my neck. I was sick, straight on to the floor in front of me. The poor pilot now became nauseous and was trying to look away, but the smell could not be ignored, and he too began to heave. There we were, thousands of feet above the rocky face of the desert, heaving, laughing and crying all at the same time. My fear had gone by now at least, but so had most of my breakfast. I just had to concentrate on keeping the rest down. When we calmed down, we continued the rest of the flight in silence and opened the small window vents. It was fucking freezing, and I mean *freezing*.

Flying over the Nevada desert was as boring as hell. My only interest was in when I was going to get my feet back on the ground and how that shit-heap stayed in the air. And then suddenly a deafening silence fell about us. We all looked at each other. Why was there no sound from the engine any more?

My heart stopped dead and I couldn't remember how to breathe. The plane's engine had stopped running and we now were flying what amounted to a very heavy glider.

'Don't worry,' said the pilot, cool as you like, 'it does this sometimes!'

He carried on in a very calm fashion, striking the start button, cranking the engine – but nothing was happening, except a little whirring sound. We continued to plummet downwards – fast, sickening, sinking. But the pilot remained cool. He cranked the engine time after time, but still no response. All the time I stared at the man's face and watched the coolness change to panic.

'Want me to get out and push?' I yelled.

All the time my breathing became more and more difficult. I

don't remember ever being this scared. I felt myself in danger of going into panic mode, but there was no way I was going to make a complete prat of myself – yet! I was saving panic for the last five hundred feet. Suddenly the engine coughed twice and re-started. I felt every muscle in my body relax and I breathed a sigh of relief.

The pilot smiled. 'Told you,' he said.

The voice of Buddy Holly left my ears. We had power again and were soon to land at our destination. I looked at The Man in all sincerity and said, 'I will *drive* home. There is absolutely no way I am ever going to fly back. I would sooner go back on a skateboard.'

'It'll take you two frigging days!' he said.

'I don't give a shit,' I replied calmly, 'you will never get me in that fucking thing again.'

He thought about it for a while, then said, 'I'll come with you.'

A car met us when we landed, I couldn't say it was an airport because it really wasn't, it was more like a home-made landing strip. The car must have been about 30 feet long, ebony black with highly polished paint-work and blacked-out windows. We got in. Wow, I thought. Deep-buttoned, off-white leather seating with black piping greeted us, with a matching carpet and a TV perched on a shelved section just above a softly-lit bar.

The drive was a long one, out to a timber shack and a huge barn painted red. The surrounding area was as rocky as a moon's landscape and all shades of red. There was little else close by the two buildings except for a water tower and a big old stainless-steel grain silo. That old silo was like an ear on a pig's arse. It just didn't belong there. The car pulled right up outside the shack and as I got out I caught sight of a huge trailer at the back end of the barn.

I noticed how quiet it was there. It was the first time I understood the phrase, 'so quiet it was deafening', the silence hummed in my ears, so strange. The heat was blistering. I could almost hear myself frying in the sun. We walked up the few steps to the door of the shack. It was not at all what I expected. Where was everyone? Our car drove off and I looked at my travelling companion.

'What's up, boss?'

He looked straight ahead and replied, 'There won't be anyone here until later tonight. The fight's tomorrow evening.'

I knew I wasn't going to fight until the next day anyway – I just wondered why we were all alone with no women draped around, and no one to pour drinks and cook food and carry bags. There were usually several people around. It was so weird.

We entered the shack. I could see immediately that inside it was hardly a shack. It appeared on first glance to be short of nothing in the way of luxury and amenities. There was a small lounge diner, a kitchen, bathroom, and three bedrooms. All the rooms were small in comparison to what I had enjoyed before but nonetheless they were comfortably furnished and short only of a television. We took a bedroom and threw our stuff on the bed, ready to sort out later. I wandered into the kitchen and opened the fridge to find that although it wasn't too well stocked, there was plenty of choice and enough for a couple of days. No beers, I thought, but soft drinks were stacked high, and plenty of ice. I poured a drink, turned on the little radio very low and stretched out on the couch as I listened to some soft country music.

As I kicked back there, I heard a vehicle approach and peeked out of the small window. It was another monster of a car. Three sharply dressed men stepped out and walked purposefully to the door. Without knocking they walked straight in.

The Man came from his bedroom, buttoning his shirt. He appeared to know all three of the men and was noticeably on his back foot in their presence. I watched as he went into grovel mode, I had never seen this before. These guys just had to be *big* money.

I was asked to go outside for a short time while the men 'discussed business'. I felt a little hurt at this suggestion. I was kind of getting used to be treated like a mini-star at these events. This brought me down with a bump. I really just felt like a bit of shit in their presence. I didn't question the request, though, and immediately left the building taking a cold drink with me.

After a while the door opened and The Man looked out with a huge grin. Things had obviously gone his way, which didn't surprise me at all – they usually did. He beckoned for me to come in. As I walked through the door, he put his arm around me. Had this happened several months ago I would have felt very uncomfortable but our relationship had moved on and I had become more educated in the ways of people's sexual preferences.

I was introduced to the men properly this time – they were the promoters of the event. We shook hands and they were off. I watched them as they disappeared back into their tank of a car without a glance back at us and I said, 'Fuck you too.'

'Well,' I said to The Man as he turned to come inside again.

'Well,' he replied and walked right past me.

'Oi! Hang on! I'm in the dark here. I need to prepare my mind for what's going down – you're not being fair to me,' I said.

He looked at me. 'When did I ever say this game was fair?' he replied.

'Look. If you want a win, and I know that you do, then I have to have every chance to pull it off, which includes peace of mind by knowing what's going down.'

The Man walked toward the door, saying, 'Come on then, but remember this is new to me too – don't go asking me loads of questions. All I can tell you is that you get three grand to fight and eight grand to win.'

'That'll do,' I said. 'What've I got to fight? A lake full of alligators?'

'Just don't go unreasonable on me when I show you what we're doing. Give it some thought before you react,' he replied.

We went down towards the rear of the big old barn. I could see nothing there but the grain silo grinning back at me, shining brightly in the sun of the mid-afternoon. We got closer and closer to the silo, it was clear now that was where we were headed.

We arrived there and the boss looked up, shading his eyes. Mine followed his. I wondered what I was looking for as I stared at the silo, like a huge funnel turned upside down with a tin can on top of it. There was a ladder fixed to the legs of this monstrosity, leading up to a platform outside with a small door hanging above it.

'That's it,' he said.

'That's what?'

'That's where you will be fighting. Inside the dome. It's the Sand Box.'

'Oh, fuck me. I gotta fight inside *that*?' I said as I leaned against one of its legs and burned my hand on the hot metal. 'I'll fry in there, it's a heat trap.'

'Come on, let's go look,' the boss replied without even acknowledging my words.

'You have got to be kidding me, boss, tell me it's a joke,' I begged.

The Man started to work his way up the ladder and I followed like a zombie, uneasy with the height of the thing, gradually allowing the reality of the thing to creep into my mind. I knew I had to do as I was told. I had no choices, they had been taken away from me as I joined the cult scene.

We reached the small platform and opened the door, entering the silo. Inside it was like Doctor Who's Tardis. It was huge, far bigger than it looked from the ground. Suspended mid-air was a platform that hung from huge springs. Someone had gone to a lot of trouble to design and make this thing. Above my head there were four CCTV cameras placed around the edge and in the middle there was a tube hanging from the ceiling.

The Man pointed out the cameras and explained that these would transmit the fight to the crowd sitting in the barn. Straight away I didn't like the idea. It was the crowd who kept me standing sometimes, even when I knew I was beaten and knocked out on my feet. The crowd somehow kept me going, only another fighter could understand that experience.

'What's the tube, then?' I asked.

'Well, above the tube are tons of sand. When the fight begins the chute will open and sand will fall from the tube, like an egg timer.'

'Fuck off!' I laughed again, nervous.

I suddenly felt the whole thing closing in on me. I couldn't breathe, I had to get out. The sweat was pouring from my body and the heat became unbearable. I rushed out the door and moved quickly down the ladder toward the ground. This time the height didn't bother me. I was more worried about the thought of being locked in that enclosure and the sand falling.

As I stormed back to the shack, The Man walked behind slowly, clearly allowing me time for thought and to come to terms with the idea. He was good like that, sensitive and understanding. He never came down hard on any of his fighters and allowed us to deal with stuff in our own time – just as long as it didn't take too long, of course.

I crashed through the door and paced up and down, moving to my own room when my boss joined me in the lounge. I needed to be on my own.

A couple of hours passed. I came out of my room very sheepishly. I knew I had acted foolishly and felt like a little kid.

'Sorry, boss,' I said. 'This is all new to me, it takes time to sink in, I guess it won't be so bad, it will only be for a few minutes.'

'It's new to me too, son. I knew you would get upset. I have to say I wouldn't fancy it a bit but you contracted for whatever came your way. We just didn't know how inventive these guys were going to get, did we?'

'Yeah, I know, I gotta swallow. I'll be all right, let's not talk about it any more. I will just do my job.'

'Fine with me, son,' he said. 'Come on, let's go outside again and I will show you what goes on here.'

We walked outside the cabin but my eyes kept being drawn to my new tomb. I was feeling sick.

The sun had gone down by now and it was quite chilly out. As we walked into the barn a huge RV drove by towards a space fenced off next to the cabin. Three men stepped out cockily. One looked across at me and gave me the stare-down. Prat. Another mountain of a man stretched as if he had travelled a long way and the third began shadow boxing. I just thought he looked stupid, really. The shadow boxer and the one who was staring laughed at me. I thought, yeah! Laugh all you want to, mate. I know what'll knock the smirk off of your faces. And I stared once again towards the silo, now standing as a huge shadow against the backdrop of the rock face behind it.

There were four more fighters to come before the event began. I guessed that the other stable of fighters were to stay in the huge trailer that was over behind the barn. I had met up with them all before at various events around California State. There were some really good men amongst them.

The Man and I continued on into the place where the crowd would watch the fighting. The seating inside was racked high and to the full breadth of the building. Although it was a shaded area it was so hot and the day's heat had remained within the open-sided building. There were huge TV screens hanging everywhere for the punters to sit and watch, set amongst the seated areas and the platforms set dotted around that were clearly where liquor would be served, although the booze wasn't around yet.

I can still picture it all so well, every arena I have ever fought in smelled the same, sounded the same and looked the same. There are the same baying voyeurs who call for blood, anyone's blood; the wannabe fighters who work in the cities all day and dream of belonging to the world I live in and have come to despise so desperately. There are the same girls darting up and down the seating areas with drinks and prize tickets, taking bets and flirting with the men, even floating off round the back or to a car to earn some extra bucks – even giving blow jobs in the stands. Still, we all have to earn our money somehow, I guess, and their way is no less principled than mine, I suppose. I guess some of the girls hate what I do. Writing this I suddenly realise that all of us who worked in the industry were whores to one degree or another: we were all selling our bodies, degrading ourselves as human beings for the carnal pleasures of those city men – those men who wouldn't piss on us if we were on fire or acknowledge us if we passed them where they live or work. What were we doing . . .? Mugs!

TWENTY

Up the Nose and
Over the Gums

The Man explained to me that there would be a total of four fights in the sand box and then there would be a girlie show which was set up on the stage area in front of the barn. There were lights everywhere on this stage, and poles, a cage and a strange-looking device covered in leather straps. I couldn't even guess what was going to go on there.

The night started at 7 p.m. sharp. First of all the fighters were paraded in front of the crowd, like slaves at an auction, just so they could all see what they were looking forward to and pick out who they were to bet on. Many would be regular fightgoers and would of course recognise most of the fighters and so know their strengths and bet accordingly. Others would be newcomers, business associates, bankers or guests of some of the larger business organisations here. They would just throw money on any one, they didn't care.

We perched ourselves on some old fencing and The Man gave me the run-down for the night. The first fight was starting at 7.30 p.m., and I was in the first tournament. I loved being first. The adrenaline was pumping nicely, the charlie was fresh up my nose and wiped on my gums. I would always be at my best when I was first up. My boss knew this and always tried to get me in the 'off position' as we called it. I was told to make the fight hard work if I was getting beat; to just hang in there as long as I could – and if I was winning then stretch it out more; take a few blows, like. After the fight I was to get back to the shack for a shower and change, then get out front and mix with the punters, do a PR job on them, help the girls – 'And behave yourself,' he added, knowing I was always a sucker for a woman's attention.

'There are some classy strippers here tonight, hands off,' he said. 'They gotta work the crowd and earn their money. If you hang around them, they lose big bucks here.'

The next day passed very slowly. None of the fighters talked much really, you daren't take the chance of getting fucked in a mind game out there. I just stayed in the shack all day and looked out occasionally to see figures slowly walking around in the heat. Some trained and some just sat and chatted to their stablemates. I was alone – except for The Man, of course, who slept most of the day away. Lazy sod.

This was a very important night for me. I had to redeem myself from my last defeat and also I needed to make a mark on the circuit to get better fight venues and bigger purses. This meeting was a great opportunity for me and after a lot of consideration I decided that the Sand Box would suit my style, it was close quarters with room to move.

Although this wasn't a huge fight meet, judging by the number of seats it was an important one. Fewer seats meant bigger ticket prices and bigger ticket prices meant a select crowd – important people who would talk about me and want to see me again if I did a good job. The Man told me that there were to be several big names from the movies coming along, including Jack Nicholson and Robert De Niro, which underlined just how important the night was in the history of the cult circuit.

Evening fell slowly. I watched as limousines and helicopters arrived one after the other, the cars lit up like Christmas trees, the choppers all brightly coloured. The passengers were not suited up but the clothes they wore were clearly designer, they were sharp. With every 'face' came an entourage of leeches scurrying behind them serving their needs. The men themselves were escorted by what seemed to be a hundred beautiful women. Once seated they were served drinks until the lights in the building dimmed and I could hear my heart shouting in my chest.

I had never felt so nervous as I did that night. The thoughts of the sand pouring down on me brought sweat to my body. I was dripping wet. I gathered myself before the parade commenced and took my first few hits of cocaine just to give me an edge. By now I was believing that I could take the drug or leave it, but in truth I was now reliant on it big-time.

We were all elegantly robed and walked in order of stable, marching in line and to the sounds of the deafening music that filled the air. We paraded in front of the stamping men and our robes were taken from us by some leggy beauties in evening gowns. This was so surreal. Here we were in the desert, on a tumbledown farm yet it had the effect and trimmings of a Las Vegas casino. We were extremely fit men, all of us – but obviously completely mad to be doing what we were about to do.

We were escorted by security men, all in dress suits and built like brick shit-houses. After our parade I got back to the shack and headed straight for the shower. I just wanted something cold and wet to pour on my heaving body. I was short of breath, coke did that to me sometimes, especially if it had been cut with speed which this stuff had.

After my shower I got back into my fighting gear. I hit another two lines and I was ready to fight the world. I had never felt so fit. I was still young, had trained hard and my body was at its best. I marched out of the shack and fixed my gaze on the silo which by now was lit from the outside with an assortment of coloured light effects and a huge strobe. The strobe affected me slightly, as the charlie affected my eyes, it made them more sensitive somehow but otherwise my senses were as keen as they ever had been. I had spent three days off of the coke so that I would get the maximum effect from it when I took it on the night, it felt so good.

I met with my opponent halfway to the Sand Box. I had fought him before twice, we had both tasted victory over each other but I knew his style and I knew I could beat him. I noticed a small trickle of blood on his top lip, clearly coming from his nose. That was to be my target. The membrane of his nose was collapsing through extended use of cocaine, he had obviously been banging it for a far longer time than me. If I worked on it it would open it up like a burst dam. When an opponent's nose is pouring with blood it gives the attacker three advantages over him:

1. He can't breathe properly and that puts the body into stress.

2. He can't resist the urge to wipe his nose and as he does so he loses both his guard and his attack.

3. It almost always demoralises a fighter when he shows first blood. It also enthuses the crowd, they love a bit of claret – and in this case I needed them on my side early on in the fight. Once they started chanting for me it would put me on top with the promoters.

I was very confident and my observations – taught to me by Denny in what seemed now another lifetime away – told me that this was to be my victory. Denny had showed me part of the psychological way of fighting. Always study your man. Take in the body language. See how edgy he is. Work with all the signs.

We reached the end of our short journey to the Sand Box. I was invited to go up the ladder first which I was glad to do. Being in the fight area first gave me another psychological advantage. I would be there when he arrived so it made it my domain; he was the intruder. I would have already had a chance to dance around in there, make myself at home and take in the work area. When he stepped inside he would see me and would not be able to afford to take his eyes off me. I, on the other hand, had time to look around and become acquainted with the place.

As my opponent came through the door, leaving the darkness behind him, I could study the frame of the man that I had to work with. The lights inside the silo were bright and shone down on us both hard. Fortunately there was some basic ventilation system operating but it was not nearly good enough to ease the discomfort of the extreme heat inside. I looked hard at my opponent, he seemed very uncomfortable with all this.

His receding hairline extended the frame of his tortured face, a face that had clearly been redesigned by his career. The drawn cheeks and lined features hinted at the extended abuse of drugs which was underlined by the thin trickle of crimson blood from his nose. His eyes were encircled by shrouds of dark skin and his thin lips were drawn tightly across his gumshield. I guess he stood around five feet seven and had the body of an athlete – not overly muscular but obviously fit. His body really didn't go with his face at all, it was like one of those kids' games where you stick a face on different bodies.

He began to dance around the platform area, jabbing and moving very swiftly. I tried not to look. I had the image of a beaten man in my head and didn't want to be impressed by any show of agility. I turned my back to him and waited for the red light to show, accompanied by a buzzer, which was our cue to go to war. I was hungry for the man's blood. I needed to see it flow to colour my own rage.

The light came on and I turned to face the man and fixed my gaze on him. The buzzer then went off and we flew at each other like men possessed. I was like shit off a shovel across that platform and slammed into the man at full thrust. I hit him as hard as I could, following through with my full body weight to carry the momentum, hoping he would go over so that I could get a few good kicks in to the head and upper arm. I wanted to inflict damage on this man quickly and have a clear and obvious win.

I wasn't thinking right. I really needed to let him have a little play so that the fight looked harder. It would do my credibility no good to show an easy fight, that would make my victory almost invalid. The man, though, showed fantastic balance and my efforts were foiled. I hadn't done enough and realised this wasn't going to go the way I had planned it but – hey! What else was new?

Suddenly I was aware of sand beneath my feet. I had momentarily forgotten that we were fighting in a glorified egg timer. I pulled back on my attack a little but kept the pressure on, following my man everywhere he went. He couldn't get away from me no matter what he tried. We were swapping blows at about an even rate and no man was on top, but I was doing all the chasing. However, these fights were not judged on points or who was the more aggressive fighter, they were won on the final result – who was knocked out or could no longer fight, and the winner just had to be me. It just *had* to be.

We fought towards the downwards flow of sand. It hit me full on the head as I passed under it. Christ, it was like being hit with a stone. It wasn't fine sand, it was more like small stones mixed with dust and it was a deep-red colour. The dust began getting down our throats. Both of us were struggling to breathe a bit and we were squinting to see through the clouds of dust. We kept having to spit, which is difficult with a gum shield. Sand had worked its way up inside the shield by now and the smallest grain felt like a rock. I eventually spat mine out; it was becoming more of a hindrance than an asset.

Suddenly the extractors must have kicked in properly and it was like a miracle being able to see again. We went into a tight clinch which I hated. I hate restrictions of any kind whether I am fighting or not, it always sends me a little crazy. I got all claustrophobic and my punches got a little wild as I struggled free. I stepped back from the grapple on my left foot and lunged forwards with a right straight, opening the little parcel of flesh in the middle of the man's face. As predicted, a fountain of claret oozed from his face, his nose poured and poured as if I had opened a tap. The balance had tipped my way.

I followed my punch with a flying nut. This was a treat to see – a speciality move that I had developed. Being shorter than most fighters I had to jump anyway when I wanted to plant the nut so I developed a move that displayed a little more elegance than a desperate launch. It was almost like a ballet move – a leap off one foot with a push from the other, hand reaching out to the back of the man's head bringing it forward to meet mine. My head would come back slightly, snapping from the neck as I would plant the nut firmly either on the opponent's snout or over an eye – whichever was going to do the most damage. In this case the eye was my target, just to give him something to really think about. His skin was resilient, though, and needed a second crack before it split.

By now we were fighting on a mound of sand. There was sand in my ears, up my nose, in my mouth and my eyes. This was getting desperate. The sand was getting deeper fast. We were both working hard to stay on our feet. It was getting tough to fight and my calves were aching now. Both of us were clearly struggling. Not through lack of strength, you understand, but through sheer effort to remain balanced. We were continually sinking up to our ankles.

The face I was looking at had become encrusted with sand, sticking to the gooey crimson fluid that was spread over it. It looked like a huge cold sore. I could no longer recognise the fighter. My head butt had landed nicely and brought the eyes up almost immediately and what with the sand and the swelling this man could barely see any more. My shortage of breath told me I had been in there long enough. This was the worst fighting experience I had ever had. Whoever thought this one up must have been a real sadistic bastard.

It was time to go home. I kicked the man straight up the nuts, brought my hands down in a double fist behind his head as he crumpled. He fell to his knees and I kicked him around the side of the head and then fell on his chest with my knees as he went over sideways. The wind rushed from his lungs in a fashion that I had never heard before. I thought he was going to be sick. While he was struggling for his life's breath I pushed sand into his mouth and eyes to blind and choke him and then punched him several times in the face. You must never back off when you believe a man is beaten or knocked out, he could be feigning. You had to make doubly sure. It's like that with professional hit men. They will shoot you twice in the body and twice in the head, they have to be sure. Their life, and at the very least their professional credibility, depends on it.

I was now buzzing, crazed with the effects of the cocaine. Nothing was going to stop me and nothing was going to hurt me. The charlie made me invincible. The man's hands were pawing at the sand in his face, he was spitting out lumps and his eyes must have been burning with pain. I just kept punching fuck out of him while he tried to breathe out of his ears – there was no other orifice left open. I had got him beaten. He lay there comatose, his body half buried in the sand. I jumped up and danced around the platform and ran over his sinking torso.

He wasn't moving a muscle and a little panic began to creep over me. Was he dead? No one came in to check like they would in the ring. Who was going to rescue him from this madman dancing around possessed? Should I drag him out of the sand and show compassion or should I pretend I didn't give a shit and just leave him there? The entertainer in me said, keep dancing. The man in me said, show some humanity. The decision was taken from me, though, as the door crashed open and two men came bursting in to the rescue. Feeling confident that he would be okay now, I got cocky again and gave one last show by kicking more sand over him.

They dragged the fighter to the door and fixed a harness around his body to lower him to the ground, after having first removed the sand that was left up his nose and in his throat. As I approached the door I heard a huge thud of machinery grinding into motion and the sand started to disappear. The floor was structured into a stainless steel louvre and as the sections opened the sand poured into a container below and was transported upwards on the outside via a conveyor system.

I was so glad to get out of that place. My victory seemed almost instantly unimportant to me when set against my relief at being free again. I scooted down the ladder and moved swiftly back to the shack. It was so cold outside now, there had been a severe drop in temperature. I crashed through the door and headed for the shower, pushing the lever almost before I had stepped inside. The gush of warm frothing water hit my face. I opened my eyes to wash them out. I sprayed the water up my nose, into my ears and drank what seemed gallons of it to clear my throat. It felt so good. I just leaned against the shower wall and slowly slid down into a sitting position.

There was a loud banging at the door, and my boss came barging in, full of the fight. You would have thought it had been *him* fighting.

I shouted: 'Pour me a drink please, boss – and plenty of ice.'

I came out of the shower and ran to my bedroom. It was so cold.

'Never mind the drink,' my boss said, 'there will be plenty out there. The crowd went wild over you. The promoters want you in their booth as soon as you are dressed.'

'Fuck 'em,' I said. 'They didn't want to know me earlier, now they want to parade me. Pour me a drink.'

'Okay, okay!' he said, 'but I'll bring some in, you can drink it while you are dressing. Don't get cocky now – the fight wasn't the important bit for you. How you conduct yourself for the rest of the evening is.'

I got dressed and finished my bourbon and coke. I wouldn't leave the room until I'd had another hit of charlie.

'There is a banquet laid out up there, fellah,' said The Man. That of course didn't mean a thing to me. I wasn't hungry, not just because I was stoned but because the adrenaline was pumping around my veins like oil from a well. My stomach was turning somersaults and my ears were ringing from a kick in the head. Still – I had to go and do my party piece.

The Man couldn't stop talking and was desperate for me to join the party in the private booth over at the main building. Once there I was given the respect I had expected on the initial meeting. The men were buzzing round me getting their fix and the girls were all over me giving me mine. These ladies were something else. They were class, just like the boss had said. These girls knew how to make their money and they didn't mind how they did it either. There were old men with ladies draped across them kissing, licking, pawing all over the place. So pathetic. It sickened me for sure. Profound thoughts struck me. Life is just a game and everyone's a player. The men thought they were winning and the ladies were convinced that they were. Everyone had what they wanted at that particular time. Nothing is forever except death – play the game and play it hard, take nothing seriously unless it's life-threatening. Every situation can be overcome once it is put into perspective. Fuck me, I'll be sounding like Confucius next.

Most of the men wanted to talk with me. I really felt on top of the world as I revelled in my fame. Jack Nicholson came over and mumbled a few words as did Steve McQueen. I was well impressed. I even spotted Joe Louis, the World Champion boxer, but he never spoke. I remember thinking what a sad man he looked. It appeared to me that everyone in the room was on cocaine (though not necessarily the celebrities). The supply was endless.

I eventually got back to the little house at about 4 a.m. Although I remember going in with a girl, that was unfortunately all I remember. I must have passed out. (I'll bet that went down well!) When I awoke she was gone. I still had my clothes on and was stretched out across the bathroom floor with the door locked.

Our car called for us that afternoon around 2 p.m. We were taken to a little town called Boulder City where we picked up a hire car. The Man and I pulled in for a bite to eat and some coffee. He made a few phone calls and then we hit the road home. Our first stop was Barstow where we stopped for a while for another feed and we then planned to head for Bakersfield where we would stop for the night. We were both still knackered after the partying.

It was after we had got ourselves settled in the motel at Bakersfield that I heard the most devastating news since my granddad died. My boss called in with a face as long as the West Coast. Berry had died. He had fought Gladiator and was caught heavily with a club across the underside of his rib cage. He'd suffered a punctured lung, internal bleeding and stuff I couldn't pronounce. In effect, he died by drowning in his own blood. I was devastated and just wanted to drive home. My boss wouldn't hear of it and he was of course quite right. I would have killed someone – and myself the way I was feeling. I was in no state to drive.

When we finally did reach home, The Man wanted me to go back to his house and stay for a while. I of course declined and said that I would sooner be in the place where Berry and I had had so many long talks into the night. In those rooms we'd put the world to rights, discussed personal problems, laughed and cried. I wanted to be there, where I was closer to him. His accident was passed off as 'a motoring incident' and all was forgotten. The lads all dealt with the death in a matter-of-fact way. It was expected at some time or another. Me? Well, I was hit hard. I had shared some very personal times with this proud and gentle man, I was so, so sad. I just cried and talked to him as if he was there. I even got drunk with him on the second night.

It was left up to me to get all Berry's things together. I wouldn't have had it any other way in fact. There wasn't much. As I cleared his cupboards and drawers I felt like a sneaky thief. I truly felt as if I was dipping in to his private stuff while he was out. Such a strange feeling. I found a large, wooden box at the top of his wardrobe, got it down and opened it carefully. Inside the box were his medals and the ribbons from his army uniform. He even had a medal of valour. This man had been a fucking hero, surviving Vietnam to die in such a futile way, for entertainment's sake. What was it all about? Who knows? Not me, that was for sure. My mind was well and truly upside down and cocaine my only escape.

I parcelled all his belongings into one box and put them into the car. I had found the address of his ex-wife and was going to take the stuff up to Ohio to give to his kid, and to tell him great stuff about his dad. I sat in the car and looked at the box thinking that that was a man's life sitting there, all in one little box. I just started to cry uncontrollably. I had never cried like this before in my life. When I look back I don't know if I was crying for Berry or for myself. How big would *my* box be? Who would send my stuff home? I had no one there who would have been interested. Would anyone even send a note to my parents? Berry was all I had. I suddenly became very angry and punched the dashboard of the car. *How dare he*? How dare he leave me alone? How dare he give me this poxy job to do? I hurt so bad.

I had faced the fiercest of men in the ring. I had looked death in the eye and had survived a plane trip that frightened the shit out of me – but there was no way that I was man enough to make that drive and tell that kid that his dad had died. I would have had to lie about the way he died, which perhaps wouldn't have been so bad because I could justify that bit – but I just couldn't face it. I convinced myself that it was best done by the boy's mum. She would know how to do it. Mums always do, don't they?

And that thought began to set me off thinking about my own mum, my family and what I was missing. I suddenly became very lonely and hit the charlie again as I drove to the mailing office to send my friend's life home to his son. After that I just kept on driving until I hit the coast up at Carmel where I found somewhere to stay for a while. I didn't tell anyone where I had gone, or if I would be back. I had the clothes I stood up in, my banking books and about 1500 dollars in cash. Apart from peace of mind, that was all I needed right now. Oh yes . . . and I had about seven grams of my old pal charlie.

TWENTY-ONE

Drugs, Sex and Jesus

I spent over a year on this huge collision course. I was completely fucked up with charlie and booze. I began to use a little trick I learned from another fighter. Whatever drink I ordered I would ask for a shot of blackcurrant in it. It disguised the blood droplets from my almost constant nosebleed that would colour any drink I had.

I took a couple of weeks out. I just spent time alone in Carmel. Most of the day I was on the beach. It was very overcast. One day a young girl came and sat with me. She looked like something from the '60s: beaded hair, headband, more beads. Her skirt was very short and showed she was wearing no underwear. She wore a thin loose top that allowed the pinkness of her nipples to peek through. She was very pretty and spoke quietly. I wasn't much for conversation though and, in any case, outside the world of horror that I was wrapped up in I was always very shy around women. I did have great respect for them, though, the way I was brought up in my culture. This girl was very different to anyone I had met. She was delicate and soft. I felt a great sense of peace coming from her that washed over me making me calm. Even my breathing became noticeably slower.

We chatted for hours about all sorts of things but ended somehow talking about the Lord and what he meant to us. I got completely wrapped up in her words. They consumed me completely. It all made so much sense. I needed something to believe in. I had completely lost my way. Everything was upside down and sideways. Nothing made sense any more. The drugs were eating my brain and owned my soul.

The girl introduced herself as 'Sweetness'. She explained that it wasn't her real name, it was given to her by her brother at somewhere called 'The House'. I was a bit puzzled but was too tired to ask for explanations. A couple of her friends came over and called her away.

'Will I see you again?' I asked.

She kissed me gently and said, 'Think of my kiss and you'll see me always.'

That was too weird for me, mate. She was beginning to scare me now. I thought she was tripping but she was serious.

She said, 'You can come with us if you want.' I said I couldn't but that I would be here tomorrow if she was around. She disappeared as quietly as she'd come.

The next day I was sat back on the beach. The same place. Six-pack by my side, just chilling and looking out to sea. I felt soft hands cup themselves over my eyes. I turned and looked up. It was Sweetness coming back to talk to me. We spent the whole day sitting, touching and, inevitably, kissing. She was like no woman I had ever held. She felt fragile. Her kiss was passionate, firm yet gentle. Her voice was soft and her words mesmerised me as I looked into those huge, liquid, bovine-brown eyes. I was falling in love. I went with her that evening, back to The House, an old, grey, wooden building housing about 12 people, situated on a small side-road in Monteray, close to the beach. Rooms were communal. There were two little girls there around two years old which gave it a real familiar, homely feeling. Joss sticks were burning and there was very little furniture to speak of. I could feel the peace as soon as I walked through their back door.

The pungent odour of dope burning filled my nostrils. Sweetness saw me sniff at the odour and asked if I objected to smoking dope.

I replied, 'Object? Lady, it became my saviour some nights!'

She held my hand like a butterfly wrapping its wings around my fingers, and led me to a small room with a blanket over the window and a mattress on the floor covered in various colours and types of material. I settled down and she stepped out of her flimsy clothes, floating downwards towards where I lay, getting down on top of me. We made love in a way I have never done before. It was something else. It was unhurried, searching and fulfilling at every stage. It was usually a 'crash-bash' experience for me – handfuls of this, mouthfuls of that – but she showed me how to explore, to visit every part of her body as she did mine. We made love all night. I'd never felt this good without snorting up. We must have smoked more dope that night than I have ever smoked. One after the other. The next day I went back to my apartment in Modesto, got the rest of my valuables, a few items of clothing and then left for The House. I said nothing to anyone – no goodbyes, kiss-my-arse – nothing.

Moving into the commune, I found a peace that I had never known. Drugs, sex and Jesus were in my life. I was off the charlie within the next two months, although I still smoked dope. (I cannot stand the smell of ordinary cigarettes, funny that.) My inner spirit was becoming my own again and my experiences with Sweetness took me to a higher plain each time. She became my spiritual guide. We spent every moment together. I learned so much about the needs, thoughts and spirit of man. I became close to the Lord and let him into my life. We would spend hours praying, talking and making love. It was all so perfect. Eventually I began to go out on the street with the group talking to people, young and old. We all moved into a bigger property as our number grew and after several months I found my money gradually dwindle to almost nothing.

I had started with about 18,000 dollars cash. I had sent a good stash home to the UK to stop it going up my nose. Berry had seen to that for me. He always looked after me and my money, trying to keep me straight. I had paid for a lot of food and fuel in the little commune. I had been slowly sucked dry of my cash. I didn't even see it happening. I was glad to get my life back, though, so I didn't begrudge it. I guess on reflection 15 or 16,000 grand was cheap for a life.

I had got into meditation and self-control, learned how to control breathing, pain levels and blood flow. It was amazing. I could get my headaches to disappear in a few minutes which was great. (I was getting quite a few of those at around this time – and stomach pains.) I started really learning about myself. I mean my *real* self. My body, secrets I had inside me that I didn't know about. This was some powerful stuff.

The leader, if you could call him that, was known as The Way – no doubt a little tag that he thought of himself. Now I look back on his name it's laughable, but at the time it was completely acceptable. He used to be a psychologist and had learned mind games – tricks you'd never see coming. He was really clever at manipulation.

As I got more and more into the Lord and meditation I saw less and less of Sweetness – until one day she turned up at The House with a new disciple, a young girl of about 18. I found them both experiencing each other sexually in my bed. I felt weird. What should I do? If Sweetness had been with a bloke I could have had a row but what could I say to a girl in there with my bird? I just didn't know how to deal with this. I walked straight in the room and Sweetness looked up slowly, smiled and held out her hand.

'Join us,' she said in her calm, quiet voice.

'You must be fucking joking,' I blurted back, spluttering with panic. I felt hurt, disgusted. I grabbed her arm and pulled her outside.

The Way came over to get between us. 'You see – this is a part of learning and acceptance,' he said and he started on about the Lord and trying to justify what they were doing. I turned and looked him straight in the eyes.

'Fuck you and fuck your Lord, you perverse bastard.'

The man inside me had risen. I was back. The others in The House stood and stared at me. I went outside and sat on the porch. I began to realise that what I had gone through was a sort of recovery programme. I was grateful it was now time to call 'time'. I thought about this stage of my life a lot later and this is my explanation for the whole affair, that it was a recovery programme – it's very simple but then I'm a simple man. This'll probably remind most of you of those experiences in life when you're in trouble and you turn to God.

Can you remember running from the police, or one of your parents and hiding, saying, 'Please, God, if you let me get away with this I'll help my mum, I'll go to church,' or some other blood-sworn promise? And then when you got away with your crime of course you got all brave again and went: 'Fuck 'em – that showed them. They can't get me!' and forgot all about your panicked promises. Well that's what I had done. I kissed Sweetness on the lips with a full embrace of gratitude for all she had done and for all we had shared. 'Thank you,' I said quietly.

I had been in trouble, my head was fucked up. I had nowhere to go with my life. A way out had appeared. I made all my promises to the Lord and to myself. Suddenly I discovered I didn't need him any more. And several months down the line I was being all cocky again, thinking 'Fuck 'em', just as I did as a child. I was my own man again, looking for a new adventure – although I remained quite into that meditation stuff. It could be useful. I remembered all the talks with the psychologist and the things he told me. I thought then that I would like to know more.

I hit the coach station and travelled down to San Diego. I didn't really like the place at first. It was full of illegal immigrants and I always felt under threat somehow there too. I couldn't settle. But I needed some money and San Diego was the place to find black-market work.

I found a small room in the old-town part of San Diego. The area was quite pretty and was safer in comparison to the rest of the district. I had a small amount of money left, about enough to see me through two months if I was careful, but I needed more. I couldn't go home skint, but first I needed to eat. I wandered down to the wharf area and found a fish restaurant.

Well – happy coincidences were at work yet again, and I managed to land a job in that very fish restaurant at which I dined that day – starting the day after. It was just coming up to Labour Day so it would be a busy weekend ahead.

San Diego started to grow on me. I made a couple of friends but kept myself to myself, really. I found out about a course in a local paper, learning Counselling Psychology and started studying. This took me through another two-year period until I became qualified to certificate standard, which is similar to a pre-degree standard in the UK. These adult education programmes soon became addictive to me and I found myself leaning towards counselling drug abusers and dysfunctional families. I made my mind up that that was what I was going to do when I came back home to the UK.

The time to return home came eventually. I was missing it terribly and I felt that after all I had been through I was at last an adult. I had a skill to share and the dedication to do the work. Since my own life was nearly destroyed by drugs I felt this compulsion to help others who hadn't found their 'Sweetness'. I made my mind up to head off home. And this time it would be for good! The life waiting for me in the UK was to be as bizarre as that which I had left behind. I began to visit a fight venue in Ilford, where good men like Roy Shaw, Danny Chippendale, Brian Hall, Steve 'Columbo' Richards and Lloyd Duncan fought, watched closely by other fighters who were to challenge them later on such as Lenny McClean, Harry Starbuck, Donny Adams and Cliff Fields. These were the men breathing life into the UK's unlicensed and bare-knuckle fighting arena. They were tough men with a mission. When I say 'tough', though, that didn't mean they had no heart. I recall a benefit boxing promotion held on Canvey Island, Essex for the unlicensed and bare-knuckle fighter Donny Adams. The benefit night followed Donny's death from a heart attack and was to raise money for his widow whom he loved dearly. The night was well attended by the fight fraternity and one man in particular made his presence known. The dominating figure of Roy Shaw appeared at the event and donated a portable television to be auctioned – however, he seemed not to be able to part with it as he kept bidding to buy it back! And then each time he bought it back, he gave it again as a donation. Eventually he paid £3,500 for it. This was the type of man you'd be dealing with; old-school values from men with pride, passion and honour in their hearts. I remember also Lenny McClean, fighting then under the guidance of a very young Frank Warren. One of McClean's training techniques as I remember was to put a rope around his waist and pull a Mini van around the perimeter road of Victoria Park in Old Ford Road, East London, with Frank Warren at the wheel.

A respected unlicensed fighter introduced me to a comedian who worked the fight venue at The Kings in Ilford. It was this comedian's misfortune and seemingly impossible job to have to warm up and entertain the partially pissed and mostly unruly punters filling the venue – some waiting for blood and some offering it. But controlling them with biting comedy and lightning repartee, he soon gained their respect and could do almost what ever he wanted with them.

The introduction to these people was probably the greatest favour anyone could ever have done for me and I always say it saved my life. I admired so much what this comic did with words. This was my very first realisation of just how futile and pointless violence was, and that there were many other ways to gain respect, dignity and above all to be liked. (I have not named either of the men here who changed my life so as not to cause them any embarrassment or 'name drop' to enhance any part of the story by using their fame. They know who they are and of my gratitude to them.)

The comedian turned my life around by teaching me a new career in entertainment. It was like a breath of fresh air, giving me a new grip on life, a new angle to explore. I was so impressed with the comedy scene I just had to join it, meeting a young Jim Davidson serving his apprenticeship while he was working as a driver for the comedian Monty Wells. I worked also with Bobby Davro at the Black Cat in Streatham where he was starting his career appearing in a drag revue which included a great old artist who worked by the name of Mrs Shufflewick. There are so many stories to tell as these great comics of today climbed their respective ladders towards fame.

I have worked with famous faces past and present and enjoyed every second, but the road that led me to where I am today has been a strange and crooked one. I've had cocktails at Buckingham Palace, rubbed shoulders with distinguished persons, partied with top UK entertainers. I've been involved in the world of both professional and amateur boxing. But eventually my experience with some of the country's less-talked-about criminals convinced me that crime and violence is just not my game – although a little skulduggery still excited me and my life's path continued to wander indiscriminately. But *that* is all another story!

.INSANITY.

CRIMINAL-LUNATIC-ASYLUM.

" BiLLY CRiBB"

Your Padded Room Awaits

Yours in Madness
and Respect

Charlie Bronson
2000

**A personal message from a pal (Charlie Bronson) who is misunderstood.
See you at your coming-home party Charlie. Keep strong!**

efits that workers are likely to be predisposed to
e action for the purposes of improving their lot.
s movements have been able to sustain popular
imarily because their leadership, to a varying
able to respond to the ideological and institutional
e occurred within capitalist society during the
conomic growth. If, during the earlier decades of
ntury, the forces of structural change operated to
f collective organization, socio-economic changes
eir disadvantage in recent years. This is shown by
level of trade union density in Britain (Gospel and

44.4
43.7
49.4
53.2
56.0
53.8
51.4
48.8

changes:
   +1.5
   +7.6
   −7.2

pment of capitalism brought about the concentration
n within large-scale industrial corporations. This was
cause of the economies of scale associated with Fordist
production. The de-skilling of work tasks encouraged
ment of occupational solidarity and it was within such
that labour unionism developed as a movement.
it had consisted of little more than collectivities of
kers who tried to protect their economic self-interests
de-based forms of collective action. But with the growth
le corporations organized upon the principles of scien-
gement, there was a rapid growth of labour unionism
i-skilled workers. These unions pursued the interests of
in the workplace and of workers in society in general. In

Even in factories where Fordist principles are most pronounced
and where trade unionism has obtained a high degree of worker
allegiance to enable it to bargain effectively with management, it has
failed to pose a fundamental threat to capitalist forms of ownership
and control. Profit margins may sometimes have been squeezed and
management may have been compelled to develop countervailing
strategies of control but, on the whole, organized labour has been less
effective than many radical writers would have hoped; certainly, in
the post-war conditions of Western capitalist society. This is because
'individualism' as a reality of everyday life will always be more salient
in personal consciousness than ideals of collectivism. This is
compatible with the predominant beliefs of Western capitalism and
constitutes the basis of liberal democracy as a pluralistic, participa-
tive political system (Mann, 1970). Political appeals are directed to
individuals in terms of their *personal* circumstances and it is by
reference to these that citizens vote and exercise their choices
between political parties.

It is these factors, coupled with feelings of personal well-being and
opportunity, that have sustained capitalism as a socio-economic and
political order. Despite the many deprivations experienced in both
the workplace and the wider society and notwithstanding the glaring
socio-economic inequalities and the injustices of class encountered
by many groups of wage earners, the development of capitalism
within the twentieth century has, in absolute if not in relative terms,
improved the opportunities and rewards enjoyed by the broad mass
of populations. This, together with the ideological impact of
capitalist ideals and assumptions, makes it rather surprising that
organized labour, in the form of trade unionism and political parties,
has been able to obtain the support that it has from the working class.
It may be suggested that a major reason for this is the very
*de*radicalization of working class movements that has occurred, since
without this their precarious legitimacy would have been even more
eroded than it has been during the post-war era of capitalist economic
growth.

Much has been written about the deradicalization of working-class
movements and the factors that underlie it. For some, the
explanation is to do with the bureaucratization of political parties and
trade unions, which has the effect that elected leaders and appointed
officials cease to represent the interests of their rank-and-file

members (Mann, 1973). This is largely because they become incorporated within negotiating processes and institutional structures, which affects their understanding of their members' interests. The outcome is the dilution of radical policies, with working-class leaders developing a vested interest in maintaining the status quo. Such a view is sometimes extended to emphasize how working-class leaders can exploit their positions for personal gain, an interpretation that has, of course, obtained greater credence since the developments in Eastern Europe of the late 1980s. In these, it seems that the abolition of capitalist orders led to the setting up of regimes in which party functionaries and so-called working-class leaders could appropriate resources for their own advantage and self-interest. That this did occur is likely to have longer-term effects for the political objectives of working-class movements in Western capitalist countries. Thus it is probably that, in order to obtain popular support, Western labour movements will need to abandon policies whose implementation would lead to centralized state ownership and bureaucratically organized forms of planning and control. The legacy of Eastern European socialism, with its tendency to totalitarianism and the curtailment of individual rights as expressed through state control over personal choice and freedom, has been to impose severe constraints upon the political objectives that Western working-class parties can now legitimately pursue. The full implications of the historical developments that have occurred in Eastern Europe over recent years, to say nothing of those within the Soviet Union itself, for working-class political movements in Western capitalist countries have yet to be assessed.

If there are those who argue that the deradicalization of working-class movements is a function of their bureaucratization and of their leaders pursuing interests removed from those of the rank-and-file, there are others who suggest that these movements have had to redefine their earlier radical goals because of the changing material circumstances and personal aspirations of their members (Marshall *et al.*, 1988). Since they are incorporated within the institutional and ideological framework of capitalist society, it is hardly surprising that this should have occurred. The economic growth generated by the class relations of capitalist corporations may exploit workers and enhance the wealth of shareholders. But this exploitative relationship continues to bring about improvements in the living

standards of the broa
ations in rates of econo
ment and, further, des
material conditions of
historical points of ti
absolute living standar
same time, despite per
tunity and the ability of
their privileged position
corporations, state insti
omic growth within cap
numbers of people to fee
within open, democratic s
with those encountered by
their families.

Because of the tendency
evaluating personal success
structurally determined ine
tween groups are seen as les
are made, they are likely to b
than those associated with the
relations. Most people are
opportunities of various group
gender, age, occupation, skill
ing to social class. Even wher
should not be assumed that th
resentment. On the contrary,
self-help in capitalist society,
claims, are likely to generate the
the disadvantages experienced by
their own failings and shortcomi
features of the socio-economic o
when workers acknowledge that
within class relations, this need no
generated – intense feelings of rese
in relatively isolated instances and,
regarded as a matter of fact, take
everyday working life (Nichols and
the overall costs of particular worki

outweigh the ben
engage in collecti
If working-clas
support, it is p
degree, has been
changes that ha
post-war era of e
the twentieth ce
the advantage o
have acted to th
the trends in the
Palmer, 1992):

1960
1965
1970
1975
1980
1982
1984
1986

Percentage
1960–9
1970–9
1980–6

The devel
of productio
necessary be
methods of
the develop
enterprises
Previously
skilled wor
through tra
of large-sc
tific mana
among ser
employee

terms of the latter, alliances with radical political parties or the setting up of union-sponsored political parties were often pursued.

While the nature of class relations in the workplace established the preconditions for working-class solidarity, concomitant developments outside work reinforced this tendency. The process of industrialization and the expansion of capitalist economic production entailed rural–urban migration and the growth of large-scale urbanism. The creation of an urban proletariat brought about the workers' dispossession of their traditional means of subsistence, which were derived from petty property ownership and their traditional productive skills. Instead, they became dependent upon the sale of their labour power as the sole source of their livelihoods. With workers concentrated within rapidly growing urban areas, networks of social relationships emerged, which often incorporated work colleagues, neighbours and others who were subject to the similar class relations of domination and exploitation. Hence, the integration of common work and non-work experiences served to foster personal identities and social networks that emphasized the values of mutual help and working-class solidarity. The setting up of workingmen's clubs, workers' educational associations, trade unions and local branches of the Labour Party enhanced feelings of class affinity as well as the necessity of collective action if self-improvement was to be pursued. In this sense, therefore, working-class collective action, as expressed in trade unionism and support for the Labour Party, has been steeped in instrumental rather than ideological motives. With very few exceptions, there is little to suggest that rank-and-file members of working-class movements in Western capitalist countries have been committed to revolutionary political change. Commitment to labour unionism and to working-class political parties has been for the purposes of improving specific and particular work and employment conditions and of extending the role of the state in the provision of health, education, welfare, housing and social services. There have been virtually no rank-and-file demands for the transfer of private ownership, in the form of the nationalization of productive industries, to more publicly accountable organizations. Certainly, this does not appear to have been the case in the countries of Eastern Europe, Britain, Italy or France, where during the immediate post-war decades, nationalization was pursued as a political goal by working-class parties, reflecting the aspirations of intellectuals, party officials and leaders rather than of rank-and-file members.

If developments until the 1960s offered favourable opportunities for the growth of labour unionism and, associated with this, flourishing working-class political parties, these have diminished during the past decades. It was mentioned earlier that the increasing strength of organized labour compelled corporate managers to implement counter strategies during the 1960s and 1970s because of the increasing frequency of wage demands, unofficial disputes and union-sanctioned strikes. Profit margins declined and the economics of scale, one of the key features of scientific management, were not fully realized because of disputes over payment systems, productivity levels and worker output. In short, organized labour was perceived to be challenging the prerogatives of management and its methods of control. Rarely, however, did it aim to take over these functions; instead, its purposes were more instrumental and geared to the personal material needs of rank-and-file supporters. Nevertheless, management in large-scale corporations was forced to implement changes that, together with other ideological and institutional trends within the capitalist order, have undermined the pre-conditions for working-class solidarity. These have brought about the fragmentation of any previous semblances of class and occupational solidarity.

One of the more important of these has been the abandonment of the more rigid forms of Fordist principles of management control and their replacement by systems that extend responsibility, autonomy and working flexibility to employees. Through 'job enrichment' and 'quality of working life' schemes, managerial strategies for improving productivity and profit margins have been directed towards the implementation of high performance work systems, total quality management, just in time management, and so on (Buchanan and McCalman, 1989). With the adoption of these practices, the more extreme forms of the division of labour have been abandoned and individual piece rate systems abolished. In their place, a greater emphasis has been put upon team work, task flexibility and group-based payment systems. As part of such initiatives, there are attempts to obtain a greater degree of worker commitment through involvement in first-line management decision-making. As a prerequisite for the adoption of these managerial practices, there is often the setting up of 'single union' plants, sometimes on green field sites, so that traditional union loyalties are circumvented. This is reinforced by recruiting younger workers, usually school-leavers, who have few trade union loyalties. Such developments, although they may not prevent the formation of limited forms of worker solidarity in the shape of close-knit work teams, nevertheless inhibit the growth of more broadly based forms of worker solidarity (Wickens, 1987). Certainly, the roots of traditional trade unionism, in both their institutional and ideological forms, are eroded as corporate leaders, in their attempts to impose organizational cultures that are intended to emphasize the common interests of management and workers, revert to repackaged forms of industrial paternalism. Inspired by Japanese management techniques, which have been imitated by their American counterparts, senior managers are persuaded to develop a range of ideological and organizational techniques whereby workers are more inculcated with corporate values and ideals (Pascale and Athos, 1982). Thus, with the weakening of trade unionism, the exploitative nature of class relations within capitalist corporations is increasingly hidden by management rhetoric, although not entirely so, if only because the material circumstance of daily work serves as a reminder to both managers and workers that organizational consensus is extremely precarious and always subject to rupture.

These trends are being reinforced by a number of institutional and ideological changes that inhibit the appeals of class solidarity. The break-up of traditional working-class communities is being brought about by large-scale economic restructuring, the decline of manufacturing industries, population shifts between and within countries, town planning, urban renewal schemes and the spatial effects of 'improving' road transport systems in towns. The decline of the traditional manufacturing industry has been particularly significant in its consequences for labour movements since it was within this economic sector that the conditions of work and employment offered the most favourable circumstances for collective organization both within and beyond the workplace. But the decline of community and neighbourhood relationships, bringing in its wake the emergence of more privatized and individualized life-styles, has had important effects. The break-down of social networks has led to the destruction of personal support systems, which has reinforced the vulnerability of sections of the working class to poverty and economic marginality (Seabrook, 1984). This, in turn, has exaggerated their dependency upon state-financed health and welfare systems, their experience of which has added to their feelings of personal subordination. The provision of state services according to Fordist, bureaucratic principles has added to working-class patterns of economic and social dependency which, during the 1970s, nurtured a growing resentment towards state institutions and their provision of services of all kinds. At the same time, deprived groups have been compelled to develop strategies for personal survival, whether they are single parents, lone pensioners, homeless youths or the mobile unemployed in search of work (Harrison, 1985). Thus, structural changes have affected the nature of personal relationships and social networks and have led to a growing emphasis upon the values of self-reliance and the overriding importance of self-interest. This, of course, was quickly identified and nurtured by the Conservative Party in Britain, the Republican Party in the United States and other bourgeois political parties in Europe. In a sense, therefore, the emergence of the new right as an ideological force of the 1980s was an *effect* of structural changes in society rather than a *cause* of them. Once the new right became accepted as a major political ideology, its ideals became incorporated within political objectives that have had far-reaching effects for the material conditions of the working class. By exploiting its appeals to individualism and personal self-interest, it has been able to challenge the underlying assumptions of the welfare state and attack the ideological roots of political collectivism upon a broad front.

In the immediate post-war era, the growth of organized labour and its increasing economic and political influence brought about the development of socio-political orders that some commentators described as corporatism (McCrone *et al.*, 1989). In many ways, this embodies what can ultimately by achieved by labour movements within the parameters of the capitalist system. Corporatism consists of structures at the levels of the capitalist enterprise and the national economy, incorporating the interests of capital, labour and the state. In essence, it is a model of socio-economic and political organization that functions on the basis of collective representation and, in fact, corporatist structures are largely unnecessary when working-class movements are weak and underdeveloped. It is only when workers' interests become articulated within influential collective movements that it is necessary for capitalist interests to form employer organizations. This is particularly so when there are state institutions that also incorporate and protect the interests of workers. Although the state may be functional to the needs of capital, it also incorporates the interests of workers, if only for the long-term stability of the capitalist order. Whether the growth of the state during the post-war decades can be explained according to its functions for capital or in terms of its responses to working-class demands, it is evident that it does provide a range of collective services that benefit workers. Hence, it can be argued that the growth of the welfare state does reflect the increasing influence of labour movements, and when this power is curtailed, as in Britain in the 1980s, it becomes possible for the activities of the state to be cut back and for its role within the economy to be severely curtailed.

The decline of corporatism in the 1980s seems to be directly associated with the weakened influence of labour movements. Representatives of organized labour are now less involved in the governmental process and their contribution to national economic management has been acutely reduced. Accordingly, it is now argued that the state's only legitimate role is to provide a range of support services to the market economy, instead of the more 'directive' function it undertook during the earlier corporatist post-war era.

Such a change in the legitimate role of the state, as highlighted in the arguments of the new right, has had ramifications for the work and employment conditions of large sectors of the working-class (Hudson and Williams, 1989). Conservative governments, incorporating many of these values within their legislative programmes, have not only curtailed the influence of trade unionism and, hence, its capacity to negotiate effectively with management, but also repealed or weakened a number of legislative measures in such areas as health and safety, employment protection and equal opportunities. Further, the demise of corporatism and prevailing political notions that capital and labour should negotiate agendas of 'shared' objectives has removed from industrial debate the ideals of worker participation, co-determination and joint negotiation. If such values do persist, they are more likely to be found in large multinational corporations than in small or medium-sized enterprises. Even in the former, managerial objectives are overwhelmingly dominant, although often concealed within rhetoric that appeals to corporate loyalty, harmony and shared values.

The dismantling of corporatist decision-making mechanisms, at both the national and the company level, has curtailed the influence of organized labour and enabled capitalist self-interest to be more vigorously pursued in an unrestrained fashion. The post-Fordist flexible firm, in terms of its internal decision-making processes, is in many ways, an expression of this. Equally, the rapid growth of sub-contracting, franchising and the use of 'self-employed' workers on the basis of fixed, short-term contracts is a reflection of the ways in which management can pursue its goals unfettered by the demands of organized labour. An outcome of such developments has been the segmentation of labour markets into 'core' and 'periphery' or 'primary' and 'secondary' sectors. If employees in the former enjoy relatively secure jobs and acceptable working and employment conditions, the latter are more likely to be subject to deprivations associated with the temporary or uncertain nature of their employment. Without the protection of influential unionism and because the state has curtailed its interventionist economic role, such employees are left to pursue their own 'self-reliant', personal survival strategies. Trends in Britain during the 1980s suggest that the consequences are greater inequalities and the emergence of sub-strata within the working class of those who are economically, politically and socially disengaged from the institutional orders of society (Brown and Scase, 1991). In most of the countries in Europe, these sub-strata consist of semi-skilled and unskilled service sector employees, who tend to be women, ethnic minorities, school leavers and pre-retired older men.

It would seem that collective working-class challenges to class-related inequalities have been highly limited, particularly during the closing decades of the twentieth century. If in earlier periods the industrialization process created large-scale productive systems, which in turn offered favourable conditions for the growth of labour organizations, this no longer seems to be the case. If the major achievements of working-class political parties has been the creation of the welfare state and the establishment of post-war corporatism, developments in the 1980s have witnessed their demise. Hence, the roles of trade unionism and of labour and social democratic political parties have changed and they are now compelled to pursue very different objectives from those in earlier decades. Their commitment to equality, welfare and wealth distribution is unlikely to be embodied in the creation of centralized state institutions of the sort set up in post-war Europe. The large-scale nationalization of privately owned assets and the formation of state capitalist enterprises are no longer legitimate strategies for labour movements. Aims that emphasize the 'peaceful transition' from capitalism to state socialism are no longer on the agenda – particularly in view of the totalitarianism, political corruption and human degradation that characterized the former regimes of the Soviet Union and the Eastern European countries. Thus, the ideological and structural changes that have occurred within Western capitalist countries are having dramatic effects upon the strategies of labour movements. Developments in Sweden illustrate some of these, as well as demonstrating what labour movements can achieve for their supporters despite the persistence of structurally generated class relations.

Sweden, of course, is distinctive among capitalist countries in the extent to which there has been the development of a highly organized and influential working class movement (Korpi, 1983). At the beginning of the twentieth century, close collaboration between trade unions and the Social Democratic Party enabled them to develop coherent programmes of industrial and political reform. The rapid industrialization of the country in the 1920s and 1930s brought about the formation of an industrial infrastructure that was conducive to the growth of *labour* rather than *trade* unionism. Although the very early unions were organized on a craft or trade basis, the expansion of union membership during the inter-war years occurred in industries where Fordist managerial practices were being widely implemented. First generation industrial employees tended to be semi-skilled, working in large corporations. This, together with the absence of broader social divisions based upon such factors as language, religion and ethnicity, led to the emergence of a well-integrated labour movement which, in the

1930s, was able to bring about the election of one of the first social democratic regimes in the world.

Almost from its very beginning, the Social Democratic Party adopted an 'accommodative' or 'reformist' strategy towards the capitalist order. Its initial programme incorporated some revolutionary Marxist objectives, but these were soon to be superseded by policies that involved control over, rather than the abolition of, the capitalist economy. Since the 1930s, successive Social Democratic governments have implemented measures which have brought about the creation of a highly developed, state-financed welfare system and the setting up of a variety of corporatist institutions (Stephens, 1979). These, in their different ways, have ameliorated the more extreme aspects of capitalist class relations without abolishing the dynamic that sustains these same relations. Thus, the competitive process, inherent within the capitalist mode of production, has brought about a high level of monopolization with a very limited number of publicly quoted companies accounting for a high proportion of total output and employment. This process has been largely aided by Social Democratic governments, who have encouraged economic concentration through their policies of 'modernization' and 'structural rationalization', arguing that this is necessary if Swedish companies are to compete in world markets (Scase, 1977). Equally, Sweden is characterized by a class structure common to that found within other capitalist countries. Patterns of economic reward and opportunity are not fundamentally unlike those of other countries, which, in view of the discussion in the preceding chapters, is not entirely surprising (Davis and Scase, 1985). Although Social Democratic regimes have made use of state institutions and their control over the political decision-making process to bring about fundamental changes within the educational system as well as to introduce and maintain a progressive, redistributive form of taxation, these policies have not brought dramatic differences compared to other countries. What, then, have been the major achievements of the Swedish labour movement as expressed through the election of successive Social Democratic regimes? Essentially, the gains have been in the establishment of the welfare state and the regulation of the capitalist economy through the creation of corporatist structures. Both of these have served to benefit the material conditions of the working class to a far greater extent than in other capitalist countries. Although class relations have not been abolished – nor can they be without the abolition of the capitalist mode of production – the pursuit of different goals, utilizing state institutions as agencies for change, has improved the material and cultural conditions of the Swedish working-class.

This can be demonstrated by reference to a recent study, which has compared the development of state welfare systems in a number of different capitalist countries. In his analysis, Esping-Andersen (1990) constructs an index of 'de-commodification' according to which countries are ranked in terms of the ease with which individuals are able to 'opt out' of the market for the purposes of obtaining pensions, sickness and unemployment cash benefits. In other words, Esping-Andersen is attempting to measure the degree to which some of the more important aspects of welfare provision are freely and universally available and provided according to non-market earning criteria. Hence, he is attempting to capture 'the degree of market independence for an average worker' (p. 50). On the basis of this, he arrives at 'de-commodification' scores for eighteen countries, ten of which are:

Sweden	39.1
Norway	38.3
Denmark	38.1
Austria	31.1
Germany	27.7
France	27.5
Japan	27.1
Italy	24.1
United Kingdom	23.4
United States	13.8

Esping-Andersen argues that there are a number of factors which explain the differences, of which strength of labour movements is but one. However, he does suggest that this accounts for approximately 40 per cent of the cross-national variance found in the degree of de-commodification. Thus, it is evident that working-class movements, not only in Sweden but also in other countries where they have been able to capture the legislative process for substantial periods of time, such as in Denmark and Norway, have been able to

Table 4.1 Relative prevalence of long-term illness by social class in Britain and Sweden

Social class	Britain	Sweden
1 Managerial and professional	0.52	0.79
2 Lower managerial and supervisory	0.94	0.75
3 Routine non-manual	1.05	1.09
4 Skilled manual	1.14	1.18
5 Semi-skilled manual	1.23	1.21
6 Unskilled manual	1.38	1.20
All	1.00	1.00
Ratio of social class 6 to social class 1	2.65	1.52

Source: The Lancet, 1 July 1989

develop welfare provisions that are non-market based and enhance individual well-being and personal citizenship. This is a major achievement despite the fact that it may have little consequence for patterns of economic and social inequalities and for class relations in general. Indeed, it can be argued that, for most people, their personal health, economic security and pension provisions are considered to be more important than issues of class inequality. National elections are won or lost by political parties in terms of their strategies for such matters rather than broader class privileges and deprivations. It can be legitimately argued that the leaders of the Swedish labour movement have pursued the interests of their rank-and-file members in a highly effective manner. As far as health and illness are concerned, it does seem that there is a generally lower prevalence of long-term illness in Sweden, certainly by comparison with Britain, and that there are fewer class differences. This is, perhaps, one of the more important indicators of social reform since general levels of health in society reflect standards of diet, housing, medical services, education and the quality of life as a whole. Table 4.1 compares patterns between Britain and Sweden, demonstrating how there are a lower prevalence of long-term illness and reduced class differences in illness patterns in Sweden.

Sweden illustrates how working-class movements are able to

develop the state provision of health and welfare services to improve the material conditions of workers, but it also demonstrates how the setting up of corporatist structures is able to achieve a similar goal. By comparison with other capitalist countries, Sweden has a variety of national, regional and local institutional structures that, in their involvement with labour market policies and economic management, incorporate the interests of capital, labour and the state. They are concerned with various aspects of education and training, technological research and innovation, the quality of working life, economic and regional planning and, perhaps most importantly, the maintenance of an 'active' labour market. As a result, and this stems from a historical objective of the labour movement, the level of unemployment in Sweden is consistently very low. Whereas in many Western capitalist countries rates exceed 10 per cent, in Sweden the level of unemployment has rarely been above 2.5 per cent in the post-war era (Therborn, 1986). This has a number of effects, including enabling organized labour to maintain its bargaining capacity in its negotiations with capitalist corporations about wages, working conditions and the nature of corporate decision-making. At the same time, it leads to high employment participation rates for women, the disabled and many other groups who are often considered in other countries to constitute a 'reserve army' or 'marginal' labour. It also enables the Swedish labour movement to prevent developments that in other countries have led to the segmentation of labour markets into primary and secondary sectors and to the emergence of impoverished sub-strata within the working-class, of the kind found in Britain.

Sweden may be somewhat atypical among capitalist countries in the extent to which a well organized working-class movement has a high degree of political influence. Although it is a capitalist country with structurally determined class relations, the everyday experience of class is even less evident than in other capitalist countries. This enables Sweden to portray itself as the 'third way': as being neither a free market economy nor a state socialist country. It is for this reason that it is emulated as a model by the newly elected political regimes of Czechoslovakia, Hungary and Poland, despite attempts by the IMF and other funding organizations to impose more liberal capitalist regimes in these countries. A socio-political system has emerged in Sweden, based upon the existence of an influential working-class movement in a capitalist country, which ameliorates the extreme excesses of class and the market but which, at the same time, allows personal freedoms to flourish and citizens' rights to be protected. Within most capitalist countries, rightist political rhetoric emphasizes the essential contradictions between the 'state' and the 'individual', but the social democratic debate in Sweden stresses how the provision of state-financed collective services is a fundamental pre-condition for the enjoyment of personal freedoms and self-development. The Swedish labour movement has been able to maintain a level of legitimacy and political support that is the envy of comparable movements in other countries and which the September 1991 newly-elected non-socialist minority government will find difficult to challenge. It has pursued – and continues to pursue – policies that have enhanced the material and cultural conditions of its rank-and-file supporters. Although from a Marxist point of view these may be conceived as reformist rather than radical and, therefore, are often considered to be irrelevant for the pursuit of basic working-class interests, they have brought about social and economic reforms which have served these same interests but without abolishing the underlying forces of class relations. This may be the price that has to be paid if the alternative is the implementation of forms of state totalitarianism of the kind that existed in the former Soviet Union and in Eastern Europe. Indeed, this raises issues about the future role of labour movements in capitalist society. This will now be considered in the concluding chapter.

5
Conclusions

At the beginning of this book it was suggested that class is generally regarded by most people as being of little relevance for the understanding of the everyday lives. In describing themselves, people tend to refer to such characteristics as age, gender, ethnicity, place of residence, occupation, etc., rather than class membership. Most frequently, notions of class are used to describe inequalities in the past or related to aspects of 'status' or 'snobbery'. As stated earlier, it is only with the considerable assistance of interviewers that respondents participating in social surveys are likely to refer to themselves in class terms and to allocate themselves to one of a number of class categories presented to them. Other than for those engaged in radical political activity or academic social science debate, it is unlikely that notions of social class will have much meaning for the overwhelming majority of people. At best, class is a vague, residual feature of social life. This has ramifications for the general and perceived relevance of sociology as a discipline, if only because concepts of class are central to most sociological analyses in Britain. Since the overwhelming majority of studies, whether they are of industrial shopfloor behaviour, family relations, health, deviance or voting patterns, tend to be discussed in social class terms, barriers are immediately erected between the practitioners of the discipline and others. A consequence is that sociological discourse becomes introspective and, usually, locked into a variety of academic debates which are perceived by others as largely irrelevant to the description and understanding of everyday reality.

The essential argument of this book is that, notwithstanding the subjective reality of class, it remains a concept that is vital for understanding the structure of present-day capitalist society. To reiterate what has been discussed earlier, the capitalist mode of production cannot exist without class relations and vice versa. Without these relations no surplus value can be produced and accordingly, capitalism is unable to reproduce itself. Without capital and labour as productive assets, structured within relations of exploitation, capital is unable to accumulate. Hence, relations of exploitation are expressed as control relations and reflected as job tasks and responsibilities within the occupational structure. Class relations, and the changes that occur within control relations, are the underlying forces that determine the nature of job tasks, the delineation of work roles and the structuring of occupations. Work tasks do not consist entirely of technical or expert skills since they have built within them dimensions of domination and subordination derived from class relations. This is why it has been argued that sociological approaches which begin with analyses of occupations and then proceed to aggregate these into social classes are dealing with the effects rather than the causes. No understanding of occupations and jobs can be complete without recognition of their origins within class relations. Equally, the structuring of organizations, whether they are directly or indirectly associated with the production or realization of surplus values, can only be understood by reference to relations of control (Dahrendorf, 1959). Profit-making organizations and state-owned institutions are little more than aggregates of employment relations within which control is exercised by those in positions of authority over others who are compelled to execute a variety of productive and/or unproductive tasks.

It is for these reasons that the analysis of social class is important for understanding the dynamics of organizational change, related as these are to the development of the capitalist mode of production (Salaman, 1981). The inherently competitive processes of capitalism, bringing about the concentration of ownership in monopoly or quasi-monopoly forms, inevitably lead to the restructuring of employment relationships. Equally, technological innovation has repercussions for the nature of work and for the delineation of job tasks. But these processes cannot be fully understood unless it is appreciated that the underlying forces are to do with the production and realization of economic surpluses. They can only be considered within the framework of class relations and how the structuring of occupations and the delineation of work roles within organizational settings are determined by these. Thus, it is clear that the analysis of class is inherent to the study of capitalist society. Western industrial societies are capitalist and, hence, their economic development is determined by the interplay of class forces of one kind or another. The fact that the prime objective of capitalist corporations is to make profits means that they are characterized by relations of exploitation and control and, hence, consist of class relations. This is the reality of economic production, irrespective of the perceptions and assumptions of participating actors. It is for this reason that social class will continue to remain central to sociological analysis. To eliminate it would be to obstruct sociologists from the analysis of the core forces of socio-economic change as they exist in capitalist society.

This is not to imply that social class will be perceived by social actors as having much bearing on their everyday lives. In a sense, why should it? There would seem to be no reason for individuals to need a sophisticated understanding of the dynamics of class for the purpose of achieving their personal goals in terms of psychological and material well-being. Indeed, most employees do recognize they are exploited – although they may rarely use such an emotive term – but view this as a taken-for-granted fact of the employment relationship (Beynon, 1980). They accept that they are hired to perform tasks that will contribute to the profits of their employing corporations and that should their labour be seen by senior management as unprofitable or unproductive, they will be fired. Most workers see nothing immoral in this and many go so far as to query the value or efficiency of non-profit-making forms of economic organization. Hence, it is unlikely that an awareness of exploitation will lead to political activism and to a personal commitment to fundamental socio-economic change. As long as employees perceive that they receive 'fair rewards' for 'fair effort', that wage differentials are reasonably legitimate, and that they are able to earn enough money to meet their personal needs, they are unlikely to become engaged in collective action directed towards the destruction of capitalism. This does not mean that workers need be satisfied with the overall distribution of economic rewards and with the pattern of wage differentials (Marshall *et al.*, 1988).

Clearly, there is discontent, which becomes expressed in forms of industrial unrest, low motivation and wage demands. But such forms of protest are generally directed towards changes *within* rather than *of* the prevailing capitalist order. Equally, it is generally recognized that some groups in society are highly disadvantaged. But the explanations for this tend to be associated with personal failure and/or the actions of governments rather than with the inherent dynamics of the capitalist mode of production. Any targets of protest, then, tend to be governments rather than capitalist corporations.

If there is collective protest, it appears in terms of various occupational, industrial, community and, sometimes, corporate interests. Thus, social protest is inclined to emphasize divisions within the working class and can sometimes reinforce ties of solidarity that cut across class boundaries. This can occur when multinational corporations threaten to close particular operating units, with the effect that local management and workers will 'unite' in their protest. More generally, corporate restructuring, the introduction of new technology and structural rationalization will elicit forms of protest that are spasmodic and localized in particular work settings. To achieve heightened levels of class consciousness among employees has been the ambition of radical activists since the nineteenth century but, with occasional exceptions, this goal has not been achieved. This is not only because of the great diversity of personal experiences encountered by those occupying similar class positions, but also for two other reasons. First, the overwhelming majority of individuals do not perceive themselves as *agents* of class in the manner that radical activists would like. Thus, their own biographical experiences, structured as these are within the context of particular intimate relationships and personal networks, will be considered by them to be more important than broader socio-political processes, irrespective of whether or not these are class related. Second, in terms of an appraisal of personal costs and benefits, the great majority of citizens in capitalist society perceive themselves as beneficiaries. They may demand more in the form of enhanced living standards and improved working conditions but, on the whole, they see themselves as enjoying greater benefits than costs. Many see themselves as exploited and view the distribution of rewards as unfair, but they take these factors for granted on the grounds that it is a price that has to be paid for better living standards and for personal non-work freedoms.

This has been a major source of legitimacy for the capitalist order, but it has been greatly strengthened by developments in Europe in the late 1980s. In the closing decade of the twentieth century, there remains no viable alternative to capitalism. Even if it is accepted that the Soviet Union and the countries of Eastern Europe were not truly state socialist, but represented repressive forms of state capitalism or bureaucratic collectivism, socio-political developments in those countries have tarnished, if not destroyed, the notion of state socialism as a model for societal development. The repressive, totalitarian nature of these countries and their socio-economic structures produced forms of society in which the majority of citizens concluded that the costs greatly outweighed the benefits. Even if the official party orthodoxy was accepted – namely, that there were no exploitative class relations – the subjective reality for most people was one of subordination and the repression of personal freedoms, individual creativity, dignity and self-respect. In this sense, the abolition of social class provided little in the form of self-enrichment. People being viewed and treated by the party as agents of class forces bringing about the construction of socialism seems to have achieved little, except to have allowed self-recruiting elites to establish state institutions of repression and control. The legacy of the Eastern European 'experiment' of the mid-twentieth century has been to reinforce the legitimacy of capitalism as a mode of production and the acceptance of class and exploitative relationships *in* work as part of a taken-for-granted reality in societies that offer opportunities for 'individuality', 'self-expression' and 'personal freedom' *outside* work. Clearly, this has ramifications for the nature of sociological analysis as well as for the strategies of radical political movements. It is necessary to consider each of these in turn.

Sociology, as an empirical discipline, rapidly expanded in the 1960s when issues of inequality and justice were at the forefront of political debate. It was a decade when social democratic ideals were on the ascent and many countries in Western Europe had labour or leftist-orientated political regimes. It is not surprising that sociologists devoted much time and energy to the study of inequalities, both historically and cross-nationally. Class analysis became a predominant mode of sociological enquiry and, as a result, the study of capitalism became central in explanations of the structuring of inequalities within different countries. The outcomes of such approaches were many but, perhaps, the following are among the more important. First, sociology became seen, although perhaps incorrectly, as synonymous with radical political ideologies, orientated to fundamental changes in the capitalist order. Further, considerable amounts of data were collected documenting the widespread patterns of inequalities in Western capitalist countries. At the same time, there was a proliferation of a variety of Marxist perspectives, which became excessively theoretical and preoccupied with the delineation of class positions and boundaries (Parkin, 1979). But, and perhaps most importantly, what sustained the validity of these approaches and maintained the momentum of sociological class analysis was the *empirical reality* of non-capitalist countries in Eastern Europe. In other words, there was a real alternative to capitalism and so discussions of class, the determination of class boundaries, issues of class consciousness, etc., could be seen, implicitly if not always explicitly, to have a broader relevance than solely academic debate. Sociology was seen by some to be part of a wider enterprise to do with the transformation of capitalism into more humane, socially just forms of socio-economic organization. Even though the countries of Eastern Europe were not viewed as models – far from it, and many commentators emphasized their despotic features – they demonstrated that alternatives to capitalism could be established. In the 1960s, they constituted relatively novel forms of social structure, highlighting the possibilities of societal planning and social engineering, and the extent to which sociological findings could be applied in the design of social institutions. Even though they may have possessed many totalitarian features, for many observers these were seen to be a function of the need to industrialize rapidly, to defend themselves against counter-revolutionary forces and to become economically self-sufficient. Hence, such 'abnormalities' as totalitarianism and political repression would be resolved as the different countries of Eastern Europe developed into higher forms of state socialism.

In the 1990s, the 'failed' experiments of the Soviet Union and Eastern Europe poses a dilemma for sociological class analysis.

Thus, it is no longer credible for sociological investigations to be undertaken as part of a theoretical programme for formulating a strategy for societal change; namely, the transformation of capitalism into an alternative socio-economic order. This is particularly so, as it seems there is a widespread recognition *and* acceptance that class exploitation is an inherent and more or less permanent feature of society – as long as the benefits for the greater majority of individuals outweigh the costs which they or others may have to bear. Accordingly, the generally implicit belief of many sociologists that class relationships and, by implication, the capitalist order *ought* to be eradicated has now to be confronted in a far more explicit manner than in the past. At least this means that those who are committed to social change must proceed to formulate agendas for action which assume the continuing development of capitalism rather than its supersedence by an 'alternative' order. If it is to be accepted that class relations will remain a feature of society, the questions that have to be tackled focus upon issues of equity, distribution and compensation within societies where the essential dynamic of accumulation will continue to be exploitative. Thus, the focus of attention shifts away from hopes for 'abolition' to more detailed discussions about amelioration and social reform. It entails a return to the consideration of the ideals of Fabian socialism and, certainly, a collusion with the non-socialist strategies that are currently being formulated by some labour movements.

It has already been suggested that it would be counterproductive for working-class political movements to establish political programmes that appeal to class and feelings of exploitation. Even though these constitute inherent features of modern capitalism, they do not generate broadly based demands for their abolition. Hence, labour movements are now compelled, largely as a result of pressures from their rank-and-file supporters, to develop strategies that give pre-eminence to 'individualism' and to citizenship (Marshall *et al.*, 1988). State socialism, with its emphasis upon centralized planning and regulation, is no longer on the agenda and, in its place, there is a renewed appeal of social democracy, with its emphasis upon the market economy *and* the collective provision of various social and economic resources. This is the model which has been developed in Sweden, which is currently being applied in the Soviet Union and the countries of Eastern Europe despite economic pressures from many Western governments. While this model accepts the reality of class and exploitation within capitalism, it also recognizes that the state, as the expression of various competing societal interests, is able to ameliorate many inequalities and injustices of the sort found within liberal economies (Korpi, 1983). Hence, it explicitly recognizes that 'the market' allows for individual freedoms and self-expression but that, without state controls, this can lead to glaring inequalities and deprivations. At the same time, it admits that state socialism, in the absence of market relationships, allows for the gross abuse of personal rights and individual liberties. It is, then, not surprising that social democratic regimes have achieved little in ameliorating class-determined inequalities in patterns of economic rewards and opportunities. As long as market principles and capitalist accumulation are regarded as necessary for economic efficiency and for protecting individual rights and liberties, class inequalities will prevail. But this does not mean that such inequalities cannot be *compensated* by a variety of state provisions of one kind or another. Although both Swedish and South African workers may be exploited and, ostensibly, members of the working class, it would be naive to assume that their material circumstances are similar and that they share common interests. Plainly they do not, and even though class inequalities in Sweden in terms of economic rewards may be little different from those found within other Western capitalist countries, Swedish workers enjoy a greater variety of compensations than their counterparts in other countries; for instance, not only in terms of health, welfare and old age benefits, but also in terms of the quality of their working lives, their community environment and the general provision of cultural and recreational resources (Vogel, 1990).

Further, the development of social democracy has led to a shift in emphasis, from trying to change relationships of class to focusing upon the circumstances – the deprivations and disadvantages – endured by *individuals* occupying various class positions. Hence, reformist policies have been directed to the different social groupings that capitalist corporations, left to their own devices, marginalize and systematically allocate to the most disadvantaged jobs. Generally speaking, women, pre-retired manual workers, school-leavers, the disabled and members of ethnic minority groups tend to be given the jobs that are the least rewarding in terms of pay, opportunities and psychological satisfaction (Brown and Scase, 1991). In Sweden, these groupings have benefited from Social Democratic legislation, although they continue to occupy working-class positions. They remain exploited but are better off than their counterparts in many other countries because there is a state apparatus that effectively 'polices' the activities of corporations to ensure that legislation to do with equal opportunities, sex discrimination and minority rights is implemented and enforced. Although such social democratic reforms do not explicitly attack the exploitative relationships of social class, they ameliorate, if only partly, the more acute forms as encountered by the more vulnerable or marginalized groups in society (Vogel, 1990).

The effectiveness of such legislation is best illustrated by the strategies that the owners and controllers of Swedish capitalist corporations adopt in order to counter the effects of the reforms. Corporations have expanded their production or provision of services in countries other than Sweden. A number of Swedish companies have evolved into multinational corporations, not only because of the need to expand their markets but also in order to avoid the high production costs associated with manufacturing in Sweden. These costs are a consequence of the influence of the labour movement and of the extent to which Social Democratic governments have introduced legislation leading to additional expenses that have to be borne by employers. These range from holiday benefits and pension rights to the design and planning of workplaces. Swedish corporations have attempted to transfer many of their manufacturing activities to other countries in order to circumvent these. That this has not led to widespread protest by the labour movement is because there has not, as yet, been a big increase in the level of unemployment in Sweden and, with it, labour market conditions in which working-class gains would be seriously undermined. But this is a possibility and a constant reminder to workers of their vulnerability in capitalist society because of their dependency upon the sale of their labour power.

In view of developments in the Soviet Union and Eastern Europe during the late 1980s and 1990s it would seem that capitalism and its inherent class relationships are now better legitimated than at any previous time. In none of the mature capitalist countries are there viable, broadly supported revolutionary movements and, as a result, *reformist* or *compensatory* strategies of the kind pursued in Sweden are likely to be the predominant strategies of labour movements. Class and capitalism are likely to remain long-term, almost permanent, features of industrial societies and, hence, debate should no longer be about the abolition of social class but about other important factors. There are three of these that may be singled out. First is the distribution of rewards as these are allocated to different occupational positions. What is an 'equitable' reward system and according to what kinds of criteria should economic inequalities be determined? In most Western capitalist countries, the present-day distribution of economic rewards appears to be irrational and, according to most moral values, offensive. Accepting the continuing existence of capital and class, how can class inequalities be more publicly accountable and equitably determined? Second is the allocation of individuals to occupational positions. How, and according to what criteria, are occupational positions to be allocated? Should not the selection and promotion policies of senior managers in large-scale organizations be subject to closer scrutiny, if only because the occupational aspirations of deprived groups in society are becoming more pronounced? Third, assuming the continuing persistence of class and capitalism, how should those who are allocated to the worst paid and most demeaning occupational positions be compensated by collective provisions of one kind or another? This raises questions about the role of the state, in terms of both its intervention in the market economy and the method of provision of its services for those who are in need.

In sum, the tackling of such issues implies the further development of the 'mixed economy', the 'third way' 'welfare capitalism' in societies where the influence of labour movements is recognized and their legitimacy is sustained. Further, it assumes a high degree of state intervention in both the productive and the distributive processes. The adoption of corporatist forms of socio-political organization, then, would seem to offer a viable strategy for labour movements that want both to ameliorate the more extreme excesses of exploitation found in liberal democratic capitalist societies and, at the same time, to avoid the oppressive totalitarianism of the former state socialist countries. None of this, of course, is new; it is to be found in the ideals of traditional Fabian socialism, the programmes of the Scandinavian Social Democratic parties and some of the political assumptions of the 1960s. What is required, however, is for Marxist sociologists to address these issues more seriously rather than, as they have over the past three decades, to dismissing them as being generally peripheral to the fundamental analysis of class relations.

Social class is part of the inherent reality of capitalist society and, for sociologists, it is an essential component of their analytical framework for understanding social structures and processes. Thus, the use of Marxist categories has been, and will continue to be, invaluable. However, to share with Marx his ideas for abolishing class must, towards the end of the twentieth century, be seen to be Utopian. In accepting both the reality and the relative permanence of class, it is now appropriate for sociologists to shift their emphasis from abstract theoretical paradigms that would seem to have little practical or political meaning. The overwhelming majority of people in capitalist society accept the personal costs of class exploitation because it offers them compensatory benefits. Eastern European state socialism failed to do this. Western capitalism is characterized by relations of exploitation but it is also distinguished by the opportunities it offers for rights of citizenship. Therein lies its paradox, the collapse of Soviet and Eastern European state socialism, and the longer-term legitimacy of social class and capitalism. It is the rise and fall of state socialism which the twentieth century has witnessed rather than the demise of capitalism. The question is no longer whether or not capitalism but of what variety or type.

Bibliography

Abercrombie, N. and Urry, J. (1983). *Capital, Labour and the Middle Classes*. London: Allen and Unwin.

Allen, S. and Truman, C. (1991). 'Prospects for women's business and self-employment in the year 2000', in J. Curran and R. Blackman (eds) *Paths of Enterprise: the Future of the Small Business*. London: Routledge.

Anthony, F. (1986). *The Foundation of Management*. London: Tavistock.

Atkinson, J. and Meager, N. (1985). *Changing Working Patterns*. London: NEDO.

Baran, B. (1988). 'Office automation and women's work: the technological transformation of the insurance industry', in R. Pahl (ed.) *On Work*. Oxford: Basil Blackwell.

Bechhofer, F. and Elliot, B. (1976). 'Persistence and change: the petite bourgeoisie in industrial society', *European Journal of Sociology*, 17.

Bell, D. (1973). *The Coming of Post-Industrial Society*. New York: Basic Books.

Bendix, R. (1956). *Work and Authority in Industry*. New York: Basic Books.

Beynon, H. (1980). *Working For Ford*. Wakefield: EP Publishing.

Braverman, H. (1974). *Labour and Monopoly Capital*. New York: Monthly Review Press.

Brown, P. and Scase, R. (eds) (1991). *Poor Work: Disadvantage and the Division of Labour*. Milton Keynes: Open University Press.

Buchanan, D. and McCalman, J. (1989). *High Performance Work Systems*. London: Routledge.

Carchedi, G. (1975). 'On the economic identification of the new middle class', *Economy and Society*, 4.

Central Statistical Office (1988). *Social Trends*. London: HMSO.

Child, J. (1988). 'Managerial strategies, new technology and the labour process', in R. Pahl (ed.) *On Work*. Oxford: Basil Blackwell.

Cockburn, C. (1986). 'Women and technology: opportunity is not enough', in K. Purcell, S. Wood, A. Waton and S. Allen (eds) *The Changing Experience of Employment*. London: Macmillan.

Confederation of British Industry (1990). *A Nation of Shareholders: Report of the CBI Wider Share Ownership Task Force*. London.

Crompton, R. and Jones, G. (1984). *White Collar Proletariat*. London: Macmillan.

Crompton, R. and Reid, S. (1982). 'The deskilling of clerical work', in S. Wood (ed.) *The Degradation of Work?* London: Hutchinson.

Curran, J. and Blackburn, R. (1991). 'Changes in the context of enterprise: some socio-economic and environmental factors facing small firms in the 1990s', in J. Curran and R. Blackburn (eds) *Patterns of Enterprise: the Future of the Small Business*. London: Routledge.

Dahrendorf, R. (1959). *Class and Class Conflict in Industrial Society*. London: Routledge and Kegan Paul.

Davis, H. and Scase, R. (1985). *Western Capitalism and State Socialism: an Introduction*. Oxford: Basil Blackwell.

Davis, K. and Moore, W. (1945). 'Some principles of stratification', *American Sociological Review*, **10**.

de Vroey, M. (1980). 'A Marxist view of ownership and control', in T. Nichols (ed.) *Capital and Labour*. London: Fontana.

Edwards, R. (1979). *The Contested Terrain*. London: Heinemann.

Erikson, R. (1984). 'Social class of men, women and families', *Sociology*, **18**.

Esping-Andersen, G. (1990). *The Three Worlds of Welfare Capitalism*. Cambridge: Polity Press.

Gallie, D. (ed.) (1988). *Employment in Britain*. Oxford: Basil Blackwell.

Gilbert, M. (1986). *Inflation and Social Conflict*. Brighton: Wheatsheaf Books.

Goffee, R. and Scase, R. (1985). *Women in Charge: the Work and Life Styles of Female Entrepreneurs*. London: George Allen and Unwin.

Goldthorpe, J. (1980). *Social Mobility and Class Structure in Modern Britain*. Oxford: Clarendon Press.

Goldthorpe, J. (1983). 'Women and class analysis: in defence of the conventional view', *Sociology*, **17**.

Gospel, H. and Palmer, G. (1992). *British Industrial Relations*. London: Harper Collins.

Goss, D. (1991). *Small Business and Society*. London: Routledge.

Halsey, A. (1986). *Change in British Society*, 3rd edn. Oxford: Oxford University Press.

Halsey, A., Heath, A. and Ridge, J. (1980). *Origins and Destinations: Family, Class and Education in Modern Britain*. Oxford: Clarendon Press.

Hamilton, M. and Hirszowicz, M. (1987). *Class and Inequality in Pre-industrial Capitalist and Communist Societies*. London: Harvester Wheatsheaf.

Hannah, L. and Kay, J. (1977). *Concentration in Modern Industry*. London: Macmillan.

Harrison, P. (1985). *Inside the Inner City*. Harmondsworth: Penguin.

Heath, A. (1981). *Social Mobility*. London: Fontana.

Heath, A. and McDonald, S. (1987). 'Social change and the future of the left'. *Political Quarterly*, **58**.

Hertz, L. (1986). *The Business Amazons*. London: Andre Deutsch.

Hudson, R. and Williams, A. (1989). *Divided Britain*. London: Belhaven Press.

Ingham, G. (1984). *Capitalism Divided? The City and Industry in British Social Development*. London: Macmillan.

Jones, B. (1989). 'When certainty fails: inside the factory of the future', in S. Wood (ed.) *The Transformation of Work*. London: Unwin Hyman.

Kanter, R. (1977). *Men and Women of the Corporation*. New York: Basic Books.

Kerr, K., Harrison, F. and Myers, C. (1960). *Industrialism and Industrial Man*. Cambridge, MA: Harvard University Press.

Korpi, W. (1983). *The Democratic Class Struggle*. London: Routledge and Kegan Paul.

Labour Research (1987). 'Big fish grab sell-off shares', *Labour Research*, September.

Lane, D. (1976). *The Socialist Industrial State: towards a Political Sociology of State Socialism*. London: Allen and Unwin.

Lockwood, D. (1988). 'The weakest link in the chain? Some comments on the Marxist theory of action', in D. Rose (ed.) *Social Stratification and Economic Change*. London: Hutchinson.

McCrone, D., Elliot, B. and Bechhofer, F. (1989). 'Corporatism and the new right', in R. Scase (ed.) *Industrial Societies: Crisis and Division in Western Capitalism and State Socialism*. London: Unwin Hyman.

Mann, M. (1970). 'The social cohesion of liberal democracy', *American Sociological Review*, **35**.

Mann, M. (1973). *Consciousness and Action among the Western Working Class*. London: Macmillan.

Marglin, S. (1980). 'What do bosses do? The origins and functions of hierarchy in capitalist production', in T. Nichols (ed.) *Capital and Labour*. London: Fontana.

Marshall, G., Newby, H., Rose, R. and Vogler, C. (1988). *Social Class in Modern Britain*. London: Hutchinson.

Marx, K. (1974). *Capital*, 3 vols. London: Lawrence and Wishart.

Marx, K. (1975). 'Preface to a contribution to the critique of political economy', in *Karl Marx: Early Writings*. Harmondsworth: Penguin.

Marx, K. and Engels, F. (1964). *Pre-Capitalist Economic Formations*. London: Lawrence and Wishart.

Marx, K. and Engels, F. (1969). *The Communist Manifesto*. Harmondsworth: Penguin.

Mills, C. W. (1951). *White Collar*. New York: Oxford University Press.

Morgan, G. (1986). *Images of Organization*. London: Sage Publications.

Murray, F. (1988). 'The decentralization of production – the decline of the mass-collective worker?', in R. Pahl (ed.) *On Work*. Oxford: Basil Blackwell.

Newby, H. *et al.*, (1985). 'From class structure to class action: British working-class politics in the 1980s', in B. Roberts *et al.*, (eds) *New Approaches to Economic Life*. Manchester: Manchester University Press.

Nichols, T. and Beynon, H. (1977). *Living with Capitalism*. London: Routledge and Kegan Paul.

Nicholson, N. and West, M. (1988). *Managerial Job Change: Men and Women in Transition*. Cambridge: Cambridge University Press.

Offe, C. (1976). *Industry and Inequality*. London: Edward Arnold.

Ouchi, W. (1981). *Theory Z: How American Business Can Meet the Japanese Challenge*. Reading, MA: Addison-Wesley.

Pahl, R. (1984). *Divisions of Labour*. Oxford: Basil Blackwell.

Parkin, F. (1971). *Class Inequality and Political Order*. London: Mac-Gibbon and Kee.

Parkin, F. (1979). *Marxism and Class Theory*. London: Tavistock.

Pascale R. and Athos, A. (1982). *The Art of Japanese Management*. Harmondsworth: Penguin.

Piore, M. and Sabel, C. (1984). *The Second Industrial Divide: Possibilities for Prosperity*. New York: Basic Books.

Pond, C. (1989). 'The changing distribution of income, wealth and poverty', In C. Hamnett, L. McDowell and P. Sarre (eds) *The Changing Social Structure*. London: Sage Publications.

Poulantzas, N. (1975). *Classes in Contemporary Capitalism*. London: New Left Books.

Rainnie, A. (1991). 'Small firms: between the enterprise culture and "New Times"', in R. Burrows (ed.) *Deciphering the Enterprise Culture*. London: Routledge.

Runciman, W. (1966). *Relative Deprivation and Social Justice*. London: Routledge and Kegan Paul.

Runciman, W. (1983). 'Capitalism without classes', *British Journal of Sociology*, 34.

Sabel, C. (1982). *Work and Politics: the Division of Labour in Industry*. Cambridge: Cambridge University Press.

Salaman, G. (1981). *Class and the Corporation*. London: Fontana.

Sarre, P. (1989). 'Recomposition of the class structure', in C. Hamnett, C. McDowell and P. Sarre (eds) *Re-Structuring Britain: the Changing Social Structure*. London: Sage Publications.

Saunders, P. (1989). *A Nation of Homeowners*. London: Unwin Hyman.

Scase, R. (1977). *Social Democracy in Capitalist Society*. London: Croom Helm.

Scase, R. and Goffee, R. (1987). *The Real World of the Small Business Owner*. London: Croom Helm.

Scase, R. and Goffee, R. (1989). *Reluctant Managers: Their Work and Life Styles*. London: Unwin Hyman.

Schein, E. (1985). *Organizational Culture and Leadership*. San Fransisco: Jossey-Bass.

Scott, J. (1985). *Corporations, Classes and Capitalism*. London: Hutchinson.

Seabrook, J. (1984). *The Idea of Neighbourhood*. London: Pluto Press.

Stanworth, M. (1984). 'Women and class analysis: a reply to Goldthorpe', *Sociology*, **18**.

Stephens, J. (1979). *The Transition from Capitalism to Socialism*. London: Macmillan.

Therborn, G. (1986). *Why Some People Are More Unemployed than Others*. London: Verso.

Vogel, J. (1990). *Lev i Norden* (Living Conditions in Scandinavia). Stockholm: Nordic Statistical Secretariat.

Ward, R. (1991). 'Economic development and ethnic business', in J. Curran and R. Blackburn (eds) *Paths of Enterprise: the Future of the Small Business*. London: Routledge.

Weber, M. (1968). *Economy and Society*. New York: Bedminster Press.

Wickens, P. (1987). *The Road to Nissan*. London: Macmillan.

Wood, S. (1989). 'The transformation of work', in S. Wood (ed.) *The Transformation of Work*. London: Unwin Hyman.

Wright, E. O. (1976). 'Contradictory class locations', *New Left Review*, **98**.

Wright, E. O. (1985). *Classes*. London: Verso.

Wright, E. O. *et al.*, (1982). 'The American class structure', *American Sociological Review*, **47**.

Index